China Changes Everything

An anthology by social justice activists, journalists and commentators

A Project of Friends of Socialist China – U.S.

World View Forum 2025

Copyright © 2025, World View Forum

Book Coordinator: Sara Flounders
Editor: Kyle Ferrana
Design and Cover Art: Lyn Neeley
Production Team: Dee Knight, Kyle Ferrana, Lyn Neeley, Creighton Ward
We want to make the ideas and information in this book available as widely as possible. Any properly attributed selection of part of a chapter within "fair use" guidelines may be used without permission.

World View Forum
New York, New York
Email: worldviewf@gmail.com

ISBN: 978-0-89567-206-3 (Paperback)
978-0-89567-207-0 (Ebook)
978-089567-208-7 (Kindle)
Library of Congress Control Number: 2025921027

First Edition November 2025

Publisher's Cataloging-in-Publication Data
Names: Flounders, Sara, Book Coordinator
Title: China Changes Everything:
An anthology by social justice activists,
journalists and commentators
Description: [New York, New York] : World View Forum, [2025]
Includes LCCN.

Subjects:
United States–Foreign relations–China–21st century |
Europe–Foreign relations–China–21st century. |
World Politics. | International Relations. | Political Science. |
POLITICAL SCIENCE / Peace | POLITICAL SCIENCE / Commentary & Opinion |
POLITICAL SCIENCE / Geopolitics | Imperialism | Political Ideologies / Democracy |
LC record available at https://lccn.loc.gov/2025000000

Cover photo credits can be found at the end of the book.

Interior design by Booknook.biz

Table of Contents

1. China's Road to Socialism

A Fundamental Difference: China – Socialist or Imperialist?   3
    By Sara Flounders

Communist Principles & Culture Drive China's Development for the Benefit Of All Humanity   15
    By Jacqueline Luqman

Completing the Original Mission: Reinvigorating Marxism in Contemporary China   27
    By Ken Hammond

2. Socialist Planning in Practice

Infrastructure:

Reflections on How China is Building Socialism   37
    By Sydney Loving

Between the Rust Belt and the Model City   47
    By Pawel Wargan

A Tale of Two Economic Systems' Transit   53
    By Betsey Piette

Steel Tracks vs War Tracks: China Builds Subways and Aids Gaza While the U.S. Builds Militarism   67
    By Lee Siu Hin

Healthcare:

If China Provides Universal Healthcare. Why Can't the United States?   79
    By Margaret Flowers

Healthcare in China: A Cooperative Project   91
   By Sue Harris

Green Development:

China Leads the World in Energy Production and Green Technology   99
   By Lyn Neeley

China's Aquacultural Revolution   111
   By Kyle Ferrana

China: Terraforming for the 21st Century   119
   By Judy Bello

3. Plans for a Future World

Contrasting Strategies of the U.S. and China: Prospects for Peace and Solving Global Problems   131
   By Roger Harris

The Race for Moondust: U.S. Imperialism vs. China   139
   By Janet Mayes

Science Fiction or Science Reality? Socialism Leads Humanity out of Artificial Scarcity   151
   By JR Hagler

4. Moving from Isolation to Prosperity

Leadership Was the Key in China's Targeted Poverty Alleviation Campaign   157
   By Dee Knight

Dismantling Western Hypocrisy on Xinjiang and Gaza   167
   By Arjae Red

Xizang's Leap from Serfdom to Socialism with Chinese Characteristics   177
   By Arnold August

5. The U.S. War Drive Against China Intensifies

The U.S. Advances Its Dystopian Plans to Destroy China   193
    By Megan Russell

China Cannot Be Contained   199
    By Margaret Kimberley

The U.S. Wants War with China   207
    By Joe Lombardo

The Greatest People's Success Story in Human History   213
    By KJ Noh

Taiwan's Residents Reject Being Washington's Proxy Against Socialist China   221
    By Chris Fry

An Analysis of the Escalating U.S. Threats Toward China   229
    By Mick Kelly

6. China's Impact on the World

Around the World, China is Turning on the Lights   239
    By Gregory Dunkel

Lips and Teeth: Korea, China, and Northeast Asia's Long Revolution   247
    By Ju-Hyun Park

Is China's Foreign Policy "Good Enough"?   261
    By Danny Haiphong

China, Yemen, and the Red Sea Passage   271
    By Ché Marino

Should the Renminbi Replace the Dollar? The Surprising Answer   277
    By Radhika Desai

7. Looking Back & Looking Forward

    The Rise of China and the Crisis of U.S. Imperialism   295
        By Gerald Horne, Anthony Ballas, Aspen Ballas,
        and PM Irvin

    Shoulder to Shoulder: British People's Solidarity   309
    with the Chinese People's War of Resistance
        By Keith Bennett

    200+ Years of U.S. Military Deployments in and   317
    around China
        By Michael Kramer

    Defend the Socialist Countries, Stand With the Peoples   325
    of the World Against Imperialism
        By Carlos Martinez

Resources for Additional Information   335

1.
China's Road to Socialism

A Fundamental Difference: China – Socialist or Imperialist?

by Sara Flounders

China's emergence as an economic powerhouse is a game-changer on a world scale today, with its Belt and Road Initiative, the Shanghai Cooperation Organization, the BRICS+ trade alliance, and numerous bilateral trade agreements. China is the top trading partner of over 120 countries, and has become an alternative to the International Monetary Fund and the World Bank and their brutal structural adjustment, deregulation and privatization programs (SAPs). Every international gathering, trade agreement and aid shipment confirms that China is a lifeline for the Global South.

China was able to end poverty for 800 million people—something neither the U.S. nor any other capitalist country has been able to do. Life expectancy is on par with the U.S., and China has achieved the fastest growth in living standards of any country in the world.

In the 1950s, when Japan and much of Europe were in ruins, the United States led the world by almost any economic measure. It manufactured half the world's goods, possessed over 40 percent of the world's income, and had by far the highest standard of living. For more than 60 years, the U.S.-based monopolies maintained their domination, but in the decades since the 2008 crisis, China has overtaken the U.S. in total production and especially in manufactured goods.

How is This Possible?

The corporate media presents the competition between the U.S. and China as a contention between two nation states, and falsely accuses the Chinese government of not playing fair. In reality, China's advantage arises from the sharp difference in two wholly different forms of organizing society.

In the United States, nearly all resources are privately owned by a handful of billionaires. Even public forests, waters, and raw minerals are ripe for exploitation for private profit. In China, the overwhelming bulk of resources—oil, gas, coal, gold, gems, rare earth minerals, and water are socially owned and used for the development of the whole society.

We will show some of the ways this difference in ownership impacts further modernization and the ability to adapt to new technology in the two societies. We will also discuss how the U.S. ruling class is reacting to challenges it faces from China and from the crisis in its own capitalist system.

Right now, the U.S. politicians and media are waging an ideological assault on China. Refuting their lies and propaganda is helpful, but the fundamental reason behind their hostility must also be exposed. This reason lies in the class and property differences between People's China and U.S. imperialism.

Cooperation in a Global Market

Ruthless competition for profit, the fundamental feature of capitalism, disrupts cooperative work that is needed to solve the enormous environmental and social problems that confront the whole planet.

In fact, a higher stage of industrial and technical development in a more complex society actually requires a higher stage of social organization. Since it employs little to no planning, capitalism can't solve the overarching problems humanity faces on a global scale.

It is beyond dispute that U.S. living standards and quality of life, measured in healthcare, education, housing, and infrastructure are in sharp decline.

High-Tech Infrastructure

Higher levels of production need a high-tech infrastructure to move what is produced to global markets. China dominates the global commercial shipbuilding market, producing over 50% of the world's new ship orders, while the U.S. share has dwindled to less than 1%. China's shipbuilding industry is backed by a vast industrial base with government support, allowing it to compete on a larger scale than the U.S.

China's workers have laid down tens of thousands of miles of high-speed rail that connect 500 Chinese cities and are still expanding to connect to neighboring countries. Meanwhile in the U.S., both freight and passenger railroads are in decline.

China has gone green, rapidly adopting solar power, and has put half a million electric city buses on its streets. Most U.S. city buses are still belching out pollution from burning fossil fuels.

A significant portion of China's free higher education starts with an emphasis on STEM (science, technology, engineering and math) education, graduating some 3.5 million STEM graduates each year. This is approximately 10 times as many as those from U.S. educational institutions. High levels of skill and advanced education are essential for intervention in today's world.

The internet is widely available even in rural China, due to government initiatives like the National Broadband Strategy. This level of internet penetration, a massive increase over the past, enables economic development and improves quality of life for rural residents.

The U.S. is Desperate to Preserve Its Hegemony

The capitalist class in the U.S. has grown frantic about the decline of its global dominance, and is therefore doubling down on imperialism. The Democratic and Republican parties both agree to blame China. The Pentagon agrees. NATO agrees. They direct new sanctions, new tariffs and new rounds of propaganda at China. In the Pacific Ocean and South China Sea, U.S. strategists are rushing to construct a military alliance similar to NATO. It will include Japan, Australia, New Zealand, South Korea and the Philippines, and is directed against China.

Every arm of the imperialist colossus is predicting and planning for war. The vicious and relentless propaganda, the expanding military budget, the relentless war "games" and military maneuvers all confirm the build-up. Think tanks and strategists promote the idea that war with China is inevitable.

Sharp Economic Differences between U.S. and China

Voices in all imperialist centers are united in slandering China, calling it an imperialist country, no different than past or present imperialist looters. Constant repetition of their propaganda attacks can make the slanders stick, even in the ranks of anti-imperialists. That's why it's important to underline the class differences between People's China and the U.S.

In a capitalist economy, run for the benefit of corporate billionaires, the CEOs and Boards of Directors must base their decisions on maximizing profit—usually, in the shortest term. If they fail, they will lose their positions. Market cycles, not human needs, drive every decision in capitalist production; what is produced is decided by what can be immediately sold for profit.

In China, whose economy is still developing and is catching up in many areas, the major productive forces are owned collectively. Since decisions are not driven by profit, let alone short-term profit, rational planning is possible.

Planned production is different from the boom-and-bust swings in capitalist economies. China has enjoyed steady development, year after year, for 75 years, without the recessions and rock-bottom depressions that have been a feature of every capitalist economy for 400 years.

The U.S. Military Budget: A Drain on the Economy

A capitalist economy depends on the state apparatus enforcing private ownership of all means of production and all resources. The police, the courts, the largest prison system on the planet, and the giant U.S.-commanded NATO military machine act as its enforcers. The U.S. military, by far the largest in NATO, has been U.S. capitalists' shortest path to the highest profits for decades, with its huge, guaranteed, multibillion-dollar annual subsidy.

In 2025, President Trump announced the largest military budget in history, more than $1 trillion. "Nobody's seen anything like it," he bragged. This means that the U.S. strategy is still to impose its military domination at the expense of funding for industrial development and infrastructure.

Federal funding has been pumped into the military for over four generations, providing huge subsidies and a guaranteed source of profits to U.S. defense corporations. But this "quick fix" has become a drag on the economy. It adds nothing of real value, and weakens civilian infrastructure by draining the resources needed for vital social programs, including those that feed, house, provide medical care, and educate the U.S. workforce.

The Chinese Revolution Shook the World

The Chinese Revolution was an upheaval that shook the world. It aroused workers and peasants globally. It achieved victory, because it was led by the Communist Party of China (CPC), which broke with the dominant imperialist powers that had looted China.

The early accomplishments made by what was then a totally impoverished country were enormous, including evicting the imperialist powers from China and opening the road to a new society. China faced enormous impediments in this task; its many contradictions led to fierce debates within the CPC.

In an all-out effort to strangle this revolution, the U.S. and its allies walled China off from Western trade and technology during its first 30 years after the revolution. During that time, the CPC reorganized agriculture as well as the basic industries that had survived decades of civil war and Japanese and Western colonial occupation.

Every step forward required a mass mobilization involving the great energy of millions of people. They collectively organized mass immunizations and literacy programs, and built basic schools, sanitation and irrigation systems, dams, and other infrastructure. They collectivized the land and enthusiastically ripped out the feudal landlord system, root and branch.

Sara Flounders

1978: Reform and Opening Up—The Compromise

However, the world dominated by monopoly capital was also changing fast, and the leadership of the CPC decided to turn toward gaining access to Western technology and trade. Beginning in 1978, China focused intensively on its development and on gaining Western investment. This necessarily opened China's economy to hostile class elements, as Western investments of money, machinery, technology and skills flooded into China, creating a new domestic capitalist class.

The compromise included concessions and profits to the capitalist class internationally and distortions of China's socialist structure. Some observers wondered if the CPC could balance the emerging contradictions and still maintain the party's socialist goals, and many in the West said that the enthusasm engendered by Western corporations' heavy investments in China had already succeeded in bringing China back into the capitalist orbit. Judging by their enthusiastic focus on China, the big corporate investors certainly must have assumed that they would be able to overturn China's socialist base.

The emergence of a class of Chinese millionaires and billionaires and a stratum that looked to and studied in the West was certainly politically disorienting. Many who had been strong supporters of China in the past assumed that the socialist base of the Chinese state was totally lost.

But both the Western capitalists and the disillusioned supporters of China were wrong.

'Socialism with Chinese Characteristics'

The most important aspect of defending China today is recognizing the socialist base of the Chinese economy and the leadership of the

Chinese Communist Party in building an economy of a new type. This is not a finished product; according to the CPC, China is building "toward socialism" or is in the "primary stage of socialism", and is not yet a fully developed socialist country with equality for all.

This phase of socialist construction is described by the CPC as "Socialism with Chinese Characteristics." It is also described as "market socialism" or "socialism with a market." China today has a "market" built on socialist pillars, and its people-oriented central planning remains decisive. Step by step, China has opened a controlled capitalist market, while holding on to state ownership of the major industries and banks.

Five Year Plans Since 1949

China still faces imbalances, insufficiencies and enormous difficulties from past imperialist looting and from U.S. military encirclement and economic sanctions today. Yet the Communist Party of China keeps firm political control over this complex and uneven process by employing socialist planning at every level of society. Major economic and social targets are set in advance and coordinated nationally, by province, by county, and by municipality.

The 14th Five Year Plan, which was focused on raising the level of the whole society and balancing historic inequality, is now ending. The 15th Five Year Plan will focus on expanding consumption and the "market" by increasing social benefits, especially in healthcare, day care, elder care, and particularly protections for migrant workers and new urban residents. These improvements in social life can simultaneously unlock service consumption, enhance social mobility and promote social equality.

Local governments are being reoriented from prioritizing mid- and low-end manufacturing toward investments in productive services and livelihood consumption. This includes funding for culture, theater, domestic tourism, improved recreational services and increasing rural residents' pensions. This approach shifts growth drivers from volatile external market demands toward a resilient domestic cycle that benefits the people.

Role of the Communist Party

The CPC now has more than 100 million members. Its cells, elected from within the ranks, are in virtually every workplace, neighborhood, school and department. The party organizations are committed to defending socialist property and determined to protect Chinese sovereignty. They are the backbone of its extensive social programs.

The CPC considers that while imperialist corporations have exploited and profited from hiring Chinese labor, this was a temporary compromise to gain access to Western technology and factories and to accumulate investment funds.

The key economic role is assigned to a state controlled by the working class. Every major industry, especially banking, remains under state control—a state controlled by a massive Communist Party. The central banks play a crucial role in subsidizing and developing key industries. The state decides where to allocate funds and what kinds of investments will be prioritized. Labor intensive, low-paid industries are now being phased out, and high-tech industries with specialized skills are the future.

The Role of SOEs

Today in China, raw materials, high-speed railroads, airlines, most forms of energy, communications and most key areas of the economy continue to be state-owned enterprises (SOE). These state-owned enterprises, a very precise category in China's state planning, have laid the foundation for China's further development over a long period of time.

The SOEs also enjoy many advantages, particularly in credit lines and interest rates granted by state-owned banks. These banks play a critical role in stimulating technological innovation in all fields, such as robotics, nuclear power, space, etc. Without the major innovations and key core technologies achieved by SOEs, there would be no economic independence and national security for China. Without their long-term commitment to a large number of social responsibilities, there would be no continuous improvement in people's lives.

Today hundreds of millions of Chinese urban workers, especially the youth, are well-informed, well-trained, highly educated, in good health, have access to good jobs and modern housing units that they own outright, and are using fast and efficient transportation facilities. A current goal is to bring these high standards to the rural and least developed areas of China.

Small production, food delivery apps, numerous restaurants and coffee shops, artisan booths and craft facilities in both urban and rural areas are largely in private hands. Much further development in many levels of production is also still a long-term goal. The majority of the workforce is still employed in a wide mix of small-scale private, co-op and township ownership plans, in the cities and in the countryside. Large-scale development of all the productive forces is far from complete in China.

Sara Flounders

Capitalism: An Impediment to Social Progress

Today in the U.S., the center of imperialism, virtually everything that we touch, eat and wear, every pill we take, every hospital we visit, every cup of coffee we drink is controlled by giant capitalist monopolies. The cars we drive, and the homes and apartments we live in are mostly mortgaged to the banks, which are all privately owned. Bank lending and government subsidies are given mainly to the corporations that have the immediate potential to make a high rate of profit.

U.S. imperialism is incapable of modernizing in order to regain its place in today's global economy, because it is totally chained to an outmoded form of production—capitalism. Ruthlessly lowering wages, cutting social benefits, infrastructure investments and education is the billionaires' only strategy. The private ownership of the means of production and the expropriation of all socially produced wealth by a handful of billionaires means fabulous wealth for a few, in the short term, but ultimately it is an impediment to the ability to modernize industry in the context of today's global supply chains.

U.S. imperialism can still threaten to destroy its opponents to impose its demands. This is a powerful threat. But the capitalists will discover that military might not backed up by industrial capacity becomes a paper tiger, growling without substance.

The interests of workers and oppressed people in the U.S. are bound up with the development of the people of the whole world. Only through increased solidarity will our class here develop the ability to solve the enormous global problems. The ability to rationally plan and invest socially created wealth into rapidly improving technology and infrastructure is decisive, and this requires socialism. Socialist economies, based on planning and cooperation, are alone capable of solving the problems that the world now faces. Therefore, stepping up to defend China, its revolution, and its accomplishments is necessary for the collective future of humanity.

Which Side Are You On?

"Which side are you on?" is the oldest formulation in the class struggle.

Political movements, parties and organizations of the working class that take sides in the global class struggle are the most able to withstand the crisis confronting their class and all oppressed peoples. Without this anchor, this basic understanding, workers and activists are cast adrift in the onslaught of each imperialist flood.

A growing number of left forces are using a Marxist lens to understand a complex world development of a new type. China's gains hold a liberating potential for humanity. If we can explain the reason for U.S. imperialism's hostility and why Washington calls Beijing "the greatest threat", we can strengthen popular resistance to the U.S. drive toward war. We urgently need to take the defense of China to a more serious and higher level. We need to challenge the attacks in the U.S. corporate media, in social media and in academia that have increased as the Chinese economy has skyrocketed past the imperialist economies.

* * *

Sara Flounders has been an anti-imperialist political activist and author committed to a socialist future for over 50 years. She is a contributing editor of the Workers World *newspaper and a leader of the International Action Center, the United National Antiwar Coalition, and the SanctionsKill Campaign.*

Communist Principles and Culture Drive China's Development for the Benefit of All Humanity

by Jacqueline Luqman

I recently spent ten days in China on a delegation with the Friends of Socialist China. The trip was organized by the China NGO Network for International Exchanges (CNIE) as part of the Fourth Dialogue on Exchanges and Mutual Learning Among Civilizations conference held in Dunhuang, hosted by the Chinese Association for International Understanding (CAIFU) and the People's Government of Gansu Province.

Convening the dialogue around the theme "Carrying Forward the Spirit of the Silk Road and Gathering Momentum for the Implementation of the Global Civilization Initiative," the three-day conference advanced CAIFU's mission of providing opportunities for people from other countries to learn about Chinese society, history, and culture. The history of and impact on society of China's socialist transformation from a feudal, agrarian, underdeveloped nation of impoverished peasants to the technological wonder and economic powerhouse it is today is a significant part of what China shares with the world. However, the intangible factors behind its socialist transformation are also seen when examining how the Communist Party of China (CPC) achieved it. Our delegation participated in the Dialogue and visited several cities in China: Shanghai, Xi'An, Yan'an, Dunhuang, and Jiayuguan City, where the culture of the Party and the Chinese people is reflected in each city's unique development. The values of the CPC that undergird Chinese society and connect the stories each of these cities tells not only explain how the ongoing development has been accomplished, but also give the world invaluable lessons on putting humanity at the center of government policy, and show us how that benefits the people of China and the world.

Communist Principles and Culture Constrain Capitalism in China

Capitalism exists in China, but the country and its economy are not reflective of "state capitalism," as some in the West have claimed. China is a communist country that engages in some capitalist economic ventures to fund its priorities. What's important to understand is what capitalism looks like in communist China and what priorities drive that engagement.

The CPC owns and operates state-owned enterprises (SOEs), which are large corporations that dominate key industries in strategic sectors of China's economy, such as energy (e.g., PetroChina, Sinopec), telecommunications (e.g., China Mobile, China Telecom), banking and finance (e.g., ICBC, Bank of China), transportation and infrastructure (e.g., China Railway, China State Construction), and defense and aerospace (e.g., AVIC, China North Industries Group).

The CPC manages those industries and establishes industrial priorities through economic planning. The CPC's social priorities are factored into how its economic plans are shaped, what is produced, marketed, and sold, and how the profits are used to benefit the people.

An example of such a venture is the Jiayuguan Iron & Steel Group Limited Company (JISCO), which we visited. JISCO was founded in

1958 and was one of the PRC's first state-owned industries. People of all levels of skill and education came from all over China to build and run JISCO, which has now grown to one of the major SOEs in China, providing the world with myriad steel products and an expanding line of other products from dairy to wine and spirits. However, the establishment of JISCO also led to the development of Jiayuguan, where the industry is located. A small, rural, and rugged area with little to no infrastructure to support the thousands of educated students, craftsmen, and workers who built the mining and manufacturing operation, Jiayuguan was transformed from a rugged company town built by the workers into a modern and cosmopolitan city.

JISCO has also expanded its operations to include real estate development, hospitality services, healthcare, higher education, power generation, and more, all under the control and regulation of the CPC. This has ensured that as JISCO has grown, the profits the company has made have not only gone to the diversification of the company's holdings, but also to the development of the city, the improvement of the quality and standard of living of its residents, and beyond.

The CPC Culture of Putting Workers First

An example of how the CPC focuses on the wellbeing of workers can be seen in the exhibition hall at JISCO Headquarters. It is dedicated to the history of the company and its numerous accomplishments, but it is also dedicated to the workers who accomplished a feat that continues to provide enduring benefit to the people of the city of Jiayuguan, to China, and to the world, all driven by the culture instilled in the people by the CPC.

Inside the main lobby of the JISCO headquarters, visitors encounter revolutionary pro-worker artwork that reflects the importance of

Communist Principles and Culture

workers and their sacrifice in building and growing the enterprise. A large bronze sculpture that represents the workers who came to the barren desert outpost to build JISCO and Jiayuguan dominates the entryway. The inscription "Hard work, Perseverance, Brave Sacrifice, Forge Ahead" reflects the culture that drove this development that those workers came from far and wide to carry out.

Beyond the beautiful and detailed artwork celebrating the accomplishment of the workers, the principles of CPC thought are accessible via kiosks at the beginning of the tour of the exhibition hall. The interactive kiosks allow visitors to learn about Mao Zedong Thought, Deng Xiaoping Theory, and the CPC's Scientific Outlook on Development. The ideals that drive the development of China and the continued expansion of that development beyond its borders are reflected here.

Furthermore, the CPC's Oath of Admission also adorns the main hallway, reflecting that the workers in JISCO commit to carrying out the Party's priorities. Even in the oath, the values and culture of the CPC are evident.

> "I volunteer to join the Communist Party of China, support the party's program, abide by the party's draft, fulfill the obligations of party members, implement the party's decisions, strictly observe the party's discipline, keep the party's secrets, be loyal to the party, work actively, fight for communism all my life, and be ready to sacrifice everything for the party and the people at any time, and never betray the party."

Visitors also see the Great Founding Spirit of the Party displayed, reflecting the key principles of the CPC:

Jacqueline Luqman

"坚持真理 (Jiānchí zhēnlǐ): Uphold the truth; 坚守理想 (Jiānshǒu lǐxiǎng): Hold firm to ideals; 践行初心 (Jiànxíng chūxīn): Practice the original aspiration; 担当使命 (Dāndāng shǐmìng): Undertake the mission; 不怕牺牲 (Bùpà xīshēng): Fearless of sacrifice; 英勇斗争 (Yīngyǒng dòuzhēng): Brave struggle; 对党忠诚 (Duì dǎng zhōngchéng): Loyal to the Party; 不负人民 (Bù fù rénmín): Live up to the people's expectations."

The success of JISCO and the beautiful city built around it testify to the enduring relevance and power of the CPC's culture—culture that is not based on imperialist lies about totalitarianism and the denial of human rights. The culture of the CPC is derived from the dogged struggle of a formerly oppressed people to fight and defeat oppression and fascism, to rebuild their country, and to improve the lives of their people through hard work, unity, and the pursuit of shared prosperity not just for themselves, but for all of humanity. This is also shown by the ongoing housing initiatives, which are a key focus of the CPC's culture of meeting the needs of the people.

Social Housing: An Ongoing Expression of the CPC's Priorities and Culture

The CPC's social housing policy is a key component of its social welfare system, designed to provide affordable housing for low- and middle-income individuals and families. Every housing plan reflects the Chinese government's commitment to ensuring housing security and improving living standards, which align with the broader CPC goals of social stability and harmonious development.

Communist Principles and Culture

China provides several forms of social housing to meet different needs and heavily subsidizes most for low-income and poor citizens. From young single workers to new families, migrant workers, and seniors, the CPC writes into its housing policy benchmarks to ensure that those with limited incomes have quality housing where they live.

There was a lot of mixed development in the five cities we visited. New high-rise apartment buildings had been built near obviously older developments, and sometimes even surrounded them. China has tried not to disturb existing housing during its incredible urban development in major cities. Still, it has not always been able to maintain the dilapidated and dangerous housing that some of the desperately poor lived in. Such dwellings have needed to be demolished to make way for the development of better housing. So while displacement is not an expected outcome of development in China, it does sometimes happen. But when it does, the government does not leave those people to fend for themselves, as is done in the U.S., where gentrification displaces the poor, usually driving many to homelessness.

The CPC is able to maintain and expand its housing programs, has eliminated homelessness, and lifted 800 million people out of crushing poverty through an intentional focus on ensuring housing for all people, with a prioritization of the poor and most vulnerable. The CPC plans housing projects for the entire country and sets construction targets, focusing on expanding affordable housing supply. Local governments then allocate land and subsidies for the social housing projects advanced in those plans. Public-private partnerships (PPP) also play a role, with private developers being required to include social housing in commercial projects. This is another fantastic aspect of the CPC's oversight of the housing market; real estate developers do not regulate themselves, and they do not dictate to the government what they will and will not do, or how much they will charge for housing. Rather, the CPC regulates the developers' actions, the housing prices, and how the housing is allocated. Affordable housing parameters—what "affordable" means—is not set by the developers like they are here in the U.S., where, in Washington, DC in particular, affordable housing might be based on a family of four with an income of $180,000, or an individual with an income of $80,000, when the average income for the poorest people in the city is less than $40,000, so none of us can actually afford housing designated as "affordable" by the developers.

Of course, there are contradictions in the Chinese system, because there is no such thing as a utopian society in any context, not even socialist or communist. Supply shortages are sometimes driven by high demand in major cities, leading to long waiting lists for the newer, modern housing under construction. But smaller cities may have excess supply; I saw some contemporary housing in a remote place like Yan'an, though most were older buildings. When I talked to a few people there, most said they didn't want too much of the newer development because they liked their "small town" feel. They preferred that as much existing housing be modernized as possible, rather than see new modern high-rise housing. So, regional desires can also differ from urban tastes.

Despite having the issues that all developing nations must face and all the negativity toward China from people in the West—particularly the U.S.—China's social housing policy plays a crucial role in reducing inequality. The CPC continues to refine the system to broaden access to affordable housing for migrant workers, young families, and single low-wage workers, contributing to social stability and economic growth for everyone. That's people-centered, human rights-driven politics, which is the essence of communism, and the foundational culture of the CPC.

CPC Development and Ideology

The central committee of the CPC and its principles were established in the mountains of Yan'an. The Yan'an Revolutionary Memorial Hall displays the development of CPC principles, thought, and policy, which is critically important to understanding the culture of China's government, its policies, and their impact on its people today.

One of the most illuminating exhibits in the museum is The Ten No's. They are the guidelines for the personal conduct of Central Committee members established during the Yan'an period. These rules established the culture of the CPC leadership and are connected to the principles of integrity, serving the people, party unity, learning from the masses, and self-reliance that are still part of the Party's guiding principles today. Even though these ten rules are not formally adopted into current CPC guidelines, the party still adheres to the Yan'an principles in carrying out anti-corruption and rectification efforts to maintain discipline and ideological commitment today under Xi Jingping.[1] Whatever criticism those in the West may have for China, the claim of a CPC full of corrupt, greedy capitalists is nothing more than projection from members and supporters of the most corrupt and anti-human governments on the planet.

Perhaps the most remarkable part of the CPC's culture is that it is not reserved for the advancement of the Chinese people alone. They share it with the world by welcoming people to visit China as tourists, by inviting people to attend conferences such as the Fourth Dialogue

---

1 The Press Office, International Department of the CPC Central Committee, "Fact Sheet on the Eight-Point Decision on Improving Party and Government Conduct," (Center for Americas, China International Communications Group, 2024).

Jacqueline Luqman

on Exchanges and Mutual Learning Among Civilizations, and most notably through the Belt and Road Initiative (BRI).

In a pamphlet from the China International Publishing Group, the different levels of impact the BRI has had over the ten years it has been implemented are outlined:

> "First, at the ideological level, the BRI is the first international cooperation initiative proposed by a developing country with global influence, puts an end to the original center-periphery international order, and is building a global partnership network of countries on an equal footing. Second, at the physical level, the BRI, jointly built by nearly 200 countries and international organizations, has connected more countries more deeply in the era of digital economy through infrastructure construction, and promoted global interconnection and close cooperation across the world, thus accelerating the modernization drive of these countries. Third, at the economic and trade level, the BRI hedges the downward pressure on the world economy through the liberalization and facilitation of trade, investment and finance, and has become the main engine driving global economic growth. Fourth, as to people's living standards, the BRI has effectively improved the well-being of the people. Fifth, the BRI is implementing the Global Development Initiative, Global Security Initiative and Global Civilization Initiative, and is effectively building a community with shared responsibilities, interests, and security development, health for all, and

of all life on the Earth, so as to build a community with a shared future for mankind."²

The recent China-Africa Changsha Declaration on Upholding Solidarity and Cooperation of the Global South is an example of China's continued commitment to these principles of its culture. The agreement was finalized in meetings held during the Fourth Dialogue on Exchanges and Mutual Learning Among Civilizations. It was announced mere days after the conference's conclusion in June of this year. The agreement states:

> "We will join hands in cementing the foundation of sovereign equality, maintaining that all countries, regardless of their size or strength, are equal members of the international community, and resolutely upholding international justice and order. We will continue to safeguard each other's legitimate rights and interests, stand side by side with mutual understanding and support amid chaos and changes, stabilize this uncertain world with the certainty of the China-Africa relationship, establish a benchmark for sincere friendship and equality in the Global South, and advocate an equal and orderly multipolar world."³

---

2 Liu Ying, "Ten Years into the Belt and Road Initiative: What It Has Brought to the World," ed. Zhang Donggang (Foreign Languages Press Company, Ltd, 2023), pp 5-6.
3 "China-Africa Changsha Declaration on Upholding Solidarity and Cooperation of the Global South," Ministry of Foreign Affairs of the People's Republic of China, June 11, 2025, https://www.fmprc.gov.cn/eng/zy/gb/202506/t20250611_11645736.html.

Jacqueline Luqman

China engages in this kind of collaboration with other countries because of the CPC's culture, which focuses on raising the standard of living of and facilitating the shared and equal development of all humanity. This culture of human-focused development and shared prosperity is still very much a part of China's model of governance today, and will continue to be the driving force behind CPC policy and China's role in the world for the foreseeable future.

* * *

Jacqueline Luqman is currently the chairperson of the Black Alliance for Peace Coordinating Committee, an international people-centered human rights group organizing against war, repression, and imperialism. Jacqueline is also a radio show host and journalist, anchoring the weekly show Darker Than Blue *on WPFW 89.3 FM, providing political commentary on the* Black Liberation Media *YouTube platform, and frequently contributing to radical independent publications such as* Black Agenda Report, Hood Communist, *and others. You can support her work on patreon.com/luqmannation.*

Completing the Original Mission: Reinvigorating Marxism in Contemporary China

by Ken Hammond

"Without revolutionary theory there can be no revolutionary movement."

—Lenin, *What Is to Be Done?*

In the summer of 2016 I was invited to teach a month-long course for MA students in History at Hebei Normal University in Shijiazhuang, the capital of Hebei Province, about 300 kilometers south of Beijing. The class was to focus on historical research methodologies and the state of historical education in the United States. The students were bright and eager to learn, very interested in how history was approached in America, and happy to discuss their own research interests in Chinese history. Over the first few days of classes, I talked about my own work as a Marxist historian, and the influence of historical materialist research methods on even non-Marxist scholars in the West. I referred to particular texts by Marx and Engels, such as the *Communist Manifesto*, the *Eighteenth Brumaire of Louis Napoleon*, and the "Preface to *A Contribution to the Critique of Political Economy*" as examples of how we could derive Marx's own working methods from these writings.

It quickly became clear that while the students had a basic recognition of the terms I was using, and had been exposed to information about Marx's writings, they had not actually read even so basic a text as the *Manifesto*. I was rather taken aback by this realization, and urged these young people to engage directly with the original writings of socialist thought and materialist analysis. We went on to have a very productive class, in which I learned as much from them as they did from me.

A couple of years later, in 2018, I was at a conference where a conversation developed among several people who had recently had similar experiences teaching in China. We exchanged ideas about why this might be the case, and sought to understand what seemed a peculiar situation in a socialist country. What seemed to make the most sense was that this was a reflection in the realm of political education of a larger phenomenon which had been characteristic of China's political culture over recent decades.

In the early 1990s, in the wake of the events of Spring 1989, as China was reviving the policies of Reform and Opening to the Outside in order to gain access to capital, technologies, information, and other resources needed for the rapid development of its economy, Deng Xiaoping famously urged the leadership of the Communist Party and the People's government to "bide their time and build their capabilities." In other words, to follow a course of accommodation with the United States and the wider world of global capitalism, to assume something of a low profile in terms of China's socialist project; not to place too much emphasis on the differences between China and the West, but also not to abandon the socialist path. This proved to be an effective strategy, and contributed to the remarkable era of growth in China's economy from 1992-2010 or so. It also, perhaps, encouraged a misconception among American political elites that China was on a path towards political transformation, and might become a subordinate component of the world capitalist system under American hegemony.

This period was also one in which there was a growing concern among some in China with what Wang Hui, a scholar at Tsinghua University in Beijing, called "depoliticized politics", the phenomenon of many ordinary people turning away from direct engagement with political affairs as they focused on improving their own life circumstances. Political affairs were instead left to those who wished to pursue them—essentially, the members of the Communist Party and government officials. One manifestation of this attitude, it seems, had been a reduction in political education, as a focus on innovation and creativity in scientific and technological fields became a more vital part of China's developmental program.

In July 2025 I returned to China for the first time since November 2019. First the Covid pandemic and then various professional and personal obligations repeatedly delayed a new visit. But in the Spring of 2025 I was invited to teach a one-week class at the School of Marxism at Shandong University, in Jinan, capital of Shandong Province. This proved to be a remarkable experience. I traveled first to Beijing, where I met with friends and colleagues at the Institute for Marxism at the Chinese Academy of Social Sciences (CASS), and at Renmin University, as well as non-academic contacts. In wide-ranging conversations one recurring theme was a concern about the need for the Party and the government to continue to exercise oversight over and restrain the activities of private capital. Everyone expressed pride in China's accomplishments, but also some anxiety about the future, and the need for vigilance in managing the processes of reform and development. The importance of dynamic leadership, and a commitment to the socialist path, seemed to be a priority. After a week of stimulating exchanges of ideas in the capital, I took the high-speed train to Jinan and settled in for a week of meetings and discussions in the classroom and around campus.

There were thirteen undergraduate students in the class, and I had been given a free hand at selecting the topics I wished to cover. I spent two days talking about my own work on China's historical political economy and the modern history of China and imperialist aggression, then two days discussing contemporary American politics, especially the role of Marx's concept of alienation in understanding the emergence of the radical far right and the phenomenon of Trump. A final class focused on eco-socialism. These were lively sessions, with students asking questions and presenting their own ideas.

It was clear from the start that this was a different conversation than the ones I had experience in 2016. Students had a much better grasp of Marxist concepts, and though they had not read widely, none having ventured into *Capital*, they were eager to engage with the material from the *1844 Manuscripts* and even the *Grundrisse* that I assigned. Only one was actually majoring in Marxism, but the others all saw an understanding of Marx as important in their own fields of interest. Several raised important points about reading texts which originated in the specific historical circumstances of mid-nineteenth century Europe. The challenges of reading Marx's style were also seen as something which needed to be taken into account. A recurring theme, central to not only the discussions in this class but to the way in which Marxist education is being approached in contemporary China, was the idea that we read Marx and Engels, Lenin and Mao, not as scripture or Classics, not to cull from their writings timeless truths which can simply be applied in any context, but rather that the focus of Marxist education must be on the dialectic of theory and practice, and on the application of Marx's analytical methodology, historical or dialectical materialism, to specific problems within the actually existing concrete material conditions. Students saw this as the essence of the concept of socialism with Chinese characteristics, socialism not as a blueprint or schematic, but as the living practice of investigation and analysis.

I talked about my earlier experience and my pleasure at finding these students so much more engaged with Marxism with two comrades at the university who were assigned to work with me. They gave me an overview of the state of Marxist education and its place within a wider process of re-emphasizing Marxism, Leninism, and Mao Zedong Thought within the Party, the government, and in society at large. The era of accommodation, of "biding time" and keeping a low profile, had come to an end with the election of Xi Jinping and Li Keqiang to leadership positions within the Party and the government in 2012. As China adopted a more confident posture in world affairs, and no longer deferred to American sensibilities in some areas, the new leadership began to stress the need, as Xi put it, to stay true to the original aspirations of the revolution, and to keep to the original mission. [不忘初心, 牢记使命 Bù wàng chūxīn, láojì shǐmìng] In other words, to always remember the socialist goals and to remain dedicated to the work of socialist construction. In a speech given on July 1, 2016, Xi made explicit the role that Marxism needed to play, noting,

> "This means we should continue to hold Marxism as our guiding philosophy, combine Marxist principles with the realities and circumstances of today's China, and push forward theoretical innovation. We should keep experimenting, so as to keep Marxism abreast of the times."

One of the clearest signals of the seriousness of this new orientation was a meeting of the Political Bureau of the Communist Party, held in April 2018, at which Party leaders read and discussed the *Communist Manifesto*. This meeting received wide coverage in the media and was meant to signal the seriousness with which the study of Marxism needed to be taken.

2018 was also the moment when institutions of higher education across China began to establish, or re-establish, schools of Marxism and Marxist studies. Over the following years more than 1,000 such schools, including the one at Shandong University, have been set up, and now enroll hundreds of thousands of students each year. Schools of Marxism offer courses in philosophy, political economy, history, and many other aspects of Marxist theory and practice. The school at Shandong University has its own multi-story building, which houses both classrooms and offices along with meeting rooms and a substantial library.

University-level schools of Marxism are an important part, but by no means the full extent, of a much broader movement of Marxist political education in China. In Beijing, the Chinese Academy of Social Sciences houses its own Institute for Marxism. This is a major research center, the second-largest unit within CASS, after the Institute of Archaeology. The Institute for Marxism supports 120 researchers, who work on a wide range of topics, including a lively interest in Marxism and socialism in other parts of the world. The Institute publishes four scholarly journals, two in Chinese and two in English. The English language journals are *World Socialism Studies* and *International Critical Thought*. The latter publishes work by foreign Marxist researchers as well. Academies of Social Sciences at the provincial or municipal level in various places also publish their own journals, including the English language review *Socialism Studies*.

Marxist political education goes well beyond the academic sphere. In tandem with the establishment of schools of Marxism at Chinese universities and the ongoing efforts of researchers and intellectual activists, there has been a significant effort to enhance the level of engagement and participation in social and economic life by the CPC in order to more effectively ensure the functioning of China's system of whole-process democracy. This involves both a renewed level of political education of cadres within the Party and a re-emphasis on the role of the Party in both guiding political affairs and in maintaining a close and dynamic engagement with the needs and interests of the people.

The Communist Party of China now has slightly more than 100 million members, which means that roughly one of every nine adults in China is in the Party. This is itself a very high level of political engagement. The CPC has, in the last decade, worked to ensure that Party members in all branches of the economy, including productive enterprises and financial institutions, and in various areas of social life, such as education or other professions, play active roles in the units to which they belong, whether as workers on the factory floor or in managerial or administrative positions. As China grapples with the challenges and contradictions of development in the context of the policies of Reform and Opening, the leadership has understood the need to manage and oversee the functioning of the system. To do this a thorough grasp of Marxist theory and materialist analytical methodologies has been seen as critical. Xi Jinping's writings, along with the contributions of many other thinkers and activists within and beyond the Party, have explored many aspects of this process. The reinvigoration of Marxism is not simply an intellectual exercise, but is central to the work of completing the original mission of the revolution.

* * *

Ken Hammond is professor emeritus of East Asian and global history at New Mexico State University. A lifelong radical political activist, he has worked and studied in China off and on since 1982. He received his PhD in history and East Asian languages from Harvard in 1994. He is currently a member of the Party for Socialism and Liberation, and works with Pivot to Peace. He returned to China in July 2025 to teach in the summer school at Shandong University.

2.
Socialist Planning in Practice
Infrastructure

Reflections on How China is Building Socialism

by Sydney Loving

This is an expanded version of an interview I gave to FightBack! News about the 2025 Friends of Socialist China delegation, which recently returned from a ten-day visit across five cities in China.

Traveling to China

The delegation was organized by Friends of Socialist China, a political project aiming to strengthen understanding and support for China on the basis of solidarity and truth. I repped Freedom Road Socialist Organization, and the delegation included folks from Black Alliance for Peace, Workers World Party, Progressive International, the Communist Party of Britain's Young Communist League, Black Liberation Alliance, Qiao Collective, Iskra Books, and others. We were invited by the China NGO Network for International Exchanges, and over ten days we visited Xi'an, Yan'an, Dunhuang, Jiayuguan, and Shanghai.

Traveling to a range of areas, we got to investigate how China is building socialism, saw the incredible advances they've made in seventy-six years of socialist construction, and had awesome dialogues about how we can better counter the negative narratives and Cold War-style lies we're bombarded with in the West. Ultimately what we found was a country led by a forward-thinking party of the people, with the purpose of carving out a better future for everybody.

China's Path of Development

To really understand how remarkable China's development is, you've got to understand the history and what life was like for most people. Before the revolution in 1949, China was totally devastated by imperialism and foreign occupation, brutal feudalism, man-made famines, warlordism, etc. Life expectancy in the rural areas was as low as twenty-four years. In Xi'an, we went to some ancient historical sites, and the terracotta generals and statues of noblewomen there were plump—because mass starvation was a feature of society for centuries. So socialism had all this to overcome.

We went to Yan'an, which was really the cradle of the revolution from 1935 to 1947. The Red Army re-grouped there after the Long March, and the CPC held its 7th National Congress there, (sixteen long years after the 6th Congress, because they were fighting Japanese imperialism and the KMT) where Mao Zedong Thought was crystalized. They fought against dogmatism and made the decision to be the party of the masses of Chinese people. When they built these political structures and elected the representatives to the Congress, they used a system of bowls and beans so people who couldn't read could vote for their chosen candidates.

Now, seventy-six years later, we saw a country with the largest economy in the world by purchasing power parity. Even smaller cities there are high-tech and increasingly green, life expectancy is over seventy-eight years, and of course, over 800 million people have been lifted out of extreme poverty—and we're not just talking by dollar amounts. We're talking guaranteed food, clothing, housing, electricity and water, healthcare, and education.

Capitalism is just not capable of that kind of project. They did it through central planning and mass mobilization. Every single city we visited showed how the Communist Party is guiding development that puts people first.

Differences in Daily Life

It really feels very different than cities in the U.S., even our biggest cities. The streets are clean, walkable, and well-organized despite how populous they are, to the point where moms and their kids would just walk across the intersections, confident that the cars would stop for them. There are lots of electric vehicles, and things are designed with the needs of the elderly, children, and workers in mind. Even at one of our hotels, the workers would all meet in the quad for a dance/exercise in the mornings. It was really peaceful but lively, with parks and gardens everywhere, and tons of free activities and access to culture and historical sites.

In Xi'an and Dunhuang especially, we saw how thousands of years of civilization are being preserved as part of people's living identity. And with internal tourism being a big deal, museums and sites were full of schoolkids, seniors, and families. To me it was clear that having history and culture belong to the people is part of the revolutionary spirit.

And unlike cities in the U.S., we saw almost no homelessness. In ten days, traveling around five cities, I saw just one person begging on the street with a QR code in the bottom of a pan. Compare that to San Francisco or New York, where you have entire neighborhoods of encampments.

Also, the technology was unreal, from little robots that take the elevator to deliver food to your hotel room to the airports where you just stand in front of a camera and it displays all your gate and flight info. Our hosts advised against us taking the always-on-time bullet train because we Westerners were too slow with all our luggage and definitely would've been late, but the normal train was awesome, too.

Touring Northwestern China

We went to Gansu Province, on the edge of the Gobi Desert, one of the most historically impoverished parts of China. But we were really blown away by what they're doing there.

In Jiayuguan, we visited JISCO, a state-owned steel company that the workers built the whole city around in the 1950s. Today, green areas cover 42% of the city, with ponds and parks. (Remember, this is the Gobi Desert.) It's a testament to the level of development of the productive forces that now JISCO even has a dairy farm and a winery with the largest indoor wine cellar in Asia. (Yes, we tasted the wine—delicious.) We also toured the Dunhuang molten salt solar power plant, which can store energy at night, and a smart grid AI control center that helps reduce carbon output across the province. We asked a worker there about the difference between how their power grid works vs. how ours works in the U.S., and he modestly said, "well our grid never goes down." That hit hard, being from Texas.

There's a big emphasis on ecological modernization. They're really transforming a desert into a livable, sustainable place. It's a testament to how poverty alleviation and environmentalism go hand in hand under socialism.

China is also proving that technology isn't inherently anti-human. In Shanghai we went to a robotics facility where they demonstrated the advancements for surgery and industry, and a Lenovo factory where they showed off how they're partnering with the school system to bring advanced tech into rural classrooms. The difference is who controls the technology, under what system, and for what purpose.

For China, development that leaves some folks behind means failure. That's why they focus on balancing the regions, uplifting the west and northwest instead of simply letting wealth accumulate on the coast. So after the success of the massive poverty alleviation projects (which even the UN can't deny) the next phase is "common prosperity".

The Electrical Grid

This is one place where the contrast with the U.S. really hits you. And it's not just about the tech; In the U.S., the grid is fragmented and everything is profit-driven, so electricity is treated as a commodity instead of a public good that human life depends on.

In terms of the grid, about 70% of transmission lines are past the lifespan they were built for. A lot of outages come from that—old poles and wires that nobody wants to pay to replace. The American Society of Civil Engineers actually gave our energy infrastructure a D+ in 2025.

Then you add fragmentation, which is why Texas set up its own system, ERCOT, basically to dodge federal oversight. That caused big problems during Winter Storm Uri in 2021 because we couldn't easily get power from other states. Generators froze, the natural gas supply failed, and they hadn't spent the money to winterize the system despite warnings after the 2011 freeze. In some places you had people getting billed for $9,000 per megawatt-hour, because the public utility commission removed the price cap on electricity during the freeze. In my city, Dallas, I remember the power being off for days and even weeks longer in the poorer neighborhoods. It was outrageous. People froze to death. Officially, 246 people died.

Puerto Rico is a colony of the U.S., and Hurricanes Irma and Maria in 2017 caused the longest blackout there in U.S. history. Some people didn't have power for nearly a year. The grid was privatized after that, but did it fix the problem? Of course not. There are still significant blackouts and much higher electricity prices than in the U.S. mainland. In 2022, a single fire at a substation knocked out the grid for the entire island. There are the same issues of deferred maintenance and the profit-driven contracts. The U.S. grid is basically held together with duct tape and prayers, and we know climate change is going to bring more extreme weather patterns—in fact, they're already here.

Now contrast that with China. Their grid is overwhelmingly public, and run by two massive SOE's: State Grid Corporation of China and China Southern Power Grid. They serve over a billion people, and because it's state-planned, they can do things to a scale and level of coordination that's difficult for us to imagine.

They built the largest ultra-high-voltage transmission system in the world. That means if you generate hydro in the southwest or solar in the northwestern desert, you can ship that power thousands of miles to wherever it's needed without huge losses. They're also rolling out the smart grids like the one we toured in Jiayuguan, that use AI to detect faults and reroute electricity in seconds. In Jiangsu province, their "self-healing" grid can restore power in under twenty seconds. Compare that to waiting hours, days or weeks after an outage in the U.S.

China's grid was tested recently, too, during the brutal 2022 heatwave and drought, when hydropower in Sichuan collapsed because reservoirs dried up. The system bent but it didn't break, and they managed rolling shortages, prioritizing residential users while they stabilized supply. Imagine Texas in 2021, but instead of mass death and chaos you had a centralized response that kept the lights on for most people.

In China, the grid is literally planned as part of their five-year national strategy. In the U.S., it's planned around whether private companies can make a profit.

And the numbers back it up. In 2024 alone, China added 373 gigawatts of renewable energy capacity. That's almost the total installed capacity of the entire U.S. electricity system. By the end of the year, renewables made up more than half their grid capacity—they're actually building the future grid at a breakneck speed.

So when that worker in Gansu told us "our grid never goes down," it wasn't bragging, it was stating a basic fact. Socialism in action.

The Role of the Communist Party in Daily Life

The Communist Party was everywhere. They just celebrated 100 million members (that's up from about 4 million members in 1949, by the way). Villages, hospitals, schools, and factories all have Party branches. In Jiayuguan we passed one of the 'party centers', where our guides told us people can go and ask questions or get help from cadres, even childcare.

Again, it's so different from political parties here. Local officials are graded on how well they serve the people, with the Party being a meritocracy in that sense. You can't buy your way into leadership like you can in political parties here in the U.S.

Actually, to rise the ranks in the Party, you have to demonstrate your dedication and service to the people. One Party member who was a teacher and an impromptu tour guide on our bus summed it up by saying it's a feeling of pride in how far they've come and in where they're going. And for good reason.

The CPC's presence isn't shadowy or abstract. It's doctors giving free checkups, committees organizing street sanitation, and workers shoring up safety conditions. It proves why they were able to defeat Japanese fascism and the KMT: because they were, and still are, deeply rooted in the masses.

Lessons for Revolutionaries in the U.S.

We know that monopoly capitalism is a dying system, so one of the lessons for everyone is that socialism works. This is real life, so it's not a utopia, and there are contradictions and improvements to be made in everything. But it's doing the most important work there is, which is lifting up people's lives and solving huge, complicated problems like poverty, climate change, and threats of war, with creativity and flexibility in changing times. If you get the chance, you should definitely visit and see for yourselves.

But it's not enough to just admire China. For revolutionaries here, we have to understand our tasks. The biggest obstacle to a peaceful, dignified future for everybody is U.S. imperialism. The same system that bombs Palestine, blockades Cuba, funds coups in Africa, and would like to wage war on China.

We are earning leadership in all the strands of the people's struggle and building a revolutionary movement at home, to create a party of the working class, rooted in the people, with the same agility and clarity of purpose that China's communists have shown for almost a century. That being said, there's no copy-pasting of China's path to development. We have to apply revolutionary science to our own conditions, time and place. Socialism is the future; in many respects, China is showing the way, but it's true for all of us. People in every corner of the world deserve to live with dignity and peace. We will get there if we fight for it.

* * *

Sydney Loving traveled to China as part of the 2025 Friends of Socialist China delegation. She is a member of the Central Committee of Freedom Road Socialist Organization and co-chairs the National Alliance Against Racist and Political Repression.

Between the Rust Belt and the Model City

by Paweł Wargan

Those of us who were born in the ruins of the socialist Eastern Bloc know how purpose-built, industrial "monotowns" are meant to look.

Rusting steel mills, cracked and potholed roads, weathered sheets of corrugated metal strewn about. Thick smog and poisoned soil. Drunks passed out on the train platform. Emaciated stray dogs. A lone child skipping down the muddy path of a panel-block neighbourhood silenced by demographic blight.

In their commodified form, packaged for mass consumption in computer games and television shows, these images of post-socialist decay serve a purpose. They beat down the idea that socialism can produce anything but misery. And they have become so firmly embedded in the popular imagination that, for many, it is difficult to believe otherwise.

Of course, many of these cities were conceived as the opposites of the dark imaginaries later built around them.

To this day, we can find shadows of the ideal in Poland's Nowa Huta, the sprawling Krakow neighbourhood built around the Vladimir Lenin Steelworks; Russia's Magnitogorsk, built around its eponymous Iron and Steel Works; or Germany's Eisenhuttenstadt, established by the socialist German Democratic Republic around a major steel mill combine.

Each aspired to be a model city—a template for the dignified life that communism envisioned for all working people. Each had green parks, good housing, abundant public services, and wide roads whose grandeur and neat symmetries recalled the genteel boulevards of Haussmannian Paris.

But capitalist restoration shattered their ambitions. Vibrant industrial cities saw their mills and factories chopped and diced and sold off at bargain prices. Economies underpinned by planned industrialisation were transformed overnight into sites of desperate labour and cheap resources, where value was siphoned upwards, to the emergent national oligarchies, then outwards to Wall Street or the City of London.

With that shift came an explosion in unemployment and an assault on society's support systems: housing, healthcare, leisure, education, catering, and so on. The model cities became grayer. The metal rusted and the plaster began to flake off the walls. People left; many died. Then, these hollowed spaces became captive to imaginaries of failure established to keep a defeated people from ever seeking their sovereignty again.

How might these cities look today had the process of socialist construction continued uninterrupted? I found one possible answer in Jiayuguan, a remote desert city in China's Gansu Province, built from the ground up around a steel plant.

In 1955, less than a decade after the Chinese Revolution, prospectors from Team 645 of the North-west Geological Bureau discovered major iron ore deposits in the Hexi Corridor of the snow-capped Qilian Mountains. Over 1,500 people would be called to the expedition, and 11 lost their lives.

With the discovery of iron, a vision emerged that would transform this barren patch of desert—once a strategic outpost on the ancient

Silk Road, the western terminus of the Great Wall, and the threshold of the Gobi Desert—into a cornerstone of regional development.

The Jiuquan Iron and Steel Corporation (JISCO) was founded in 1958 as part of revolutionary China's ambitious drive to establish the basis of a modern, industrialised economy.

It was a gruelling effort. At the heels of a century of humiliation, protracted civil war, and long struggle against Japanese occupation, China lacked basic technologies and know-how. Workers who came to the region dug the earth with their hands, trudged through waist-high mud, and carried heavy equipment on their backs. They faced the desert's biting cold and punishing heat. It took the nascent industry more than a decade to break even.

But development continued, and the steel plant soon began reshaping the political geography of the region. The administrative boundaries were redrawn to create Jiayuguan City, carved from parts of surrounding counties and placed under provincial jurisdiction.

Now, where once there was desert stands China's fourteenth-largest steel producer. It has an annual capacity of over 11 million tons of crude steel—double the total steel-making capacity of Britain. JISCO has manufactured everything from the steel Apple logo on the back of the iPhone to the lattice shell and steel trussed columns of the "Bird's Nest" National Stadium in Beijing.

The state enterprise has expanded its activities far beyond metals, to agricultural products and industrial manufacturing equipment, packaging and logistics, housing and healthcare, education and even wine.

The largest wine cellar in Asia is found at the Zixuan Winery near the Jiayuguan steel mills. The winery was the first in China to receive both national and international organic certifications, winning several awards in the process. (Having first tried Chinese wine as recently as a decade ago—and knowing that wines are notoriously slow to improve given the frequency of harvests—I was taken aback by the delicious, plummy and well-rounded merlot made here.)

JISCO also manages the city's power grid. Its Smart Grid and Localised New Energy Consumption Demonstration Project, powered almost entirely by artificial intelligence, automatically distributes energy, optimising for consumption patterns in real-time.

Despite JISCO's expanded production capacity and Jiayuguan's rising living standards, energy consumption has decreased thanks to investments in efficiency—a decoupling of growth from energy use that many experts in the West say is impossible.

JISCO's industrial waste is collected and used to make the tiles that cover the city's broad pavements and public squares.

Alongside the industry, Jiayuguan City continued to develop. In many ways, the process mirrored efforts to build socialist industrial towns across the Eastern Bloc. But there is a crucial difference: Jiayuguan's development was never interrupted, never subjected to the shock therapy of capitalist restoration.

Today, Jiayuguan is so unlike how we might expect a purpose-built industrial city to look. It is clean. Its green boulevards are lined with trees and neatly-trimmed hedges. Broad cycling lanes line the city's well-paved roads, and new apartment blocks—buildings that might well be considered luxury housing in the West—rise against the backdrop of mountain peaks to house the city's growing worker population. Trees cover some 40 per cent of this desert land and many of the city's scenic parks are built around large, cerulean lakes.

On my last day in Jiayuguan, I told a local teacher that it was moving, coming from a part of the world that had lost its socialist path, to see a place where the story of the model city continues to be written. Jiayuguan offered proof that the images of decay and despair that many have come to associate with industrial cities in Eastern Europe were not products of their socialist past, but symptoms of their capitalist present.

"China not only learned from the experiences of Eastern Europe," he told me. "China saved socialism." I asked how he felt about the changes his city had seen in the past few decades. His eyes smiled and he responded with seven words that we who call ourselves communists desperately wish to hear from all humanity: "I am satisfied, and I am proud."

* * *

Paweł Wargan is a researcher and writer from Poland. He serves as political coordinator for the Progressive International, a global coalition of left organisations. There, among other roles, he leads the People's Academy—a Marxist political education program. His writing has been published in Monthly Review, Morning Star, Verso, Tribune, *and* Peace, Land, and Bread, *among other publications.*

A Tale of Two Economic Systems' Transit

by Betsey Piette

While I have yet to visit China, one of its technological achievements that particularly interests me is the expansive transportation system, which includes the "bullet trains" connecting Beijing to dozens of other major Chinese cities, and the metro subways developed within those cities to meet the transportation needs of workers. Five of the ten largest metro networks in the world are in China. I was motivated to write about them after witnessing the recent, contrasting changes to U.S. transit systems.

In late 2022, my partner and I decided to sell our house in a Philadelphia border suburb and rent an apartment in the city. We made several trips through Philadelphia, armed with a map produced by the Southeast Pennsylvania Transit Authority (SEPTA), that showed all the transportation routes available in each area of the city. We wanted to be within walking distance of a train or bus that would give us access to Center City.

We found an apartment complex within a short distance of not one, but two Regional Rail lines and five bus routes. Fast forward to today, after the cuts in Pennsylvania's funding for SEPTA, only one of those bus routes remains. As of January 1, 2026, the closest Regional Rail line into the center of the city will no longer exist. Ours is not an isolated area; we live close to a major university, and across from a K-12 school.

A Tale of Two Economic Systems' Transit

As I write this essay, the first round of SEPTA's threatened draconian cuts went into effect on August 24, 2025. Thirty-two of their 150 bus routes were eliminated, and 16 others were shortened. The 88 remaining buses, trolleys and subways now have reduced services with fewer daily trips. Starting September 2, fewer trains will run on the subway/elevated rail system. Fares will increase to $2.90 one way—one of the two highest of all U.S. metro areas. Beginning in January 2026, five Regional Rail lines will be eliminated, and all metro and regional lines will stop service at 9 p.m. every night.

Philadelphia, and its surrounding counties, are the sixth-largest urban area in the United States with a population of 4 million people. The cuts impact over 50,000 high school students who depend on public transportation to get to school. Philadelphia is a college town, so the impact on universities will be huge. Millions of workers in the region are left without means of getting to and from work. Seniors will be unable to get to doctor appointments. Thousands of SEPTA workers face layoffs as the cuts take effect.

Yet in 2026, as the first U.S. capital, Philadelphia will be the center of events celebrating the 250th anniversary of the signing of the Declaration of Independence. The city is scheduled to host several major sporting events including six FIFA World Cup matches, the 2026 Major League Baseball All Star Games, the first and second rounds of the National Collegiate Athletic Association Men's Basketball Tournament, and the 108th Professional Golfers' Association Championship. Just how participants will get to and from these events, given SEPTA's deep cuts, remains a mystery.

Philadelphia is Not Unique

SEPTA claims that the lack of $213 million in support from Pennsylvania makes cuts up to 50% through 2026 a necessity, on top of a 20% increase in fares. It is possible that the state legislature, or even the city, will find a solution to the cuts, but the transit crisis in Philadelphia is not unique.

Over 45% of people, especially in rural and suburban areas in the U.S., lack access to public transit services. Where services exist, there are an inadequate number of routes, infrequent service, and antiquated trains and rail structures. Cities throughout the U.S. opened very little transit access in 2024, adding just 29 kilometers (18 miles) of light rail and no new metro rail service.[4]

U.S. mass transit systems, including those in Boston, Washington, and the Bay Area face imminent funding gaps. Mass transit in Chicago, the third-largest U.S. city with a broader metropolitan population of 9.5 million, has a deficit of hundreds of millions of dollars. If the Illinois legislature does not act, half the branches of the Chicago Transit Authority L will stop, and 74 bus routes will be eliminated.[5]

This all comes at a time when President Donald Trump's administration has reduced federal support for public transit with a 98% cut to transit capital investment grants, bringing a halt to projects intended to provide improved subways, bus lines and rapid transit.

---

4 Yonah Freemark, "Transit Project Openings in 2025: A Global Review," *The Transport Politic*, January 12, 2025, https://www.thetransportpolitic.com/author/yonah-freemark/.

5 Thomas Fitzgerald, "SEPTA's Massive Cuts Are Here and It's 'Bad on so Many Levels,'" *The Philadelphia Inquirer*, August 24, 2025, https://www.inquirer.com/transportation/septa-cuts-take-effect-sunday-20250824.html.

A Tale of Two Economic Systems' Transit

Discretionary funding for Amtrak's national network, including the Northeast Corridor, has been eliminated.

At the same time, Trump proposed a 13% increase in defense spending for fiscal 2026, increasing Pentagon spending to over $1 trillion. Just .002% of the military's budget would cover SEPTA's shortfall. Expenditures for the U.S. military, Homeland Security, and the Immigration and Customs Enforcement could pay for transit systems across the U.S., but under our capitalist system, this isn't going to happen.

More Roads, More Cars, More Pollution

Through April 30, 2025, U.S. states committed $202 billion in highway and bridge funds to support over 96,000 new projects, increasing roadway lane-miles by 28,500. More highways lead to more cars on the road, producing more pollution. With significant backing from the oil and gas industry, it is no surprise that Trump is pushing for an expansion of natural gas production, a major contributor to rising levels of greenhouse gas emissions. At the same time, Trump has eliminated tax breaks for electric vehicles.

China Surges Ahead

Over a year ago, I happened to watch a YouTube video produced by Living in China about the advances that China was making in mass transit.[6] This piqued my interest, and I wanted to know more.

In July, the Philadelphia Workers World Party hosted an event

---

6 *America CAN'T Compete with China's Infrastructure!*, Living in China, February 3, 2023, 00:10:23, https://www.youtube.com/watch?v=ul5rqQGaLQ4.

in Philadelphia with Dee Knight, author of *Befriending China: People-to-People Peacemaking*, in which Knight writes:

> "[Shanghai's] Underground, the metro hums along; more than 20 lines rival the extent of New York's MTA, and humble it for cleanliness, courteous service and safety. All the stations have escalators, elevators, and super clean floors. They also have moving barriers between the passenger platforms and incoming and outgoing trains, to protect the riders."[7]

Knight described the bullet train that nearly "flew" from Shanghai to Beijing in just four hours—covering about the same 793-mile distance from New York to Chicago:

> "These bullet trains now connect all of China's major cities, following the gigantic infrastructure projects of recent decades. The U.S. has no bullet trains, and cannot seem to find the financing for them, especially since the profit potential in military production is so much higher. Europe has some very good fast trains among about a dozen cities, but none is as fast as those in China."[8]

China has built the most extensive and fastest-expanding transit system in the world, starting in 1969 with the Beijing Subway. With over 50 cities operating networks and more under construction, today

---

7 Dee Knight, *Befriending China: People-to-People Peacemaking* (Solidarity Publications, 2025), 31.
8 Knight, *Befriending China: People-to-People Peacemaking*, 34.

A Tale of Two Economic Systems' Transit

China's urban rail transit has become a cornerstone of its infrastructure development. China has five of the world's ten largest metro systems, surpassing two of the oldest transit systems in the world—London's Underground, inaugurated in 1863, and New York City's Subway Metro, built in 1906.[9]

China's systems include the **Shanghai Metro**—topping the list of the world's longest rapid transit rail systems. It began operation in 1993, serving both urban and suburban municipal districts for one of China's largest cities, handling 10 million passengers daily. It stretches 365 miles, including 508 stations across 20 lines. The system plans to add additional lines and connect two other systems in Jiangsu province in the coming years.

Constructed in 1969, China's 345-mile-long **Beijing Subway** is the second-longest rapid transit system in the world. It now encompasses most districts in Beijing, with 18 lines that serve 334 stations, carrying just over 9 million passengers a day, with a total of 3.25 billion passengers per year—making it the world's busiest rapid transit system.

Beijing, as China's capital city with over 22 million residents, is a major hub attracting tourists and hosting numerous international and national sporting events, including both the Summer and Winter Olympics in 2022. To meet Beijing's growing needs for transit, there are plans to add 650 more miles.

Opened in December 2004, the **Shenzhen Metro** is the world's fifth-largest metro system. The massive underground network currently

---

9 Zee Media Bureau, "Top 10 Largest Metro Networks In The World Including Delhi Metro: 831 Km, 508 Stations, 20 Lines And More; Check Full List," *Zee News*, July 15, 2025, https://zeenews.india.com/photos/mobility/top-10-largest-metro-networks-in-the-world-including-delhi-metro-831-km-508-stations-20-lines-and-more-check-full-list-2932259.

stretches for over 300 miles, in the city of Shenzhen in Guangdong Province. The newest lines opened in December 2024, expanding the network to 369 miles. In 2017, Shenzhen also became China's first city to electrify 100% of its 16,000 buses, cutting carbon emissions by 48%.

Opened in 1967, China's fourth-largest transit system is the **Guangzhou Metro**. The 150-mile-long subway has 16 lines serving 302 stations. Daily passenger counts average around 6.2 million. Since 1997, the Guangzhou Metro has offered free rides to transit workers and their immediate families.

Opened in 2005, the 140-mile-long **Nanjing Metro** rapid transit system is located in the Jiangsu Province of China, servicing the city of Nanjing. The system has 6 lines with 121 stations and includes 202 rail cars. The daily passenger count was as high as 2.248 million. Future plans include expansion lines to connect to He County and Anhui Province.

In addition, China's high-speed rail network connects major cities across the country. The largest globally, it spans just under 25,000 miles.

An article by *HROne* titled "Public Transportation in China" addressed the rapid gains that China has made in public transit: "As of 2023, the nation is home to over 1,000 cities with public transit systems that include buses, subways, and light rail" that "served approximately 12 billion passengers in 2022." *HROne* notes that public transit in China has helped alleviate congestion while reducing pollution.[10]

The article references a study by the multinational professional services network Deloitte that found that "investments in public

---

10 HROne Team, "Public Transportation in China: An Efficient Journey," *HROne*, March 26, 2025, https://hrone.com/blog/public-transportation-in-china-an-efficient-journey/.

transportation can yield considerable economic returns, with every dollar spent potentially generating up to four dollars in economic activity."

The demand for skilled workers in China's public transportation is projected to rise by 20% in the next five years.[11] The affordability of China's public transit—with fares as low as 30 to 80 cents (U.S.) helps households save up to 25% of their monthly incomes by reducing reliance on cars. Jusha.travel notes that the HSR, by linking smaller cities and regions to major hubs like Beijing and Shanghai, has reduced travel times by up to 70%. This has enabled labor mobility, tourism growth, supply chain efficiency, and saves roughly $20 billion annually in congestion-related economic losses.[12]

China's public transit systems have had a positive impact on the environment, with the widespread use of electronic buses. The rate of electrification of China's railways is 75.2%—significantly reducing carbon emissions by 30% over the last five years, according to a recent report by the China Academy of Transportation Sciences. China plans to electrify 80% of buses and taxis by 2025 through government subsidies of over $14 billion.[13]

Motivation for Transport Developments— U.S. Versus China

No essay on China's mass transit systems, especially when compared to those in the U.S., would be complete without understanding what motivated these developments.

---

11 HROne Team, "Public Transportation in China: An Efficient Journey."
12 "Jusha," Jusha, 2025, https://jusha.travel/.
13 HROne Team, "Public Transportation in China: An Efficient Journey."

In the U.S., war and spending for infrastructure development are closely linked. Historically the U.S. government prioritized improvements in supply chain infrastructure, including transit, when it benefited the U.S. military. The Civil War, for example, significantly increased the use of railroads. In January 1862, President Abraham Lincoln gave the U.S. Military Railroad, established through the U.S. War Department, the authority to seize control of the railroads for military use. The USMRR restricted its authority to Confederate rail lines captured during the war, giving the Union a strategic military advantage over the Confederacy.

Construction on the first transcontinental railroad began soon after the war and was completed in May 1869. The expanded rail system played a significant role in the westward expansion of U.S. imperialism, including the theft and occupation of Indigenous lands and the genocide of Indigenous peoples, and the near-annihilation of the native buffalo.

The First Transcontinental Highway

In 1956, during the Cold War with the Soviet Union, President Dwight D. Eisenhower signed legislation to fund construction of the interstate highway system, officially known as the National System of Interstate and Defense Highways. Between then and 1990, around 45,000 miles of new interstate roads were constructed, using $119 billion in federal funds.

As an Army Lt. Colonel in 1919 after World War I, Eisenhower had observed the First Transcontinental Motor Convoy, a military experiment in moving troops from coast to coast in the U.S. that confronted a patchwork system of paved and unpaved roads, aging bridges too low for trucks to pass under, and mountain roads too narrow for two-way traffic. During World War II, Eisenhower observed the far superior German Autobahn system, which included national highways connecting all parts of that country.

'Red Scare' Highways

When Eisenhower was president, the construction of the first mammoth coast-to-coast highway construction in the U.S. was fueled by the "Red Scare"—the perceived threat of nuclear war after the Soviet Union developed an atomic bomb as protection against the U.S., which had used this weapon in Japan in 1945. In 1954, Eisenhower appointed West Point-trained engineer Lt. Gen. Lucius Clay to promote the highways. The "Clay Committee" pushed the multibillion-dollar plan by generating public fear and arguing the highways were essential for emergency evacuation of large cities and quick movement of troops in the event of a nuclear attack.

Touted as "modern marvels," the interstate highways resulted in the forced removal of over 475,000 households to make way for construction of the system. A majority of those displaced lived in low-income urban communities with high concentrations of Black, Latine, Indigenous and immigrant people.

Military interests served to promote domestic infrastructure development during the rise of U.S. global imperialism, but over time, military spending became a drain on resources vital for domestic programs. Nowhere is this more evident than in the current state of U.S. infrastructure. As the U.S. nears its 250th anniversary, capitalism's decline is evidenced by the inability to develop infrastructure expansion to benefit the population.

Betsey Piette

China: Human Needs Prioritized

The People's Republic of China, now 75 years old, has prioritized the human needs of its population, in planned efforts to lift people out of poverty. It has invested heavily in mass transit and electronic vehicles including trains, buses, cars and scooters. Rather than driven by profit or the need for military expansion, the evolution of China's public transportation system stemmed from the need for rapid urbanization coupled with the centralized planning that propelled China following the 1949 revolution.

During the period between 1949-1978, resources were directed toward development of industry and agriculture. Transportation in China consisted of overcrowded buses, limited rail infrastructure, and reliance on bicycles and foot traffic. Economic reforms in the 1980s depended on migration to urban cities like Beijing and Shanghai that became overwhelmed with traffic congestion and pollution.

A shift after the introduction of market-oriented policies came in the 1990s as the government increased infrastructure spending. The Communist Party of China had already prioritized metro systems, building Beijing's first subway line in 1969, with rapid expansion in the 2000s. The Beijing Olympics in 2008 spurred modernization, with investments in high-capacity transit, and smart technologies. Long-term government planning, including the Medium-and Long-Term Railway Network Plan of 2004, opened the way to build the world's largest high-speed rail network.

The systems created since then in over 50 cities are not only a testament to China's engineering prowess, but also a critical solution to the challenges of urbanization, traffic congestion and pollution. China's planners understand that mass transit effectively alleviates traffic congestion and reduces pollution, thus contributing to more sus-

A Tale of Two Economic Systems' Transit

tainable cities. While some of the systems are aging, and accessibility and overcrowding remain problems, China continues to innovate and invest in sustainable solutions.

These are all questions of priority. Do the needs of the people—transportation, health care, education, and so on—come first, as they do in China, or does the drive for profits from the military-industrial complex, as it does in the U.S.?

In a letter to the editor of the *Philadelphia Inquirer* in September of 2025, regarding the SEPTA cuts, W.B. Lowry, a student at Temple University Beasley School of Law, suggests that it may be time to internationalize the fight for Philadelphia's transit network by reaching out to the People's Republic of China for a grant to fund SEPTA:

> "As the United States undertakes a retreat from its position of global leadership, many observers are wondering if we are at the cusp of the "Chinese Century." China is funding infrastructure projects all over the world as part of its "Belt and Road initiative," and China's dynamic domestic infrastructure projects make a stark contrast with America's crumbling public roads and our woefully inadequate national railway network. There is a real opportunity for China to cement its status as a world leader by stepping up to help SEPTA riders, who have been abandoned by our own government. There are also the historic ties between the city of Philadelphia and China: Temple University was one of the first American schools to establish academic ties with China in the late 1970s and maintains a vibrant academic relationship with Chinese universities today.

The question remains whether our request will be enough to motivate our state government to finally do its job, but SEPTA is too important to the region to let it collapse without exhausting every possible avenue to secure funding."[14]

* * *

Betsey Piette is a managing editor and regular contributor to Workers World *and an organizer for the Workers World Party in Philadelphia, where she has lived since 1985. She is active in the Philadelphia Palestine Coalition, Mobilization4Mumia, and other community groups struggling against capitalist oppression. In 2012, she won Cuba's 10th annual "Thinking Against the Mainstream" international essay contest for her essay "Drilling into the abyss: Why hydraulic fracturing is not a solution for global energy needs or global warming."*

---

14 W.B. Lowry, letter to the editor, *The Philadelphia Inquirer*, Septermber 7, 2025, https://reader.inquirer.com/infinity/article_popover_share.aspx?guid=50ae587d-7a70-40fb-8d0a-549ada8813fb.

Steel Tracks vs War Tracks: China Builds Subways and Aids Gaza While the U.S. Builds Militarism

by Lee Siu Hin and Kening Zhang

While both the U.S. and China face immense challenges in governing vast nations and maintaining complex infrastructure, the outcomes and priorities they exhibit are strikingly different. The following is a first-person account by Mr. Lee Siu Hin, compiled and edited by Kening Zhang.

Every time I take a flight from Shanghai to Los Angeles, or Ürümqi to New York City, what gives me the biggest shock is the comparison between the filthy, unsafe, and inefficient New York City Subway and the cleaner, safer, and more modern Chinese metro systems in Shanghai and Ürümqi.

According to the New York City Council, the NYC subway's operating budget is $10.79 billion for 2025.[15] The system has 665 miles (1,070 km) of track, which means approximately $16.2 million is spent on each mile of subway track ($10.1 million/km)

---

15 New York City Council Committee on Transportation & Infrastructure, "Report on the Calendar Year 2025: Adopted Budget and the 2025-2028 Financial Plan of the Metropolitan Transportation Authority," New York City Council, March 2025, https://council.nyc.gov/budget/wp-content/uploads/sites/54/2025/03/Metropolitan-Transportation-Authority.pdf.

annually.[16] According to Chinese media reports, the operating budget of the Shanghai Metro in 2024 was approximately $73 million for 557 miles (896 km), or approximately $131,100 per track mile ($81,400/km).[17] The average operational cost per mile for the NYC subway is over 120 times that of the Shanghai Metro. Even the NYPD's 2025 budget of $5.75 billion for subway security is a whopping 7.88 times the entire annual budget of the Shanghai Metro.[18]

Even though the NYC subway system allocates disproportionately large sums of money for security, there were still ten murders in the subway in 2024, according to the NYPD.[19] There were also at least thirty hate crimes against Asian Americans on the NYC subway in

---

16 Metropolitan Transportation Authority, "Comprehensive Annual Financial Report for the Years Ended December 31, 2018 and 2017," Metropolitan Transportation Authority, June 26, 2019, 156, http://web.mta.info/mta/investor/pdf/2019/2018_CAFR_Final.pdf.

17 Shentong Metro Group's (operator of the Shanghai Metro) revenue in 2024 was 586 million yuan, up by 45.89% compared to the previous year. Its net profit was 51.8186 million yuan, down by 24.94% year-on-year. The gross profit margin decreased by 2.20 percentage points. (*Sina Finance*, March 27, 2025, https://baijiahao.baidu.com/s?id=1827745466045792228&wfr=spider&for=pc.)

18 轨道文化 (Track Culture), "28家地铁公司营收及利润排行榜出炉 (Revenue and profit rankings of 28 subway companies have been released)," 轨道文化 (Track Culture), May 16, 2025, https://mp.weixin.qq.com/s?__biz=MzIwNjg0MDIzMg==&mid=2247579703&idx=2&sn=a02a4dbb63a1697a2a698f38723b2d93&chksm=96585d20ebcf1cbc0721116de352e468faf5ab9b-29f972b6b8ab3dcbbe21d9f77d4f803ae75f&scene=27.

19 Ben Brachfeld, "Are N.Y.C. Subways Dangerous? What the Statistics Show After Recent High-Profile Attacks," *People*, January 6, 2025, https://people.com/subway-crime-statistics-show-incidents-down-despite-high-profile-incidents-8769805.

2021,[20] and a hate killing of a Chinese woman in a subway station in January 2022.[21] Violent crimes in the Chinese subway system are virtually unheard of.

Because I fear for my safety, I never stand near the edge of the subway platform and always choose to ride in the car where the conductor is located. Public transportation is considered one of the most important services a city offers and one that should have the public's trust in the government, since everyone needs to use it for work or travel.

A city should provide a reliable, safe, and clean metro or bus system for everyone to improve quality of life, save commuting time and money, and reduce their carbon footprint. This stark contrast in safety outcomes reveals the institutional logic behind resource allocation: **capital interests consistently outweigh public safety investments, and the military-industrial complex diverts funds meant for people's livelihoods. Even massive security expenditures cannot conceal systemic failure.**

This stark contrast in public transportation reflects a broader divergence in national priorities between China and the United States.

It's not only Shanghai that is a showcase of China's urban development. Ürümqi, the capital of the Xinjiang Uyghur Autonomous Region in western China, is also a city with well-developed infrastructure and a clean and safe subway system. It is completely different from the image painted in the hostile, anti-China narratives

---

20 Jose Martinez, "2021 Saw Another Surge of Anti-Asian Hate Crimes in Subway," *The City*, January 4, 2022, https://www.thecity.nyc/2022/01/04/2021-saw-another-surge-of-anti-asian-hate-crimes-in-subway/.

21 Rafu Staff, "Subway Killing Shocks Asian Americans Coast to Coast," *The Rafu Shimpo*, January 20, 2022, https://rafu.com/2022/01/subway-killing-shocks-asian-americans-coast-to-coast/.

of the U.S. and the West. Their image of Xinjiang is of an open-air concentration camp with horrific genocide. The truth is, Ürümqi **is cleaner, safer, more developed, and enjoys greater ethnic harmony than New York City.**

The reality of Ürümqi, with its modern infrastructure and visible development, presents a direct challenge to the prevailing narrative in Western media. New York exemplifies the U.S.'s infrastructure failures, reflecting systemic inefficiency, waste, and corruption. In contrast, the Chinese government is people-centered and emphasizes efficient public service. While China is not free from corruption or bureaucratic inefficiency, it nevertheless demonstrates greater effectiveness in serving its citizens compared with the U.S.

Another good example is MacArthur Park, a low-income immigrant community west of downtown Los Angeles, where we have organized many activist projects in the past. For the last thirty-five years, except for the construction of one new LA Metro line and a few new and expensive commercial buildings and condos, it has seen little change, and in many ways has deteriorated, because the surrounding buildings and community are also deteriorating. Last July, ICE and the military made a sweep through the MacArthur Park area, sending fear and insecurity through the community. On the other hand, in Shanghai's Huaihai Road district, over the past thirty years, many old neighborhoods have been rebuilt or refurbished, making it more livable and transforming it into an attractive commercial center.

The U.S. has a capitalist-centered economy, so everything is geared to maximizing corporate profits as the ultimate goal. Subsidizing the military-industrial complex and fueling endless bloody wars around the world has also effectively become part of the U.S.'s economic planning. According to the National Priorities Project, the actual U.S. military budget is **$2,700 billion**, equaling 50% of the entire U.S.

government budget based on Trump's Fiscal Year 2026 proposal.[22] It is larger than the world's next four largest defense budgets (China, Russia, Germany, and India) combined.[23]

The question arises: how is this funding allocated?

It is used for mass surveillance, targeting inner-city immigrant communities of color, and providing weapons to far-right Ukrainian forces and the Israeli military in operations that result in civilian casualties, including children, around the world. As a result, the U.S. lacks the financial, technical, and human resources to rebuild its aging infrastructure and industrial base.

In contrast, there is the success of China's countless infrastructure projects over the past several decades—not only the gigantic power stations, hydroelectric dams, and intercity high-speed railroads, but also many other urban public projects that bring better living conditions to everyone. These include clean and convenient subway systems, affordable housing for the poor, jobs with living wages, crime- and hate-free communities, rural development, and green technologies.

It's not just that the U.S. can't and China can, but rather **it is the fundamental difference between the Chinese government prioritizing people's needs, and the U.S. making corporate greed its ultimate goal.**

---

22 War Resisters League, "Where Your Income Tax Money Really Goes FY2026," *War Resisters League*, March 2025, https://www.warresisters.org/store/where-your-income-tax-money-really-goes-fy2026/.

23 Pallavi Rao, "Ranked: Top 15 Countries by Military Budgets in 2025," *Visual Capitalist*, June 27, 2025, https://www.visualcapitalist.com/ranked-top-15-countries-by-military-budgets-in-2025/.

How Racism Continues to Shape U.S. Policy

This doesn't mean there have been no new developments in New York or Los Angeles over the past thirty years, but it does indicate that these developments have mainly happened in the wealthy white neighborhoods at the expense of the poor people of color who are their neighbors. This process is called "**gentrification**", the displacement of lower-income communities by wealthier residents. A good example is the South Bronx neighborhood in New York City, where a mixed low-income African-American and immigrant community will soon be filled with expensive apartments. This type of development will affect nearby property values, causing rental prices to shoot up. The future of the South Bronx is to no longer be a haven for immigrant communities.[24]

The anti-communist capitalist elite of the U.S., who have driven gentrification in pursuit of profit, often with racialized impacts, cannot accept that China is spending massive resources to build infrastructure to benefit its low-income and ethnic minority communities; therefore, they are promoting claims of "genocide" against China in an attempt to undermine the significance of the development occurring in Xinjiang.

Most ordinary Americans have never been to China, but they have been traumatized by the negative experience of racist gentrification across their own country. Therefore, they will find it difficult to understand that China's massive urban development in Xinjiang's Ürümqi and Kashgar is greatly improving living standards, benefiting local economies, and strengthening multi-ethnic unity.

---

24 Ed García Conde, "The gentrification and luxury takeover of the South Bronx waterfront," *Welcome2TheBronx*, September 29, 2021, https://www.welcome2thebronx.com/2021/09/the-gentrification-and-luxury-takeover-of-the-south-bronx-waterfront/.

The ultimate goal for the U.S. anti-communist and anti-China groups is to split Xinjiang off from China and turn it into a war-torn failed state like Syria. U.S. imperialists have consistently prioritized the wealthy at the expense of the poor, and are now channeling resources and support to Israel, enabling its ongoing bombardment and displacement of Palestinians in Gaza.[25]

Aid to Gaza: U.S. Hypocrisy vs. China's Genuine Commitment

On the surface, the U.S. appears to be one of the largest donors to Gaza, providing $635 million to the UN Relief and Works Agency for Palestine Refugees in the Near East (UNRWA) in 2024.[26] However, a significant portion of the funds has been used to pay high salaries to international staff at humanitarian agencies that oversee what the U.S. and Israel refer to as Gaza "humanitarian operations." It has also spent millions of dollars coordinating costly airdrop operations with other countries, some of which tragically resulted in civilian casualties in Gaza,[27] [28] or building a floating pier in Gaza (which failed within days of construction) to help Israel keep any genuine humanitarian

---

25 Ché Marino, "Fund people's needs in the Bronx, not genocide in Gaza!," *Workers World*, January 25, 2024, https://www.workers.org/2024/01/76536/.

26 United Nations Office for the Coordination of Humanitarian Affairs, "Occupied Palestinian Territory 2024," OCHA Financial Tracking Service, 2024, https://fts.unocha.org/countries/171/donors/2024.

27 Einav Halabi and Elisha Ben Kimon, "At least 5 Gazans crushed to death by botched US aid airdrops, Palestinians report," *Ynet News*, March 9, 2024, https://www.ynetnews.com/article/s1qda0u6t

28 Taqwa Ahmed Al-Wawi, "Airdropped Aid Is Crushing Starving People in Gaza," *The Intercept*, August 22, 2025, https://theintercept.com/2025/08/22/gaza-aid-airdrops/.

agencies from sending aid over land to Gaza from Egypt, the easiest and most efficient route.

Even more cynically, a large part of the U.S. Gaza "humanitarian" funding is now being spent to hire former Israeli Mossad members to create the so-called Gaza Humanitarian Foundation (GHF).[29] The U.S. thereby blocks genuine international humanitarian agencies from operating in Gaza, instead hiring private contractors to assist the Israeli Occupation Forces (IOF). This support enables the IOF to perpetrate what constitutes femicide and ethnic cleansing. Between May 27 and July 31, 2025, the IOF killed at least 1,373 Palestinians who were trying to get food aid—859 were killed in the vicinity of the GHF food distribution sites and 514 others were killed along the routes taken by the food convoys, according to the United Nations.[30]

This is not spending money for "humanitarian aid." Instead, it is U.S. investment in sustaining Israel's occupation and policies of mass violence in Gaza.

Aid to Gaza from China and other countries of the Global South takes a human-centered approach. While China donated $2 million to the UN agencies in 2024, far less than the U.S., China's aid didn't go to help with genocide. Gaza's aid system is not broken; rather, it functions precisely as intended by the U.S.[31] There are many Chinese grassroots movements sending aid to Gaza. For example, my friend Yousef, a

---

29 Max Blumenthal and Wyatt Reed, "Israeli Mossad named as funder of Gaza Humanitarian Foundation," *The Grayzone*, May 29, 2025, https://thegrayzone.com/2025/05/29/israeli-mossad-gaza-humanitarian-foundation-aid/.

30 United Nations, "Gaza: Nearly 1,400 Palestinians killed while seeking food, as UN warns airdrops are no solution," *UN News*, August 1, 2025, https://news.un.org/en/story/2025/08/1165552.

31 Ahmad Ibsais, "Gaza's aid system isn't broken. It's working exactly as designed," *Al-Jazeera*, May 28, 2025, https://www.aljazeera.com/opinions/2025/5/28/gazas-aid-system-isnt-broken-its-working-exactly-as-designed.

Gazan who escaped to China with help from his Chinese friends, has organized a family-run humanitarian project to feed people, with help from his mother, who is still in Gaza. Our organization, *Panda Aid*, is working with Palestinian humanitarian organizations to send medical aid and donated funds to support food kitchens in Gaza.[32]

These are efforts by Chinese community activists to support the people of Gaza. Meanwhile, the U.S. is diverting resources away from its own communities at home to fund racist campaigns and Israel's genocide in Gaza, all while baselessly defaming China's infrastructure projects and development initiatives in Xinjiang.[33] Meanwhile, the New York City Subway is worse than the subway systems of not only Xinjiang, but of many other cities around the world, including Cairo, Istanbul, and Bangkok.

There's no doubt that, as the saying goes, "the U.S. bombs, China builds."[34] That's why America's infrastructure is crumbling and never gets rebuilt; the money is funneled into other priorities. This isn't an accident—it's by design.

It is not that Trump single-handedly ushered in the racist MAGA movement; rather, long-standing structural racism and authoritarian tendencies within the U.S. system created the conditions for its rise.

* * *

---

32 Panda Aid, "Insan Sebil Slam (ISS)-Panda Aid Gaza Joint-Project Promotional Video (English Caption)," *Palestine Watch*, July 14, 2025, https://www.palestinewatch.net/post/insan-sebil-slam-iss-panda-aid-gaza-joint-project-promotional-video-english-caption.

33 Liu Xin, Fan Lingzhi and Xie Wenting, "How blood-stained West orchestrated 'genocide' defamation against Xinjiang step by step," *Global Times*, June 08, 2021, https://www.globaltimes.cn/page/202106/1225747.shtml.

34 Sharon Black, "U.S. bombs, China builds," *Struggle La Lucha*, June 28, 2025, https://www.struggle-la-lucha.org/2025/06/28/u-s-bombs-china-builds/.

Lee Siu Hin is a Chinese American immigrant rights activist born in Hong Kong, China, and from Los Angeles, California, USA. He is the founder of the China-US Solidarity Network *(CUSN), the* National Immigrant Solidarity Network *(NISN), and* Panda Aid. *He is a long-term organizer in community, labor, anti-war, and immigrant rights activities, committed to grassroots struggles. He was also a long-term unpaid reporter, producer, and war correspondent for Pacifica Radio KPFK in Los Angeles, and has worked in war zones in the Middle East, Europe, and Africa. He travels frequently between China and the U.S. to build the China-U.S. activist international solidarity movement.*

Healthcare

If China Can Provide Universal Healthcare, Why Can't the United States?

by Margaret Flowers

Healthcare in the United States is overly expensive, deeply unequal, and of poor quality. Most people in the U.S. have either experienced financial or other obstacles to getting the medical care they need, or have a close friend or family member who has had this experience. When compared to other wealthy nations, the U.S. is an outlier for spending the most per capita on healthcare while delivering the worst outcomes. In contrast, China spends less than 3% of what the U.S. spends per capita, while providing nearly universal coverage and improving health outcomes. These differences are largely due to opposing philosophies on the responsibility of governments to provide for their populations.

One distinctive difference between healthcare in the U.S. and China is that the U.S. does not have an actual healthcare system. Rather, the U.S. has a complicated mess of public systems, which are privatized in part or almost completely, and private insurance plans and health facilities, which largely do not communicate with each other or coordinate their activities to benefit the public. The healthcare sector is entirely market-driven and focused on making maximum profits for its corporate executives and shareholders.

This fact was made tragically salient in December of 2024 when

Brian Thompson, the CEO of United Healthcare, one of the major insurance companies, was murdered in New York City on his way to a meeting with investors. The public response to his death was less than sympathetic. Instead, many people criticized United Healthcare for its policies of denying coverage of lifesaving care for its enrollees. As United Healthcare attempted to make changes to its policies to recover its public image, shareholders in the corporation took the company to court,[35] claiming that its new "consumer-friendly" policies were hurting them financially. In the U.S., publicly-traded corporations, including those in the healthcare sector, have a legal responsibility to maximize profits for their shareholders even though it comes at a cost to human health and life.

Profiteering from healthcare in the U.S. began in the early 1970s under the Nixon Administration with the passage of the Health Maintenance Organization (HMO) Act, which permitted private investment in HMO plans and mandated employers to offer these plans to their employees. In the 1980s, healthcare privatization and profiteering took off as the government encouraged and trained private investment groups to enter the healthcare sector.[36] Another pivotal moment in U.S. healthcare history was the passage of the so-called Affordable Care Act in 2010. For the first time, a tiered healthcare system was codified into law, along with massive government subsidies for health insurance corporations. The law not only required people to buy health insurance or pay a penalty, but also created government-run

---

35 Josh Russel, "UnitedHealth sued over plummeting share price in the wake of CEO's murder," *Courthouse News Service*, May 7, 2025, https://www.courthousenews.com/unitedhealth-sued-over-plummeting-share-price-in-the-wake-of-ceos-murder/.

36 Donald L. Barlett and James B. Steele, *Critical Condition: How Health Care in America Became Big Business—and Bad Medicine* (Crown, 2005).

marketplaces where government representatives sold private insurance.

The mandate to purchase health insurance was a concession to the industry, purportedly in exchange for greater regulation. However, since 2010, to counter these regulations, healthcare corporations have increased their power through mergers, acquisitions, and "vertical integration" or ownership of multiple parts of the industry, from insurance to health facilities, including owning physician practices, laboratories, imaging centers, hospitals, and nursing homes. In this environment, private venture funds are now taking over. Hospitals are shuttering essential services such as obstetrics and pediatrics to open more lucrative specialty centers in orthopedics and cardiovascular interventions. Hospitals that don't turn a profit, especially in rural communities and poor urban areas, are being closed down and either abandoned or converted into commercial spaces.

The Commonwealth Fund's 2024 health insurance survey[37] highlights some major failures of healthcare in the United States. They found that only 56% of working-age adults had adequate health insurance. Of those who had health insurance without adequate coverage, 57% "avoided getting needed health care because of its cost," and 41% of these experienced a worsening of their health condition as a result. 44% of underinsured adults held medical or dental debt. In fact, in the U.S., medical illness is the leading cause of personal bankruptcy, and about three-fourths of those who go bankrupt had health insurance at the start of their illness.

Given this crisis, there is widespread public agreement that the United States requires a drastic change in how healthcare is financed

---

37 Sara R. Collins and Avni Gupta, *The State of Health Insurance Coverage in the U.S.*, The Commonwealth Fund, November 21, 2024, https://www.commonwealthfund.org/publications/surveys/2024/nov/state-health-insurance-coverage-us-2024-biennial-survey.

and delivered. In fact, people in the U.S. have advocated for a national universal healthcare system for more than 100 years, but efforts to create such a system have been stopped by powerful, racist, right-wing professional and industry interest groups. Decades ago, it was the physicians' group, the American Medical Association, and racists from the Southern U.S., particularly the "Southern Dixiecrats," who blocked reform. More recently, think tanks affiliated with both major political parties and lobbyists with the medical-industrial complex have convinced members of Congress to reject even modest proposals such as "Medicare for All" legislation.

Open Secrets, a lobbyist watchdog group, reports that in 2024,[38] the pharmaceutical and healthcare sector was the industry that spent the most on lobbying politicians. The insurance sector ranked third highest in spending. Studies have found that private health insurance lobby groups also spend large amounts of money—more than $100 million each year—to influence voters through social media campaigns that erode trust in public healthcare systems.[39] Common falsehoods promoted by the industries are that a universal public healthcare system would be more expensive, limit people's choices, and diminish the quality of healthcare. Of course, data from nations that actually have universal healthcare systems prove otherwise.

The medical-industrial complex also works to convince voters that the United States is too big and too diverse for a "one size fits all" healthcare system. China stands out as a shining example that proves

---

[38] Open Secrets, "Industries," https://www.opensecrets.org/federal-lobbying/industries?cycle=2024

[39] Kendra Chow et al., "Generating Opposition to Universal Health Care Policies in the United States: An Analysis of Private Health Industry Advertising on Meta Platforms," PLOS Global Public Health 5, no. 7 (2025): e0003244, https://journals.plos.org/globalpublichealth/article?id=10.1371/journal.pgph.0003244.

the foolishness of such thinking. China has a landmass similar in size to the U.S. and a highly diverse population, roughly four times larger than the U.S. population. After the People's Republic of China (PRC) was founded in 1949, it took on the task of building a national universal healthcare system as part of its social and economic programs with impressive success.

Political analyst K. J. Noh reports that at the start of the Chinese Revolution, China was a poor country where, because of the West's Opium Wars, 10-20% of the population was addicted to opium. In a major public health victory, addiction was eradicated within four years.[40] Another impressive public health accomplishment is that through a forty-year effort, China succeeded in ending extreme poverty, which impacted almost 800 million people. The World Bank reports that China accounts for nearly three-quarters of the global reduction in extreme poverty.[41]

China has accomplished these impressive feats because its fundamental approach is to prioritize basic public needs rather than corporate profits. Noh explains that China uses a framework of "one income, two assurances and three guarantees": everyone has an income, they are assured food and clothing, and they are guaranteed basic medical care, safe housing, and an education.

Through a centralized healthcare system that includes both Traditional Chinese Medicine and Western medicine, China has attained

---

40 Margaret Flowers, "The West Would Rather Burn The Planet Than Let China Shine," *Popular Resistance*, October 15, 2024, https://popularresistance.org/the-west-would-rather-burn-the-planet-than-let-china-shine/.

41 The World Bank and the Development Research Center of the State Council, People's Republic of China, *Four Decades of Poverty Reduction in China: Drivers, Insights for the World, and the Way Ahead*, The World Bank Group, July 20, 2022, https://openknowledge.worldbank.org/entities/publication/c0d9423b-f682-5f14-b40b-22b99af80b97.

China Provides Universal Healthcare

nearly universal healthcare coverage. The Chinese National Healthcare Security Administration reports that for the past four years, more than 95% of Chinese residents were enrolled in their basic medical insurance program. For the low-income and rural populations, the percentage covered is 99%.[42]

Health outcomes have dramatically improved over the past 76 years. The average life expectancy in China was around 43.5 years in 1950, and rose to almost 78 years in 2024.[43] Life expectancy in China rose by almost seven years between 2000 and 2021, while life expectancy in the United States fell during that same time period. In China, neonatal and maternal mortality rates are lower than those in the United States and are still declining, while the rates in the U.S. are increasing. The homicide rate in China is roughly one-sixth, and the suicide rate is roughly one-half, of what they are in the U.S.

A study published by the United States National Institutes of Health called the impressive rise in life expectancy during the first 30 years of the Chinese revolution one of "the most rapid sustained increases in documented global history."[44] The authors credit four reasons for this: an expansion of primary care services and public health programs, investment in basic infrastructure to provide clean water and other sanitation needs, improved nutrition, and better education.

---

42 Xinhua, "China's basic medical insurance covers 95 pct of population," State Council of the People's Republic of China, July 24, 2025, https://english.www.gov.cn/news/202507/24/content_WS6881c72cc6d0868f4e8f463b.html.

43 Macrotrends, "China Life Expectancy (1950-2025)," https://www.macrotrends.net/global-metrics/countries/chn/china/life-expectancy.

44 Kimberly Singer Babiarz et al., "An exploration of China's mortality decline under Mao: A provincial analysis, 1950-80," *Population studies* 69, no. 1 (2015): 39-56:10.1080/00324728.2014.972432, https://pmc.ncbi.nlm.nih.gov/articles/PMC4331212/.

China has made these achievements while spending a fraction of what the U.S. spends on healthcare. In 2024, China spent $356 per person on healthcare,[45] which is 5.78% of its Gross Domestic Product (GDP), while the U.S. spent $15,610 per person,[46] which is more than 18% of its GDP. Healthcare spending in the U.S. is an outlier even among other wealthy Western nations due in large part to high administrative costs, lack of control over the prices of goods and services, and the profit margins baked into the industry.

A big difference between China and the United States is that China controls the medical corporations, while in the U.S., medical corporations use campaign donations and offers of high-paying jobs in the private sector to buy influence over politicians and government officials. A look at the pharmaceutical sector demonstrates the difference this makes: in China, the national government keeps the costs of medications low by purchasing them in bulk and using this leverage to negotiate fair prices, while in the U.S., pharmaceutical lobbyists have prevented this practice.

An example of this was the national fight over drug prices for Medicare enrollees in 2003. Instead of promoting bulk purchasing, the head of the Center for Medicare and Medicaid Services (CMS), Thomas Scully, pushed an insurance scheme to cover drugs and hid the true cost of the proposal from Congress. Following the passage of a law to allow this insurance, referred to as Part D of Medicare, Scully resigned from CMS and took a lucrative position as a pharma-

---

45 CEIC, "China Consumption Expenditure per Capita: Health Care and Medical Services," https://www.ceicdata.com/en/china/expenditure-per-capita/consumption-expenditure-per-capita-health-care-and-medical-services.

46 Sean P. Keehan et al., "National Health Expenditure Projections, 2024–33: Despite Insurance Coverage Declines, Health To Grow As Share Of GDP," *Health Affairs* 44, no. 7 (2025): 776–87, https://www.healthaffairs.org/doi/10.1377/hlthaff.2025.00545.

ceutical lobbyist.[47] What this did was allow pharmaceutical prices to continue to rise unchecked while creating a new insurance product that seniors could purchase, a win for both the drug and insurance corporations. The high cost of medication continues to be a crisis in the U.S., where patients routinely forgo filling prescriptions or skip doses to save money.[48]

Another big difference is transparency in prices. When patients walk into a hospital in China, they can look up the cost of tests and treatments on a computer screen.[49] They know exactly how much they will be charged. This would be impossible in the U.S. under the current arrangement because the cost of a test or treatment can vary widely depending on whether a patient has health insurance (prices are higher for the uninsured) and what type of insurance the patient has (each company negotiates prices with the hospital).[50] Patients in the U.S. also face high out-of-pocket costs, which vary depending on which insurance plan they have and whether or not the facility where they go is in their covered network or not.[51] Often, information

---

47 Olga Pierce, "Medicare Drug Planners Now Lobbyists, With Billions at Stake," *ProPublica*, October 20, 2009, https://www.propublica.org/article/medicare-drug-planners-now-lobbyists-with-billions-at-stake-1020.

48 Emily Harris, "Survey: Millions of People in the US Forgo Medications to Reduce Costs," *JAMA* 330, no. 1 (2023): 13–13, https://doi.org/10.1001/jama.2023.10395.

49 *People vs Profits: China and US Health Care Systems Compared*, BreakThrough News, 2025, https://www.youtube.com/watch?v=T12WJ2AlITw.

50 Preethi Rao et al., "Barriers to Price and Quality Transparency in Health Care Markets," *Rand health quarterly* 9, no. 3 (June 30, 2022): 1, https://pmc.ncbi.nlm.nih.gov/articles/PMC9242565/.

51 The Brookings Institution, "Everything you need to know about surprise billing," https://www.brookings.edu/collection/everything-you-need-to-know-about-surprise-billing/.

about which facilities are covered is out of date, and patients may go to a "covered" facility only to find that the department where they received care was subcontracted to a private entity that is not in their network. If the facility is not part of their insurance network, patients are responsible for the full cost of care.

Healthcare in the United States is complicated and opaque, which benefits the corporations but creates great uncertainty and stress for patients, while patients in China have an efficient and transparent system, which provides them with greater choices for care and the security that their medical needs will be taken care of without leaving them financially destitute. This is the difference between a capitalist economy in the U.S. and an economic system that China refers to as "socialism with Chinese characteristics". In the U.S., society competes with corporations for basic necessities such as healthcare, housing, and education, while in China, basic necessities are viewed, according to Noh, as "a whole-of-society responsibility requiring a whole-of-society response."

Given the propaganda about China in the United States, it may come as a surprise to learn that China is a deeply democratic society where the political power of the wealthy is restricted. The PRC's Constitution places all state power in the hands of the people through local and national people's congresses. The Communist Party of China (CPC), which leads the government, creates five-year plans for social and economic development. These five-year plans are developed through a process of extensive public input. Each year, the National People's Congress, which has almost 3,000 delegates, meets to review the country's progress and make decisions about changes that need to be made.

It is through these five-year plans that China has successfully eradicated poverty, built a high-quality education system, constructed an extensive and efficient transportation system, and become a world leader in renewable energy. People in China experience significant material gains in their quality of life, unlike in the United States, where the social safety net is unraveling and infrastructure is failing, as documented in China's annual report on human rights violations in the U.S.[52]

In the 2024 report, China found that both wealth and social inequalities are worsening in the United States. More than 40 million people live in poverty. Credit card debt and defaults on loans are at record highs. Food insecurity impacts 13.5% of households. More than 700,000 people in the US do not have a home, and that number is rising at record rates. Rather than housing people who need it, more cities are making the problem worse by implementing policies that criminalize homelessness. It is common for city governments to order police to dismantle homeless encampments, confiscating and discarding people's possessions in the process, including medications and personal documents.

China's human rights report notes that the United States is the only wealthy nation that does not have a universal healthcare system. In the U.S., there are also gross disparities in health outcomes based on race. According to the report, "African Americans have a life expectancy nearly five years shorter than that of white Americans, an infant mortality rate more than twice as high, and a maternal mortality rate nearly three times greater."

While people in China are experiencing improvements in their quality of life, the United States is a country in decline. In fact, one

---

52 Xinhua, *Full text: The Report on Human Rights Violations in the United States in 2024*, State Council Information Office of the People's Republic of China, August 17, 2025, http://english.scio.gov.cn/m/scionews/2025-08/17/content_118029304.html.

could argue that the much-vaunted "American Dream" is being realized in China, while people in the U.S. are living a nightmare. Perhaps this is some of the impetus behind U.S. belligerence toward China; the U.S. has a history of targeting nations that are succeeding in order to maintain its own dominance.

However, the world is changing. A multipolar world is rising alongside a growing demand for a new form of world governance based on cooperation, diplomacy, and respect for international law. These are fundamental changes that are required to tackle the many crises in the world, and China is one of the countries working to put the world on this new path.

Demands for change are growing in the United States. As people organize to create a new society and new systems in the U.S., it will be important to learn from others around the world about how to solve our many crises. China provides time-tested examples of solutions to the healthcare crisis and more. Rather than invest trillions in new weapons in an attempt to defeat China militarily, people in the U.S. would do well to demand those dollars be invested in addressing our many needs at home. Rather than cut connections to China through greater tariffs and policies that restrict academic collaboration, people in the U.S. would benefit from greater cooperation with China. We have much to learn and gain by doing so.

* * *

Margaret Flowers, M.D., is a retired pediatrician and Physicians for a National Health Program (PNHP) advisory board member. In 2009-10, Flowers volunteered as a Congressional Fellow for PNHP. She co-founded the Health Over Profit for Everyone campaign and the Maryland Health Care is a Human Right campaign. Flowers writes about health policy, and is also the director of Popular Resistance, *where she advocates for a wide range of social, economic, and environmental issues and hosts the radio program* Clearing the FOG.

Healthcare in China: A Cooperative Project

by Sue Harris

China's ability to cooperate is the key to its success in the field of healthcare among many other fields. On an individual basis, cooperation is the ability to empathize with other people and a knowledge of cause and effect in order to reach a common goal. It is the same with nations. In healthcare, how do you achieve longer life expectancy for everyone, lower infant mortality rates and fewer deaths due to communicable diseases? The healthcare system in China is not considered a business. Its goal is not profit. Healthcare is about saving lives and preventing illness.

The recent Covid pandemic is a good example of how China behaved cooperatively to stem the spread of this disease and developed the means to prevent and treat it. When cases of Covid-19 were identified in Wuhan, there was an immediate lockdown, and a quarantine was established. State-owned industries ensured a steady supply of food and fuel at normal prices, increased the supply of rice, flour, oil, meat, and salt, and cracked down on price gouging and hoarding. Several field hospitals were built quickly. There was guaranteed free treatment for Covid.

On the community level, to combat pandemics and deliver healthcare, China relies on a united, well-organized population, long accustomed to cooperating in times of need. China still maintains an important base of urban and rural civil organizations developed in the

1950s. From the early stages of China's Wuhan lockdown—where the Covid pandemic was first identified—members of these committees mobilized to conduct door-to-door temperature checks and deliver food and supplies, especially to elderly residents.[53]

In China, when cases of Covid started to appear, before a vaccine had been developed, the government and civic organizations took non-pharmaceutical actions that stopped the spread of the disease:

1. Intercity travel restrictions
2. Early identification and isolation of cases
3. Contact Restrictions
4. Social Distancing

This limited the early spread of Covid and bought time for the rest of the world. Very few cases have been exported from China.[54]

The pharmaceutical system in China is designed for finding medicines that cure all human beings, and teaching others how to produce them, not for cornering the market with exclusive patents. Western capitalist countries, like the U.S., Canada and members of the European Union, bought up most of the world's supply of Covid medication, well beyond what they needed, in order to sell them to other countries. They bought billions of doses and sold the first batch to other wealthy countries. They stopped at that point and told the rest of the world to wait until they got around to distributing the rest. High-income countries had ordered nearly 4.2 billion doses, while lower-middle and low-income countries ordered less than 700 million.

---

53 Lee Siu Hin et al., *Capitalism on a Ventilator: The Impact of COVID-19 in China & the U.S.* (2020).

54 Calvin Deutschbein, "China Pushes Back U.S. Empire of Lies," *Workers World*, July 31, 2020, https://www.workers.org/2020/07/50348/.

The wealthy countries bought up most of the doses, and the poorer countries did not have enough.

China, however, has sent or donated millions of vaccine doses around the world—especially to the Global South. According to Chinese Foreign Minister Wang Yi, by mid-February, China had donated vaccines to 53 developing countries, including Somalia, Iraq, South Sudan and Palestine. It has also exported vaccines to 22 countries. In addition, it has launched cooperative research and development projects with more than ten countries. Also at the WHO's request, China will contribute 10 million doses of vaccines to COVAX.

As of February 14, according to the *Global Times*, at least 40 countries had ordered or donated at least 561 million doses of Chinese vaccines; some of the main buyers include Peru (38 million), Mexico (35 million), Indonesia (122.8 million), Philippines (25 million doses with an additional 0.6 million donation), Turkey (50 million), Brazil (120 million) and Chile (60 million). Other buyers include Colombia, Uruguay, Myanmar, Malaysia, Thailand and Laos—and Morocco, Egypt, Seychelles, Zimbabwe, Senegal and Equatorial Guinea in Africa.

In Europe, Serbia received Chinese vaccines, making it the second-most vaccinated country in Europe, following the U.K. Hungary became the first EU member state to receive Chinese vaccines (which are not yet EU-approved for use). China's vaccine success across the world shows the true meaning of global solidarity.

Chinese vaccines are more suited to countries of the Global South. They do not need to be stored in very cold freezers as the Western vaccines do. They are also cheaper. In addition, the cooperative research projects between China and other countries create global solidarity and increase independence and competence. To quote Dr. Alex Mohubetswane Meshilo of the South African Communist Party:

> "The African continent as a collective, and the various African states, individually, must unshackle themselves from the legacy of colonialism [and] build a people based healthcare system, having due regard for the relevant African conditions."

There is a Chinese story about how a fisherman helped a village that didn't have enough food. The village was near a river that had plenty of fish in it. Instead of catching the fish quickly and donating them to the village, he taught many of the villagers how to fish. That ensured that the village would have a perpetual supply of food. "Teach people to fish" is a common expression used in China.

China cooperates with other socialist countries, such as Cuba, a leader in the field of health, sharing information rather than hoarding it. In this way, everyone benefits. According to an article in *Black Agenda Report* by Danny Haiphong, China and Cuba's medical internationalism is a shining example of global solidarity.[55] It is this internationalism that may provide the key for human survival or even human progress in the future.

* * *

---

55 Danny Haiphong, "China and Cuba's Medical Internationalism Is a Shining Example of Global Solidarity," *Black Agenda Report*, April 1, 2020, https://blackagendareport.com/china-and-cubas-medical-internationalism-shining-example-global-solidarity.

Sue Harris is a videographer and a psychotherapist. As a member of Peoples Video Network she went to Iraq to study the effects of sanctions on children, and then made the video The Children Are Dying. *She later directed* Poison Dust, *a video about the effects of depleted uranium on the environment. With PVN, she videoed hundreds of demonstrations in support of the oppressed and put them on Youtube. She continues to write for* Workers World *newspaper. With colleagues, Dr. Harris published* Interpersonal Psychoanalytic Theory for the 21st Century: Evolving Self, *which won the American Legacy Book Award in 2025 for books on mental health. She continues to practice and write, maintaining her interest in movements for social change.*

Green Development

China Outpaces the World in Energy Production and Green Technology

by Lyn Neeley

China's gains in renewable energy production have skyrocketed. According to the *New York Times*, "Not only does China already dominate global manufacturing of solar panels, wind turbines, batteries, [electric vehicles] and many other clean energy industries, but with each passing month it is widening its technological lead."[56]

The biggest driver of China's economic growth is innovation and clean energy technology, accounting for 40% of its gross domestic product expansion last year. China's climate goals may well be reached sooner than expected: peak carbon dioxide (CO_2) emissions before 2030 (when global CO_2 emissions reach their highest level and begin to decline), and carbon neutrality before 2060 (when the amount of CO_2 released into the atmosphere equals the amount being removed).

For decades, China, a socialist country based on centralized planning, has been preparing for and investing in renewable energy infrastructure. Energy planning is coordinated by technical experts that predict demand instead of reacting to it.

Scientific training and education are top priorities for the Communist Party of China's leadership. A majority of undergraduates and

---

56 David Gelles et al., "There's a Race to Power the Future. China Is Pulling Away.," *The New York Times*, June 30, 2025, https://www.nytimes.com/interactive/2025/06/30/climate/china-clean-energy-power.html.

China's Energy Production and Green Technology

three-quarters of China's doctoral students major in math, science, engineering or agriculture. China has nearly 50 graduate programs on battery chemistry and metallurgy alone.[57]

China's investment in research and development and in a skilled workforce has grown rapidly. The number of clean energy patents filed by China rose from 18 in 2000 to over 700,000 in 2024, over half the world's total.[58]

China has automated its factories, installing more robots each year from 2021 through 2023 than the rest of the world combined, and seven times as many as the U.S. As a result, the cost of China's renewables keeps falling and global demand is growing.

Production costs are low in China's state-owned industries. Instead of driving to make a profit, the country prioritizes meeting people's needs and improving the quality of life. According to a recent article from *Project Syndicate*:

> "China supplies the majority of the world's refined lithium (70%), cobalt (78%), graphite (95%), rare earths (91%), and manganese (91%). In terms of green-tech manufacturing, China accounts for 80% of solar panel production, 50-70% of the wind turbine market, and over half of electric vehicles. And in terms of deploy-

---

57 Keith Bradsher, "How China Built Tech Prowess: Chemistry Classes and Research Labs," *The New York Times*, August 9, 2024, https://www.nytimes.com/2024/08/09/business/china-ev-battery-tech.html.

58 Max Bearak and Mira Rojanasakul, "How China Went From Clean Energy Copycat to Global Innovator," *The New York Times*, August 14, 2025, https://www.nytimes.com/interactive/2025/08/14/climate/china-clean-energy-patents.html.

ment, it is undertaking three-quarters of the world's renewable-energy projects.⁵⁹"

The increase in China's renewable energy markets is expanding its global political and economic relationships. China is exporting electric vehicles (EVs), building wind turbines and solar farms, and setting up clean energy projects in countries like Brazil, India, Indonesia, Kenya, Zambia, Sudia Arabia, Thailand, Morocco, Hungary and Cuba.

Electric Vehicles

As of this writing, China has produced 70% of the world's electric vehicles and 98% of the world's electric buses.

Chinese EVs are cheaper and more advanced than EVs made anywhere else. A Chinese EV now costs less than $10,000 because of the efficient manufacturing processes and an increase in the amount of government subsidies for EVs from $76.7 million in 2018 to $809 million in 2023.

The world's largest producer of EVs is the Chinese company BYD (Biyadi). It has developed a battery that can be charged in five minutes and driven for about 250 miles. Patrick George, the editor in chief of *InsideEVs*, said BYD EVs were a generation ahead of the rest of the world.⁶⁰

---

59 Mark Blyth and Daniel Driscoll, "Trump's Global War on Decarbonization," *Project Syndicate*, August 21, 2025, https://www.project-syndicate.org/commentary/trump-global-war-on-decarbonization-green-technologies-by-mark-blyth-and-daniel-driscoll-2025-08.

60 *We Tried BYD's 5-Minute 'Megawatt' EV Charging In China — It's Mind-Blowing*, InsideEVs, May 7, 2025, 00:07:45, https://www.youtube.com/watch?v=u-sUxO7y4z_E.

China's Energy Production and Green Technology

BYD and CATL (Contemporary Amperex Technology Co. Limited) are the leaders in making EV batteries. Theirs are lighter, longer-lasting, faster to charge, cheaper, and safer, and cars using them are more convenient to drive. Both companies make lithium-ion batteries that use more inexpensive minerals: iron and phosphate, combined with lithium, rather than nickel and cobalt, which Western producers use.

Solar Power

China dominates the global solar power industry. It produces over 80% of the world's solar panels and controls most of the entire supply chain, from raw materials to finished products. This success comes from a combination of government support, lower production costs, and massive manufacturing scale. It has driven down global solar panel prices but also created significant supply chain dependencies worldwide.

Government support, high manufacturing volume and lower production costs all contributed to China exceeding its 2030 solar and wind capacity goal by the end of 2024, six years early. China increased its solar energy production by 45% in one year.

In 2024, the Ürümqi solar farm became the largest solar facility in the world. A planned facility on a Tibetan plateau was announced in July, and is expected to be even larger. Smaller solar farms further increase China's solar capacity and boost China's power production much higher. Entire rural provinces are blanketed in rooftop solar panels. In 2024, distributed solar accounted for 43% of China's new capacity added that year.

Lyn Neeley

Hydropower

Hydropower is the primary renewable energy source in China, which is the world's leading producer of hydroelectric power, generating around 30% of the total world output. Half of the world's ten largest dams are in China, including the Three Gorges Dam, which is presently the world's largest dam and greatest producer of hydroelectricity to date. Currently, an even larger dam is under construction in Tibet.

Plans are underway for the new mega-dam project to be built along Tibet's Yarlung Zangbo River in the Himalayan mountains in Medog county (Motuo in Chinese). It is the highest major river in the world, and therefore the one with the most hydroelectric potential. The $137 billion project will harness the power of gravity in the river's steep descent of 2,000 meters over a 50-kilometer stretch. This massive hydroelectric project will generate 300 billion kilowatt-hours (KWh) of electric energy per year, enough to power 50 million homes and three times the power of the Three Gorges Dam.

The new Motuo mega-facility includes twenty-eight dams at various stages of completion and several tunnels to divert portions of the water down steep slopes through one of the tallest mountains in the world, the Namcha Barwa mountain. The tunnels increase the elevation drop, allowing gravity to maximize the amount of energy produced, and minimize the impact on mountain ecosystems by reducing the number of large reservoirs that displace local habitats.

In addition to reducing carbon emissions, the dam will help prevent climate change disasters in downstream regions by controlling the river run-off. This will distribute water more evenly throughout the year, preventing flooding during wet seasons and drought during dry months. According to a research article in the *Communications*

Earth & Environment journal on the environmental impact of the dam, "[t]ransboundary cooperation is strengthened through adaptive reservoir management, ensuring energy security for China and flood protection for downstream nations. This integrated approach highlights the potential for harmonizing sustainable hydropower expansion with ecological and geopolitical resilience in international river basins."[61]

The Western press has made numerous criticisms of the Motuo project, some regarding the potential need to relocate people currently living in the path of the dams. In China, as in any country with an extensive history, all new infrastructure, no matter beneficial or essential to society, must inevitably displace someone. However, the Chinese government has faced similar challenges in the past, and has demonstrated that it prioritizes the collective well-being of the affected communities. The Three Gorges Dam, for example, required the displacement of 1.3 million people, yet entire new cities and towns were built to relocate them to. According to a report from the 2004 United Nations Symposium on Hydropower and Sustainable Development, 40% of China's investment in the Three Gorges Dam financed preferential policies for relocated residents, carried out simultaneously with the dam construction from 1993 to 2004.[62]

---

61 Fengbo Zhang et al., "Hydropower System in the Yarlung-Tsangpo Grand Canyon Can Mitigate Flood Disasters Caused by Climate Change," *Communications Earth & Environment* 6, no. 1 (2025): 323, https://doi.org/10.1038/s43247-025-02247-8.

62 Lu Youmei, *Hydropower and Sustainable Development in China*, United Nations Symposium on Hydropower and Sustainable Development (United Nations, 2004), 6, https://www.un.org/esa/sustdev/sdissues/energy/op/hydro_luyoumei.pdf.

Lyn Neeley

Innovations in Clean Energy

Chinese workers and scientists have created the first seawater electrolysis system that produces hydrogen directly from ocean water using offshore wind power, a renewable energy source. Hydrogen is a clean, versatile fuel that traditionally could only be produced using an expensive high-energy process to first desalinate ocean water.

Chinese researchers have designed a material that reflects the sun's rays and can be welded together in planks. When attached to the exterior of buildings, the planks reduce temperatures inside, cutting down the need for air conditioning and reducing carbon emissions. The plank material is made of gelatin and DNA from organic matter, which can be made biodegradable, and converts ultraviolet (UV) radiation into visible light. This plank technology opens the way for further innovative and sustainable cooling materials.

At the end of 2023, China had produced 1.27 million registered drones—huge pilot-free cargo planes that run on solar power, battery power or combined solar and hydrogen power. They can carry a 500-kilogram (1,100-pound) load as far as 500 kilometers (310 miles) with a maximum range of 1,800 kilometers (1,118 miles). They can be used for transportation, fire and rescue teams, flood control and disaster relief work, and are 70% quicker and 30% cheaper than conventional cross-sea transport.

Trump Vows to 'Drill, Baby, Drill'

The International Energy Agency expects that by 2035, renewable power will surpass coal and natural gas sources, and that by 2025, oil, gas and coal will supply below 60% of global energy needs.[63] In China, renewable energy has become a cornerstone of the economy. Shifting from a reliance on imported fossil fuels to renewable clean energy has made China an independent leader in the global green industrial revolution.

President Trump's vision of energy dominance, on the other hand, is based on the U.S. being the world's largest producer of oil and the largest exporter of natural gas. He is using tariffs and pressuring countries to buy more U.S. fossil fuels, especially liquified natural gas.

Trump's re-election fundraising dinner at Mar-a-Lago hosted over 20 executives from companies like Chevron, Exxon and Occidental Petroleum. In exchange for large campaign contributions, he promised to allow increased drilling, pause restrictions on gas exports and reverse new rules aimed at cutting motor vehicle pollution. Fossil fuel companies invested $96 million in Trump's recent re-election campaign and another $243 million in lobbying Congress in 2024.

British multinational oil company BP has increased its production of oil and gas by 20% and cut more than $5 billion from its previous green investment plan. Its new carbon production target is 60% higher than the net zero plan they promised at the 2015 Paris Agreement. General Motors is investing $888 million to start producing V-8 engines at a factory near Buffalo, N.Y., where they had recently planned to build electric motors.

Trump also recently canceled a Revolution Wind offshore wind turbine project in Rhode Island and Connecticut. The project was 80% complete, with 45 out of 65 turbines already installed. Local politicians say the move threatens 1,000 union jobs and the states'

---

[63] International Energy Agency, *World Energy Outlook 2024* (International Energy Agency, 2024), 396, https://iea.blob.core.windows.net/assets/140a0470-5b90-4922-a0e9-838b3ac6918c/WorldEnergyOutlook2024.pdf.

climate goals and may drive electricity prices up throughout the region.

The U.S. capitalist political and economic system is not set up to build an energy grid for the future. Large-scale infrastructure projects can take decades to build and depend heavily on private investors who expect to turn a profit within three to five years.

Results of a budget committee investigation uncovered hundreds of documents from energy companies showing that big oil has privately acknowledged its efforts to downplay the dangers of burning fossil fuels. U.S. Senator Sheldon Whitehouse (Rhode Island) said: "The fossil fuel industry is running perhaps the biggest campaign of disinformation and political interference in [U.S.] American history, and they're backing it up with immense amounts of political spending. ... The consequences in the White House are enormous and having a huge effect ... but people aren't aware."[64]

People Before Profits! Land Back Now!

In 2017, China built the largest floating solar farm at that time on a lake formed by a collapsed coal mine in Huainan, Anhui Province. It was a symbol of China's transition from coal to clean energy, repurposing abandoned mining land for renewable power generation.

In contrast, U.S. industries trespass on sovereign Indigenous land to construct solar plants, wind farms, power transmission lines and copper mines for lithium extraction for electric batteries—without consulting with leaders of the Indigenous nations and tribes.

---

64 Dharna Noor, "Big Oil Is Waging 'Biggest Campaign of Political Interference in US History', Senator Says," *The Guardian*, March 6, 2025, https://www.theguardian.com/us-news/2025/mar/06/big-oil-investigation-congress-republicans.

U.S.-based industries are still heavily reliant on profits from the fossil fuel economy. The U.S. government, while beginning to invest in renewable fuels, is moving in on Native reservations and sacred lands.

The Colorado River Indian Tribes (CRIT), which includes the Mohave, Chemehuevi, Hopi and Navajo Nations, is suing the Bureau of Land Management for constructing a solar plant on 4,000 acres of their ancestral homelands. They have been fighting the plans since 2006. The CRIT explained they are not against solar power, but they object to not being consulted—and to the effects it will have on the ecosystem, cultural resources, groundwater and the Colorado River.[65]

In February, members of the San Carlos Apache Nation in Arizona asked that work stop on the $10 billion construction of a copper mine on the reservation's sacred territory. Tribal member Verlon Jose said, "We do not disagree with renewable energy. We are for renewable energy. You know what the fix to this issue is? They could have rerouted it. But they didn't listen." Native activist, ecologist and author Winona LaDuke added, "In the endless pursuit of energy, once again, Native people are in the eye of the storm." She called mines and other projects that could imperil tribal sovereignty "the next Standing Rock."[66]

* * *

---

[65] Louis Sahagún, "Native Americans Challenge Construction of Mojave Desert Solar Plant," *Los Angeles Times*, December 12, 2014, https://www.latimes.com/science/sciencenow/la-sci-sn-native-americans-solar-20141212-story.html.

[66] Maxine Joselow, "'On Stolen Land': Tribes Fight Clean-Energy Projects Backed by Biden," *The Washington Post* (Tucson, Arizona), March 4, 2024, https://www.washingtonpost.com/climate-environment/2024/03/04/tribes-clean-energy-biden-sunzia/.

Lyn Neeley

Lyn Neeley taught high school science, biology and ecology in New York City for twenty years. She is now retired and a community organizer in Portland, Oregon. She is a member of the Workers World Party, where her work focuses on political education.

China's Aquacultural Revolution

by Kyle Ferrana
edited by Natalia Burdyńska

The audiences of typical television networks and major newspapers in the Western world today may detect, in their coverage of the People's Republic of China (PRC), a faint but insistent vexation over the fact that the PRC remains at peace. Wars are ongoing in almost every region of the world, including very near a few of China's borders,[67] yet the PRC itself has stubbornly refused to drop any bombs nor so much as fire a bullet at its regional rivals. Any action taken by the Chinese government or even vessels of the Chinese coast guard that can in any way be construed as hostile is magnified many times by the press, such as its use of water cannons to defend territorial claims in the South China Sea,[68] which sometimes receives equal coverage as news of actual bombings and massacres in Yemen, Lebanon, and Gaza, despite a lack of casualties. For years we have been told that China is ready for war, or preparing for war, and that the People's Liberation Army (which has not fought a war for several

---

[67] The prolonged civil war in Myanmar in particular, but neighboring regions have also seen a concerning increase in military skirmishes, such as between Cambodia and Thailand and between Pakistan and India in the summer of 2025.

[68] Jim Gomez, "Philippines Condemns Chinese Coast Guard's Use of Water Cannon on a Research Vessel," *AP News* (Manila, Philippines), May 22, 2025, https://apnews.com/article/south-china-sea-sandy-cay-philippines-a9f7522ee0d3c71fddce8a3e81543107.

decades) is poised to attack Taiwan, or perhaps even somewhere else, at a moment's notice.

The truth is that China is at war, just not the kind of war that Western governments, especially the United States', wish to see it fight. China's wars are not with other countries, but with poverty, with climate change, and with hunger. They are the types of wars that are not only unsensational to the Western press, but even embarrassing. China's extraordinary—in some cases, even exponential—progress in the production of zero-emissions energy, electric vehicles, and high-speed railways, for example, is putting the United States to shame,[69] as its "Magnificent Seven" tech giants plow hundreds of billions of dollars into the production of largely fossil fuel-powered AI data centers. Gasoline consumption and carbon emissions from China are now falling years ahead of schedule as electric vehicles rapidly replace internal combustion engines and renewables rapidly replace coal, despite China's continuing role in manufacturing an enormous share of the entire world's consumer products. Exports of renewable energy technology from China to its partner countries are also already having measurable effects in reducing their emissions.[70]

Even less attention is paid to China's efforts to fight hunger and promote sustainable food production, though in many ways this struggle is far more crucial. Carbon emissions are not the only threat to our planet's environments. Deforestation, desertification, and overfishing are also rapidly bringing entire ecosystems to the point of collapse,

---

69 David Gelles et al., "There's a Race to Power the Future. China Is Pulling Away.," *The New York Times*, June 30, 2025, https://www.nytimes.com/interactive/2025/06/30/climate/china-clean-energy-power.html.

70 Lauri Myllyvirta, *Analysis: China's Clean-Energy Exports in 2024 Alone Will Cut Overseas CO2 by 1%* (Carbon Brief, 2025), https://www.carbonbrief.org/analysis-chinas-clean-energy-exports-in-2024-alone-will-cut-overseas-co2-by-1/.

and more species to the brink of extinction. The demand for pasture land and seafood is a critical driver of the reckless depletion of the Earth's natural resources, and if this demand cannot be reduced or met in a sustainable manner, the collapse will eventually take the form of ubiquitous hunger and mass starvation. Already, according to statistics tracked by the World Bank, the average prevalence of undernourishment in the world has begun increasing, from a minimum of 7% in 2018, to 9% in 2022. China has avoided this trend, reaching the lowest level of undernourishment of any country or region in the world in 2010 and remaining there to this day.[71] [72]

A serious effort to make food production sustainable in China is currently underway, and has made remarkable progress in the realm of aquaculture. China consumes an enormous quantity of fish and seafood, far more than any other country;[73] yet the amount that it draws from the ocean is now decreasing, thanks to a generations-long effort to expand domestic fish farming. Since 1983, the last year that the volume of fish and seafood produced by capture fisheries (wild fish caught in the ocean) was greater than the volume produced by aquaculture,

---

71 World Bank, *Prevalence of Undernourishment (% of Population) - China, World, India, Sub-Saharan Africa, Latin America & Caribbean, North America, Middle East, North Africa, Afghanistan & Pakistan, Euro Area*, SN.ITK.DEFC.ZS, Food and Agriculture Organization (The World Bank Group, n.d.), accessed August 26, 2025, https://data.worldbank.org/indicator/SN.ITK.DEFC.ZS?locations=CN-1W-IN-ZG-ZJ-XU-ZQ-XC&name_desc=false.

72 According to prominent Indian economist Amartya Sen, China enjoys a considerable lead over India in food distribution due to its farther-reaching social security programs. (Jean Drèze and Amartya Sen, "China and India," in *Hunger and Public Action*, ed. Jean Drèze and Amartya Sen (Oxford University Press, 1991), https://doi.org/10.1093/0198283652.003.0011.)

73 Food and Agriculture Organization of the United Nations (2024), *Fish and Seafood - Production (Tonnes)* (Our World in Data, 2022), https://ourworldindata.org/grapher/fish-seafood-production?time=2022.

the output of Chinese aquaculture has increased by approximately 2,000%. Wild fishing by Chinese vessels now accounts for a smaller volume than it did in 1996, and Chinese aquaculture now produces more than five times as much as wild fishing per year, as of 2022.[74]

Neither is aquaculture development limited to China's coastal areas. According to Singapore-based magazine *Aqua Culture Asia Pacific*, China's far-west region of Xinjiang—in fact the region of the Earth farthest from any ocean—boasts a thriving and expanding network of aquaculture farms, supported by the government and managed by farmers' cooperatives, that cultivate over a hundred different species of fish.[75] In 2023, Chinese aquaculture firm Xinjiang Shi Shi Xian completed a pilot program to create saltwater fisheries in the autonomous region, allowing marine fish to be cultivated even at the edge of the Taklamakan Desert.[76]

Today, not only does China produce more in aquaculture than the rest of the world combined,[77] but the rate of its expansion has also remained steady for three decades, and shows no sign of slowing down.

---

74 Food and Agriculture Organization of the United Nations, via World Bank (2025), *Seafood Production: Wild Fish Catch vs. Aquaculture, China* (Our World in Data, 2022), https://ourworldindata.org/grapher/capture-fisheries-vs-aquaculture?country=~CHN.

75 Aqua Culture Asia Pacific, "Aquaculture Thrives in NW China's Xinjiang," *AQUA CULTURE Asia Pacific*, July 26, 2024, https://aquaasiapac.com/2024/07/26/aquaculture-thrives-in-nw-chinas-xinjiang/.

76 Kinling Lo, "China's Food Security: Xinjiang Develops Seawater Aquafarming in Desert Region amid Agriculture Focus," *South China Morning Post*, August 31, 2023, https://www.scmp.com/economy/china-economy/article/3232825/chinas-food-security-xinjiang-develops-seawater-aquafarming-desert-region-amid-agriculture-focus.

77 Weijun Chen and Shiyang Gao, "Current Status of Industrialized Aquaculture in China: A Review," *Environmental Science and Pollution Research* 30, no. 12 (2023): 32278–87, https://doi.org/10.1007/s11356-023-25601-9.

Additionally, Chinese aquaculture is becoming increasingly industrialized, preserving water through standardized recycling, preserving land by combining fish farms with rice cultivation, and reducing the emissions involved by farming more fish species with lower carbon footprints.

At the same time, the government is aggressively scaling back wild fisheries. Goals for the reduction of domestic fishing fleets, announced in 2017,[78] were exceeded by 2020, with 40,000 fishing vessels (about 15% of the total) taken off the water so far.[79] Fuel subsidies to Chinese fishermen are being replaced with retirement subsidies, and more regulations and limitations on wild fishing are being put in place.[80]

It is difficult for an average Westerner to learn these facts, because doing so requires actively and consciously seeking them out. They are not part of the narrative that Western governments wish their presses to print. China must everywhere and at all times be increasingly hostile, warlike, and ready to strike at the drop of a hat; the story of rogue Chinese fishing fleets running amok across the world's oceans can never become *less* true. The size and audacity of these fleets must

---

78 中华人民共和国农业农村部 (Ministry of Agriculture and Rural Affairs of the People's Republic of China), "农业部关于进一步加强国内渔船管控 实施海洋渔业资源总量管理的通知 (Notice of the Ministry of Agriculture on Further Strengthening the Control of Domestic Fishing Vessels and Implementing Total Amount Management of Marine Fishery Resources)," 中华人民共和国农业农村部 (Ministry of Agriculture and Rural Affairs of the People's Republic of China), January 16, 2017, http://www.moa.gov.cn/govpublic/YYJ/201701/t20170120_5460583.htm.

79 Chun Zhang, "China's Five-Year Plan for Fishing Focuses on Aquaculture," *Dialogue Earth*, March 24, 2022, https://dialogue.earth/en/ocean/chinas-five-year-plan-for-fishing-focuses-on-aquaculture/.

80 Kaiwen Wang et al., "Fisheries Subsidies Reform in China," *Proceedings of the National Academy of Sciences* 120, no. 26 (2023): e2300688120, https://doi.org/10.1073/pnas.2300688120.

always be on the rise, at least in the minds of Western audiences, never mind that the opposite is happening in reality.

Aquaculture is not without drawbacks. There are many critics of aquacultural fish farming, who often point to adverse environmental effects or the need to provide farmed fish with wild-caught feedstock. However, as Chinese aquaculture matures, such issues are also being capably addressed with equal attention. For example, a recent report by the Global Mangrove Alliance found that from 2000 to 2020, China had mitigated the damage aquaculture had wrought upon its mangrove-rich wetland areas, and through careful protection and afforestation efforts had increased its mangrove area by 1.8% per year, making it one of the few countries in the world with a net increase in mangrove area, as well as the world leader in scientific achievements in mangrove research.[81] The solution to wild feed requirements is, inevitably, more farming, allowing the feedstock to eventually be cultivated as well.

The benefits of fish farming are also not limited to sustainability and food security. By pioneering large-scale aquaculture, China can provide a roadmap for other seafood-consuming countries to do the same. The preservation of the world's oceans and preventing the extinction of myriad fish species must be a collective effort; even if China ended its wild fisheries entirely, other countries with less sustainable fishing fleets may fill the gap, expanding their fishing ranges to absorb the territory China's fleets have abandoned. An ocean is by nature too vast to be contained, and legal restrictions have little to no effect internationally, with a plethora of bad actors taking advantage

---

81 Global Mangrove Alliance, *Report on China Mangrove Conservation and Restoration Strategy Research Project*, Research (Global Mangrove Alliance, n.d.), 17–18, 2020, https://www.mangrovealliance.org/resources/report-on-chinas-mangrove-conservation/.

of under-patrolled waters. Yet if competition can finally give way to cooperation, these problems can be eliminated to the benefit of all. Increasingly, the government of the PRC, at least, is pursuing internationalism and global cooperation in maritime affairs: in its 14th Five-Year Plan, it expressed a commitment to building a "maritime community of common destiny" (海洋命运共同体).[82]

Presently, China is one of several countries with overlapping territorial claims in the South China Sea. Curiously, despite the outsized attention paid to clashes between Chinese and other countries' vessels in this region by the Western press, the disputed territory is relatively unremarkable, containing no inhabited islands. A discerning reader may ask, upon learning to what lengths the claimants will go to contest these waters: what is it about the South China Sea, then, that these countries are interested in?

For China, the answer clearly lies in the South China Sea's strategic location. Surrounded as China's only coastline is by the allies and military installations of an increasingly belligerent United States, the South China Sea represents the only conduit for maritime trade that does not have a gun pointed at it. Were control of these waters to pass to a U.S. ally such as the Philippines, the threat of closing this conduit would have severe consequences for the economic lives and safety of China's population of 1.4 billion people.

Control over the South China Sea would bring little benefit to the Philippines' trade routes, on the other hand, as the Philippine

---

[82] 中华人民共和国中央人民政府 (Central People's Government of the People's Republic of China), "中华人民共和国国民经济和社会发展第十四个五年规划和2035年远景目标纲要 (Outline of the 14th Five-Year Plan for National Economic and Social Development of the People's Republic of China and the Long-Term Objectives for 2035)," 新华社 (Xinhua News Agency), March 13, 2021, https://www.gov.cn/xinwen/2021-03/13/content_5592681.htm.

archipelago has numerous unobstructed coastlines and broad access to the Pacific Ocean. Instead, the Philippines' interest in the region has more to do with securing territory for its wild fisheries. If China's interest in fishing the disputed regions of the South China Sea were to dry up, a lasting peaceful arrangement between the two countries may become far more likely. In the final analysis, international conflict is often driven by economic concerns, and the division of scarce resources; sustainability is therefore a preventative measure against wars with other countries, which are after all not the wars that the People's Republic seeks to fight.

* * *

Kyle Ferrana is a writer, editor, tenant unionist, and political activist based in Portland, Oregon. He is the author of Why the World Needs China *(Clarity Press, 2024) and a contributor to* Monthly Review, The International Magazine, *and* Peace, Land, and Bread. *He currently serves as a writer and organizer for the U.S. Committee of the Friends of Socialist China and for the Oregon China Council.*

China: Terraforming for the 21st Century

by Judith Bello

When I was growing up in the 1960s, science fiction was enormously popular. "Terraforming" was a key concept in stories about space travel, but rarely if ever related to our own Earth. Terraforming means changing the land, the atmosphere, and/or the flora and fauna to create an environment that can support life. Notably, in those days, "life" referred to human life in a world where alien life forms were not prioritized. Terraforming requires that you make changes to a complex system so as to create a self-sustaining ecosystem with the characteristics that you would like to see. For instance, terraforming Mars would entail warming the frozen surface and triggering some sort of growth cycle, beginning with plants to produce oxygen, and ultimately to create food for imported animals and the humans themselves.

In real life, terraforming requires a very sophisticated understanding of environmental elements and how they interact. Having a positive relationship with our own environment requires the same understanding of and respect for the integrity of environmental processes that would be necessary to adapt another land or another planet to our needs.

The science fiction plot of colonizing a new planet is often a metaphor for colonization on our own planet. While they might not use the techniques of terraforming in their home land, the colonizers would surely want to manage conquered lands to meet their convenience and tastes. This practice does not necessarily entail the deep understanding of natural processes that is required for successfully interacting with what appears to be a hostile or difficult environment in a new land or on a new planet.

Capitalist and Colonialist Visions of Terraforming

Capitalism and colonial expansion were so pervasive in Western culture that no one questioned the context of these stories. Terraforming was a tool for colonization, and colonization is what "civilized nations" do. There was no need to terraform your own planet or your own location because it had already produced your life. Even stories in which the earth's environment had been destroyed had their characters looking to terraform a new planet instead of recovering their own.

The Israeli initiative to mold the land of the Palestinians to their vision is an attempt at terraforming with colonial intent. When the Israeli settlers arrived, the land was flourishing with olive and citrus groves. Modern technologies existed, but had not been applied to the extent of disrupting the environmental balance. The people there had an ancient culture with deep roots in the land. The new population, mostly from northern Europe, preferred their own agricultural products. They saw in the warm dry climate an opportunity for luxuries like year-round swimming pools and lush vegetation supported by irrigation.

Accustomed to the presence of large bodies of fresh water, they did not see the limitations of the fresh water supply or the value of the olive and citrus groves that had flourished in the region for millennia. They bled the underground aquifers that had sustained the native population dry, damaging the Sea of Galilee and the Jordan River, ultimately creating a world that required the continuous acquisition of new water sources. For political reasons, they have uprooted the orchards that thrive in this environment and planted trees from their homelands over the ruins of depopulated Palestinian villages.

Elon Musk, who owns several cutting-edge technology companies based in the United States, appears to espouse the original science fiction model of terraforming other planets. Every year, while public school budgets are being cut, the healthcare system is overloaded, and Social Security and the rest of the social safety net are threatened, he collects billions of dollars from the U.S. government to support his apparent dream of colonizing Mars.

Despite this, Musk is not actually investing in terraforming technologies. He has not even developed the technology to go to the moon, much less Mars. In a world where solar and wind power are suppressed to make way for gas and oil, where the possibility of using technology to mitigate global warming is dismissed by many political forces, Musk is powering his AI facilities with massive gas turbines that pollute local communities with toxic fumes. When actual terraforming—supporting the environment to enrich our lives—is left to oligarchs like Musk, it is relegated to the final phase of a fantastic dream.

Along Comes China, Terraforming for Life

By 1949, the Chinese revolution had ended thirty-five years of chaos and civil war in China, fifteen years of brutal Japanese colonization, and 200 years of British and American subjugation. The revolutionary government and five hundred million people found themselves hungry and tired and surrounded by a postwar wasteland. Members of the Communist Party of China rolled up their sleeves and went to work.

Fortunately, they didn't begin with nothing. They had deficits in resources, education and scientific development, but their work was founded on 3,000 years of civilizational development. Remnants of ancient social structures and physical infrastructure already existed, from medical and educational systems, historical and philosophical works, and community solidarity to canals, irrigation ditches, and grain stores. These were the foundations that restoration could be built upon.

However, the arid land of western China was less inviting; in the modern era, it had become isolated from world trade routes by poverty and colonialism. The Silk Road had become a memory, buried in the dust and sand of the Taklamakan Desert. When the people's government came to power, the dream of a new Silk Road came into focus, and the old Silk Road became a point of interest.

Fifty years ago, the government initiated the work of restraining the two great deserts: the Gobi in Inner Mongolia and Gansu, and the Taklamakan in Xinjiang. They began to build the Three-North Shelter Forest Program, or the "Great Green Wall," tree by tree. The Great Green Wall was a people's project. Thousands volunteered for the work of restoring the land. Peasants, farmers, and workers, both young and old, flooded the boundaries of the desert with pickaxes and shovels, planting seeds and seedlings… and they failed. Initially, they did not choose varieties of trees that would grow well in the dry conditions at the edge of the desert. The developed world laughed. But survival is a powerful incentive, and they persevered. After some experimentation, they found varieties more likely to succeed in these regions.

There were other problems, especially in sandy areas, where the ground was not stable enough for roots to take hold. This particular issue was eventually resolved by utilizing rice straw to make squares in which to plant. The rice straw held the soil in place creating a stable area for a plant to take root. Irrigation ditches and canals have been built to bring water to the surface from underground aquifers.

Trial and error, innovation, and technological and scientific advances eventually paid off. Little by little, the great sandy Taklamakan Desert was restrained. Along the road from Kashgar to Hotan, there are now bands of flourishing trees, rice straw checkerboards, and areas of scrub and brush growing along rickety fences. Highways cross the sandy wasteland and are not buried by the shifting dunes. The process has been expedited by water from the oasis where the ancient city of Hotan is once again a thriving center of agriculture and trade. While it is still a work in progress, the desert is no longer expanding.

Xinjiang Close Up

I visited the Xinjiang Uyghur Autonomous Region (XUAR) of China in early September of 2025 with a small delegation of six people including our guide. We spent nearly ten days in the region, first a couple of days in Ürümqi, then a couple of days in Kashgar, and finally a few days in Hotan. There is a great deal of security everywhere in Xinjiang due to issues with the Turkistan Islamic Party, a violent far-right relative of ISIS and Al Qaeda. The areas I visited, however, were quiet, friendly working class neighborhoods for the most part.

The XUAR lies north of Tibet in the shadow of the Kunlun mountains—not the highest in China, but a place of mythical significance, that feeds the oasis at Hotan as well as groundwater reservoirs under the desert. Peaches originally come from this region, where they were once deemed the food of the gods. To the north, high mountains bring glacial waters into the region beyond the desert. My delegation had a stopover in Altay, a stunningly beautiful city in the mountains in the far north, on our way back to Shanghai. This apparently desolate region is endowed with great wealth.

Ürümqi is a bustling hub of industry in the region. A woman who worked at my hotel led me through a gated residential area on the way to find a bank one day. There were gates both for people and cars at each end of a long block, lined with shops on the street level with apartments above them. The gates were manned by security guards who appeared to be local. On one side of the street the sidewalk gate was open, but on the other it was closed. The guard would lift a barrier to allow cars through one at a time. The area was bustling with shoppers; fruits and vegetables and even live chickens in cages were set out on the sidewalk to draw their attention. We also visited an oil company conference and a wonderful cultural museum.

Kashgar is an old Uyghur city near the western border of China, not far, in fact, from Afghanistan and Pakistan. Currently Kashgar has been restored as a tourist center, with a level of hustle and bustle I found a little disquieting. As we walked through the narrow cobbled streets of the "Old City," we saw a group of women dancing down the street followed by men and women riding horses and camels. The old architecture was interesting, but the people don't live in the Old City any more, preferring the nearby high-rises on quiet streets behind the tourist area.

From Kashgar we took the train to Hotan, a city on the southern Silk Road, or the "Old Tea Horse Road" in Chinese. The train was an old-fashioned sleeper with private cabins with bunks in some cars and open dormitories in others. We rode in a private cabin during the day and the scenery was stunning. The patches of sandy desert were broken by farmland bounded by mature trees with irrigation canals and ditches in all the green areas. In some areas desert sands were covered with a patchwork of rice straw squares, and in others young trees or shrubs clung to mesh and picket fences. Stands of mature trees came and went in the background as we traveled.

Hotan, which rests on a substantial oasis, has been continuously inhabited for at least three thousand years. When we arrived by train, there was a large statue of NeZha, a defiant young "Demon Orb" recently popularized in Chinese media, standing by the door. The city has a modern look, with cultural remnants of ancient times embedded here and there. In a thriving night market, inside a long building, there were a few traditional gift shops but mostly specialty foods like ostrich eggs, sheep testicles, snails and turtles and all kinds of oddities. The main bazaar was a huge open air market selling local crafts, foods and more.

Also in Hotan, we walked to a huge public square with a central statue of a Uyghur official greeting Chairman Mao when they first integrated the region into the People's Republic of China. At dusk, the trees surrounding the square were illuminated with festive lights and tinsel, balloons drifted in the air, and the statue in the center of the square was lit up. Several groups of people gathered in different areas of the square with boom boxes and danced to their music. In one group there were dozens of people, with more gathering as time passed, doing an aerobic dance to techno music. In other groups, couples were dancing traditional Uyghur dances, ballroom dancing, and more. A basketball game was going on one side. Everywhere we went, we were invited to join the fun.

Aquaculture and Prosperity

Today, with 1.4 billion mouths to feed, the Chinese government has continued to experiment and innovate. They found that the desert and the glacial waters coming from the towering mountain ranges surrounding Xinjiang provided a fertile environment for growing fish. Salmon thrived in the fresh mountain streams. Desert lakes and water tanks filled from the underlying aquifer could be seeded with fish and shellfish from far-away lakes and oceans, and with a little technology, their progeny would thrive.

Aquaculture is a growing resource and business opportunity in China's great deserts, making high-quality protein and delicious fresh seafood available to once impoverished populations, and supporting a high-end export business as well. I visited a fish farm outside of Hotan and had a brief conversation with their communications worker, a very pleasant young man who provided tea and fruit during our conversation, which took place in a quietly affluent corporate office.

I was aware that the aquaculture business around Hotan was not fully developed and expected to meet with a local farmer with a couple of water tanks, but this was a large corporate undertaking initiated in late 2023 and already operational with fifty-six tanks amounting to 2,240 square meters of fresh water and another seventy-two temporary tanks for imports. The tanks are moderated by a complex technological system. Hotan is a great location for this type of aquaculture, since it is situated on a freshwater oasis with the water table only ten meters below the ground, so there is no risk of undermining local water resources.

This aquaculture corporation specializes in large fish like bass, blackfish and silver cod, suitable for sale to restaurants. So far, they only have permission to sell locally, but they expect to be exporting very soon. Meanwhile, they use their temporary tanks to house king crab and fancy shellfish imported from other parts of China to boost interest locally. The enterprise is a private company with two large investors from Beijing, and also some government investment. Most of the local employees are Uyghurs, who are a minority in China but make up most of the population in Hotan. These jobs provide them with opportunities to integrate with the more developed business culture and scientific development in the east. Overall, the business is a win for the local community, bringing jobs and prosperity as well as a source of quality nutrition, and is a model for more fish farms in similar contexts. On the day I visited, the company was expecting to entertain a delegation of investors from Tibet who are interested in developing a similar startup there.

The Great Green Wall and desert aquaculture are two ways in which China is terraforming the desert to enhance the well-being of local populations and increase the long-term balance of natural resources. It is a model for other regions where vast areas of desertification have made life difficult for humans and other living beings. Natural processes can be augmented to bring about prosperity and a greener and healthier Earth, and China is leading the way.

* * *

Judith Bello is the editor of the United National Antiwar Coalition (UNAC) blog, End the Wars at Home and Abroad, *as well as several other blogs including the West Asia Sovereignty Support Movement. She is a consultant in web publishing, and hosts numerous websites. Judith was design editor for the book* Sanctions – A Wrecking Ball in a Global Economy.

3.

Plans for a Future World

Contrasting Strategies of the U.S. and China: Prospects for Peace and Solving Global Problems

by Roger D. Harris

Washington increasingly defines the U.S.-China relationship as one of "strategic competition."[83] Even before Donald Trump returned to the presidency, Joe Biden's ambassador to China remarked, "I don't feel optimistic about the future of US-China relations."[84] Indeed, the U.S. has been preparing for war with China for some time.[85]

This contrasts with the Chinese approach of cooperation for mutual benefit to solve the most pressing global problems. In short, each country's leadership presents different paradigms—the Chinese strategy emphasizes collaboration and community consistent with a

---

83 The White House, "National Security Strategy of the United States of America," The White House, December 2017, https://trumpwhitehouse.archives.gov/wp-content/uploads/2017/12/NSS-Final-12-18-2017-0905.pdf.

84 Associated Press, "US-China Relations Are Defined by Rivalry but Must Include Engagement, American Ambassador Says," *U.S. News* (Washington), December 15, 2023, https://www.usnews.com/news/us/articles/2023-12-15/us-china-relations-are-defined-by-rivalry-but-must-include-engagement-american-ambassador-says.

85 Peter Apps, "US Prepares for Long War with China That Might Hit Its Bases, Homeland: Peter Apps," *Reuters* (London), May 19, 2025, https://www.reuters.com/world/us-prepares-long-war-with-china-that-might-hit-its-bases-homeland-peter-apps-2025-05-16/.

socialist orientation, while the U.S. strategy reflects a capitalist fundamentalism rooted in competitive social relations.

The Chinese understanding is that the U.S.-China association is the most important bilateral relationship in the world. As President Xi Jinping explained: "**How China and the U.S. get along will determine the future of humanity.**"

This assessment is predicated on the acceptance of a high degree of integration between the two countries' markets. Entwining their economies is seen as mutually beneficial, as each country can benefit from the other's development.

Overarching this bilateral relationship from the Chinese perspective is a posture of friendly and cooperative relations, and a belief that a "common prosperity" can be built on the following three principles:

1. **Mutual respect**; not crossing the red lines of either of the two global powers.
2. **Peaceful coexistence**; a commitment to manage disagreements through communications and dialogue.
3. **Win-win cooperation**. Beijing explicitly criticizes Washington's posture as a "zero-sum mentality." In the U.S. framework, one side's gain is automatically the other's loss. Instead, China promotes "win-win" relations based on mutual benefit. For example, increased trade with China has boosted the purchasing power of U.S. households.[86]

---

86 Blog Admin, "Despite Job Losses, Lower Prices from Trade with China Have Left US Households Massively Better Off.," News, *USAPP*, August 14, 2019, https://blogs.lse.ac.uk/usappblog/2019/08/14/despite-job-losses-lower-prices-from-trade-with-china-have-left-us-households-massively-better-off/.

That the U.S. and China occupy such dominant positions in the world suggests concomitant accountabilities. According to China, **major countries have major responsibilities to humanity**. Chinese officials argue that global existential challenges—pandemics, nuclear proliferation, and climate change—cannot be solved without U.S.-China cooperation. For instance, the U.S. and China together contribute to 40% of the planet's current greenhouse gas emissions.

China takes exception to the U.S. definition of bilateral relations as antagonistic competition. This U.S. stance toward China is bipartisan. Upon assuming office in 2021, Biden—despite previous campaign rhetoric—largely continued Trump's earlier confrontational policies, escalating tariffs and export controls. In 2024, he quadrupled tariffs on Chinese electric vehicles to over 100% and tightened investment restrictions. Trump, back in office in 2025, threatened 200% tariffs on rare-earth magnets. The two major U.S. parties compete over who can be tougher on Beijing.

Thinking Through the Unthinkable

The military dimension is even more ominous. Roughly 400 U.S. military bases encircle China, from Japan and South Korea to the Philippines and Australia.[87] Biden expanded the Quad, advanced the AUKUS pact, reinvigorated Five Eyes, and inaugurated a trilateral "mini-NATO" with Japan and South Korea.

China, in contrast, maintains no bases anywhere near the U.S. mainland—a point Chinese officials highlight to question who is truly threatening whom. From Beijing's perspective, U.S. actions reflect

---

87 John Reed, "Surrounded: How the U.S. Is Encircling China with Military Bases," *Foreign Policy*, August 20, 2013, https://foreignpolicy.com/2013/08/20/surrounded-how-the-u-s-is-encircling-china-with-military-bases/.

containment and even provocation. They note the U.S. would never tolerate a similar military buildup on its own borders.

In fact, the U.S. Army even commissioned the RAND Corporation's research report *War with China—Thinking Through the Unthinkable*,[88] paying the best minds that money can buy with U.S. taxpayers' money to game Armageddon. The study ominously warned that even if the U.S. ultimately prevailed, the conflict would devastate both sides and be nearly impossible to contain. Any conflict over Taiwan, the South China Sea, or another flashpoint could rapidly escalate, draw in other nations, or even trigger nuclear exchanges. U.S. military strategists openly acknowledge the peril that once conflict erupts, each side would face strong incentives to strike first. Yet, the U.S. continues planning for war.[89]

U.S. Hegemony Versus China's Shared Destiny

The superpower rivalry extends beyond economics and security to ideology. In his official national security strategy, Joe Biden described "the contest for the future of our world." He vowed that his administration will "seize this decisive decade to…outmaneuver our geopolitical competitors," meaning chiefly China.[90]

---

88 David C. Gompert et al., *War with China: Thinking Through the Unthinkable* (RAND Corporation, 2016), https://www.rand.org/content/dam/rand/pubs/research_reports/RR1100/RR1140/RAND_RR1140.pdf.

89 Ben Norton, "'We Are Preparing for War' with China 'Threat,' Says US Defense Secretary Pete Hegseth," *Geopolitical Economy Report*, June 6, 2025, https://geopoliticaleconomy.com/2025/06/06/preparing-war-china-threat-us-defense-secretary-pete-hegseth/.

90 The White House, "National Security Strategy," The White House, October 12, 2022, https://bidenwhitehouse.archives.gov/wp-content/uploads/2022/10/Biden-Harris-Administrations-National-Security-Strategy-10.2022.pdf.

Biden then promised to impose "American leadership"—in effect, domination, because the world did not vote to make the president of the U.S. a planetary potentate. Perversely, the U.S. is already the world leader in having the most mass shootings, the highest national debt, and the largest incarcerated population. The U.S. also currently leads the world in the sale of military equipment, military expenditures, and foreign military bases.

Whistling in the dark, Biden concluded that "our economy is dynamic." In fact, the U.S. economy is dominated by the non-productive FIRE (finance, insurance, and real estate) sectors, while China has become the industrial "workshop of the world." Statista projects that China could overtake the US as the largest economy by 2030.[91]

In contrast to Trump's tariffs on the world, China's Belt and Road Initiative (BRI) is a global infrastructure development program, which has invested in over 150 countries. In Beijing's view, such projects demonstrate an alternative path to global leadership: instead of military domination or sanctions, a great power should contribute to other countries' growth and stability. Major countries, Xi suggests, **achieve peace through prosperity**—by helping solve the underlying development problems that often lead to conflict.

The global reception to China's initiatives—BRI, BRICS, and its Global Development and Security frameworks—has been largely positive, as they provide an alternative to a U.S.-dominated world order.

Not surprisingly, Washington fears these alternatives. According to the official U.S. national security strategy, Beijing's multipolar vision

---

91 Statista.com, "Gross Domestic Product (GDP) at Current Prices in China and the United States from 2005 to 2020 with Forecasts until 2035," Statista. Com, 2025, https://www.statista.com/statistics/1070632/gross-domestic-product-gdp-china-us/.

Contrasting Strategies of the U.S. and China

"tilts the global playing field to its benefit."[92] In contrast to the U.S. and its Western allies, whose wealth grew through colonial exploitation,[93] China has elevated 800 million people out of poverty without resorting to imperial wars.[94]

Although U.S. imperialism continues along an increasingly rapacious trajectory under Trump, the current occupant of the White House has revived diplomatic efforts for global denuclearization involving China and Russia. This initiative should not be mistaken for a U.S. move toward peace but rather a pragmatic realization that, as China and Russia advance, Washington's interest is in preserving its strategic military advantage before it is overtaken.

The U.S.-China contest for the future is not merely about tariffs and military bases; it is a rivalry between two competing visions of world order. The Chinese paradigm of global cooperation stands in opposition to the U.S.'s zero-sum model. In today's contentious geopolitical climate, China and by extension the Global South pose a countervailing space to U.S. imperial hegemony, displaying both maturity and confidence that the rationality of "win-win" peaceful development will prevail.

* * *

---

92 The White House, "National Security Strategy."

93 Immanuel Ness, *Southern Insurgency: The Coming of the Global Working Class*, Wildcat (Pluto Press, 2015), https://www.plutobooks.com/9780745335995/southern-insurgency/.

94 The World Bank, "Lifting 800 Million People Out of Poverty – New Report Looks at Lessons from China's Experience," The World Bank, April 1, 2022, https://www.worldbank.org/en/news/press-release/2022/04/01/lifting-800-million-people-out-of-poverty-new-report-looks-at-lessons-from-china-s-experience.

Roger D. Harris is a member of the human rights organization Task Force on the Americas (https://taskforceamericas.org/) and is on the executive committee of the US Peace Council (USPC—https://uspeacecouncil.org/). Research for this paper was informed by a USPC delegation to China with our counterpart, the Chinese People's Association for Peace and Disarmament.

The Race for Moondust: U.S. Imperialism vs. China

by Janet Mayes

There is much fanfare surrounding the National Aeronautics and Space Administration's (NASA) Artemis III project, which boasts that it will land the first woman and the first person of color on the moon within the next two years. The mission depends on the success of centibillionaire Elon Musk's super rocket, the SpaceX Starship, designed to ferry astronauts from lunar orbit to the moon's surface.

In 2021, SpaceX won a $2.89 billion contract with NASA to develop the super rocket. So far its performance has been lacking. In 2023, the rocket's unsuccessful explosive launch spewed brown grime and dust onto populated areas in Texas's Boca Chica area,[95] which Musk calls "a wasteland." The blasts are destroying the fragile surrounding ecostructure, replete with endangered species.[96] In March of 2025, their super rocket again exploded, spewing debris on The

---

95 Livia Albeck-Ripka, "SpaceX's Starship Kicked Up a Dust Cloud, Leaving Texans With a Mess," *The New York Times*, April 21, 2023, https://www.nytimes.com/2023/04/21/us/spacex-rocket-dust-texas.html.

96 Eric Roesch, "SpaceX's Texas Rocket Is Going To Cause A Lot More Damage Than Anyone Thinks," *ESG Hound*, April 16, 2023, https://blog.esghound.com/p/spacexs-texas-rocket-is-going-to.

Bahamas[97] and temporarily grounding flights at Florida airports.[98]

Several months later, Starship finally achieved a "largely successful" test flight. But Artemis III is still behind schedule, now expected to launch no earlier than 2028. The China National Space Administration, meanwhile, has already successfully tested a lunar lander.[99]

A Global Clean Energy Solution or a Multibillion-Dollar Market?

What is this really all about? The United States is hellbent on building mining stations on the moon before China does because of another kind of dust: moondust, replete with helium-3, touted to be the fuel for an emerging technology that will provide clean, abundant energy.

In 2021, Beijing's Research Institute of Uranium Geology announced that China's lunar Chang'e 5 mission had identified this precious mineral on the moon. Helium-3 fusion technology promises to produce clean energy: nuclear energy without radioactive waste. Fossil fuels and even current nuclear power plant technology would become obsolete.

Three space missions bringing back the helium-rich moondust

---

97 The Bahamas, "Statement from the Government of The Bahamas on Space X Starship Operations," Bahamas.com, March 7, 2025, https://www.bahamas.com/pressroom/statement-from-the-government-of-the-bahamas-on-space-x-starship-operations.

98 Mauricio Maldonado, "SpaceX Debris Grounds Flights at South Florida Airports," *CBS News*, March 6, 2025, https://www.cbsnews.com/miami/news/spacex-debris-grounds-flights-at-south-florida-airports/.

99 Kenneth Chang, "SpaceX's Giant Mars Rocket Completes Nearly Flawless Test Flight," *The New York Times*, August 26, 2025, https://www.nytimes.com/2025/08/26/science/spacex-starship-test-launch.html.

would provide the entire planet with energy for a year.[100] One cargo bay load (about 25 tons) on a space shuttle would power the entire U.S. for a year, representing a value of about $3 billion per ton.

"The country that controls the source of energy that keeps technological civilization running will control the Earth," said an article in *The Hill* in 2022, elaborating that "[t]he moon could become the Persian Gulf of the mid- to late-21st century. Clean and abundant fusion energy would change the world in ways that can barely be evaluated." China, along with Russia, plans to complete construction of a lunar base by 2035. Then it will mine the helium-3 rich crystal "Changesite-(Y)," which is contained in vast quantities on the moon's regolith (layer of unconsolidated rocky material covering bedrock). *The Hill*'s analysis described the crystal mineral sample returned by the Chang'e probe as "exceedingly tiny, about one-tenth the size of a human hair. ... The helium-3 that it contains has the potential to change the world."[101]

Since China has accelerated plans for lunar exploration and future mining, the panicked imperialist countries, particularly the U.S., cannot sit by and just watch. They are horrified at the possibility that China could be the first country to gather the moondust that contains helium-3. If they lose this space race, imperialist governments and corporations will lose the opportunity to corner the multibillion dollar market for this potentially planet-saving technology, and sell it for a profit.

---

100 Jia Hepeng, "He Asked for the Moon-and Got It," *China Daily*, July 26, 2006, https://www.chinadaily.com.cn/cndy/2006-07/26/content_649325.htm.

101 Mark R. Whittington, "China Has Returned Helium-3 from the Moon, Opening Door to Future Technology," *The Hill*, September 18, 2022, https://thehill.com/opinion/technology/3647216-china-has-returned-helium-3-from-the-moon-opening-door-to-future-technology/.

In preparation for landing people on the moon before China does, NASA has engaged several private companies to gather moondust samples which, according to *SpaceNews*, is "part of an effort by the agency to establish a precedent for ownership and use of space resources." For example, in 2020, NASA hired Masten Space System to gather small lunar samples, which NASA will then own. "Today's Lunar Regolith Purchase is small measured in dollars," Masten tweeted, "but monumental in impact on unlocking the value of space for humanity."[102] After it filed for bankruptcy in 2022, it was acquired by Astrobotic Technology, which retained the Masten team contracted by NASA.[103]

In May 2025, Interlune, a startup company founded by, among others, two former executives of Jeff Bezos's spaceship company Blue Origin, revealed that it had signed a contract with the U.S. Department of Energy to harvest three liters of helium-3 from the lunar regolith and return it to Earth.[104]

The ultimate value, of course, is mammoth profits for the U.S., its imperialist allies, and its private companies if they control the mining, transporting and fusion processing of helium-3. Given the fragile condition of Western economies, it is a space race the imperialists cannot afford to lose.

---

102 Jeff Foust, "NASA Selects Four Companies for Lunar Sample Purchases," *SpaceNews* (Washington), December 3, 2020, https://spacenews.com/nasa-selects-four-companies-for-lunar-sample-purchases/.

103 Brianna Wessling, "Astrobotic Acquires Masten Space Systems for $4.5M," *The Robot Report*, September 13, 2022, https://www.therobotreport.com/astrobotic-acquires-masten-space-systems-for-4-5m/.

104 Emma Gatti, "Lunar Helium-3: Separating Market from Marketing," *SpaceNews*, June 4, 2025, https://spacenews.com/lunar-helium-3-separating-market-from-marketing/.

Janet Mayes

A Mountain of Lies Exposed

The U.S. and its imperialist allies rationalize spending billions of taxpayers' dollars to beat China to the moon by repeating unsubstantiated lies and the standard China-bashing. These tactics are well-documented; for example, articles by Sara Flounders ("Accomplishments belie U.S. propaganda")[105] and Arjae Red ("Imperialist media can't stop lying about mosques in China"),[106] as well as Carlos Martinez's book *The East is Still Red: Chinese Socialism in the 21st Century* have all exposed similar lies.

U.S. officials and media figures often claim that China must be prevented from "ruling" the world, and frequently lie in support of this accusation. In 2022, warning of a new "space race" with China, NASA chief Bill Nelson was quoted by the *Global Times* as being "very concerned about" the joint Chinese-Russian lunar research base, and baselessly accused China of wanting to "occupy the moon."[107] The *Washington Examiner*, a right-wing U.S. news outlet, attacked China in 2023 with the fabricated, ominous statement: "If the West turns away from space, China, which cares little for human rights … will forge ahead. A Chinese-dominated space frontier is not a future that anyone should want."[108]

---

105 Sara Flounders, "Accomplishments Belie U.S. Propaganda," *Workers World*, June 9, 2023, https://www.workers.org/2023/06/71505/.

106 Arjae Red, "Imperialist Media Can't Stop Lying about Mosques in China," *Workers World*, June 22, 2023, https://www.workers.org/2023/06/71812/.

107 Fan Anqi and Zhang Changyue, "NASA Chief Urged to Drop Cold War Mentality after His Lashing out at China's Space Progress," *Global Times*, July 3, 2022, https://www.globaltimes.cn/page/202207/1269666.shtml.

108 Mark Whittington, "A Smear of Christianity, Capitalism, and the Colonization of Space," *The Washington Examiner*, April 12, 2023, https://www.washingtonexaminer.com/op-eds/2762067/a-smear-of-christianity-capitalism-and-the-col-

The Race for Moondust

China's Humane Approach to Battling Climate Disaster

Actually, it is clear that a "Chinese dominant space frontier" is a future that everyone *should* want. If our planet is to survive the climate disaster, it is imperative that the imperialists lose the race to the moon.

Far from seeking to profit, China's approach to international energy production is in fact geared toward protecting the planet. As Martinez explains when discussing China's "green energy" solution in his abundantly-researched book, Socialist China's international humanitarian policies are aimed at saving the globe from climate catastrophe.

China is not driven by the profit motive, and will not seek world domination by harnessing helium-3 technology. As *Workers World* Managing Editor Deirdre Griswold wrote: "China's economic planners have the power to make decisions that cost a lot of money, but will benefit the people—and the world—over the long run."[109]

In the meantime, in addition to developing the fusion technology, China has begun the construction of a "Space Solar Power Station" (SSPS), a space-based power generation system used to collect solar energy before converting it into electricity and then into microwaves. It is expected to launch into low orbit in two years. By 2050, it is estimated that the solar plant will be able to generate more kilowatt-hours of energy in one year than are contained in all of the oil within the Earth. China's goal is to provide free clean energy, not reap profit.[110]

---

onization-of-space/.

109 Deirdre Griswold, "China Takes Another Big Step Away from CO2," *Workers World*, January 24, 2017, workers.org/2017/01/29359/.

110 J. Hagler, "Socialism Leads Humanity out of Artificial Scarcity," *Workers World*, February 28, 2025, https://www.workers.org/2025/02/84155/.

A 21st-Century Gold Rush

In 2020, NASA, the U.S. Department of State, and the newly re-established National Space Council created the Artemis Accords. Its principles, according to the State Department, "establish a common political understanding regarding mutually beneficial practices in the exploration and use of outer space, including activities conducted in support of NASA's Artemis program."[111]

The document sounds benign, promising cooperation among signatory countries, all sorts of safety protocols, and preservation of lunar historic sites, such as the first Apollo landing site. However, a sleight of hand embedded in the Accord's wording about "safety zones" actually grants control of lunar mining sites to whichever countries and corporations lay down a stake first—except for China!

Both China and Russia have criticized the concept of "safety zones" laid out in the Accords, and according to an article in the *Space Policy* journal, "Whilst the use of Safety Zones is ostensibly proposed for small scale In Situ Resource Utilisation (ISRU) activities focussed on lunar water production, messaging around the Artemis Accords has indicated that there may be an intent to use them to set precedent for longer term, larger scale commercial resource activity."[112]

Not surprisingly, 24 of the 50 signatories to the Accords are members of NATO, and the others fall within the economic and strategic influence of the U.S., such as Israel and Japan. The U.S. Congress in

---

111 US Department of State, "Artemis Accords," U.S., Department of State, n.d., accessed August 30, 2025, https://www.state.gov/bureau-of-oceans-and-international-environmental-and-scientific-affairs/artemis-accords.

112 Ben McKeown et al., "Artemis Accords: Are Safety Zones Practical for Long Term Commercial Lunar Resource Utilisation?," *Space Policy* 62 (November 2022): 101504, https://doi.org/10.1016/j.spacepol.2022.101504.

fact voted against inviting China to sign, being against cooperating with their chief competitor.

Bezos versus Musk

Centibillionaire Jeff Bezos, founder and current executive chairman of Amazon and owner of the *Washington Post*, did not win the contract for his spaceship company, Blue Origin, to ferry astronauts to the moon. But he has not been deterred from profitable lunar ventures. He is developing "Blue Alchemist" technology, a process that would produce solar cells and transmission wire using simulated moon regolith. Blue Origin claims that the resulting solar cells could operate for over a decade in the moon's "harsh" environment.[113]

Bezos and Elon Musk are also rivals in their long-term goals to send their rocket ships to Mars. In early 2023, Bezos' untested rocket ship New Glenn landed a launch contract with NASA for the Escape and Plasma Acceleration and Dynamics Explorers (EscaPADE) mission to study Mars' magnetosphere.[114] The moon will become the launching pad for these ventures.

Musk, the notorious owner of Tesla and X, and briefly President Trump's closest advisor, infamously advocates detonating atomic

---

113 Jon Fingas, "Blue Origin Made Solar Cells by Smelting Simulated Moon Dust," *Engadget*, February 13, 2023, https://www.engadget.com/blue-origina-solar-cells-moon-soil-173908801.html.

114 Claire A. O'Shea, "NASA Selects Blue Origin to Launch Mars' Magnetosphere Study Mission," National Aeronautics and Space Administration, February 9, 2023, https://www.nasa.gov/news-release/nasa-selects-blue-origin-to-launch-mars-magnetosphere-study-mission/.

bombs over Mars' polar regions to make it more livable![115] His SpaceX super rocket was originally designed for colonization of Mars, where, he envisions, a self-sustaining colony could escape the possible demise of humanity on Earth.

It is possible that Trump's decision to deeply cut Artemis funding from NASA's budget as part of his "One Big Beautiful Bill" was influenced by Musk's focus on Mars. But even the Republican-dominated U.S. Congress could not fall into line with Trump on this issue. While not explicitly stating that they were afraid to lose future control of the hugely profitable helium-3 mining, they succeeded in restoring some of the funding for Artemis. The NASA funding amendment to the Bill was written by Senator Ted Cruz of Texas. According to Cruz's Senate committee, the amendment "dedicates almost $10 billion to win the new space race with China and ensure America dominates space. Makes targeted, critical investments in Mars-forward technology, Artemis missions and Moon to Mars program, and the International Space Station."[116]

Panic ensued after the passage of the Bill. In an opinion piece published by *Scientific American*, Matthew Beddingfield writes: "This conflict and dizzying back and forth regarding America's moonshot project suggests a question: Are we committed to Artemis and the broader goal of understanding space? Or to put it another way: Do we

---

115 Mike Wall, "Elon Musk Floats 'Nuke Mars' Idea Again (He Has T-Shirts)," *Space*, August 17, 2019, https://www.space.com/elon-musk-nuke-mars-terraforming.html.

116 Bud McLaughlin, "U.S. Senate 'Directive' Would Revive Artemis IV & V, Protect Huntsville's NASA Jobs and Ensure American Dominance in Space," *Yellowhammer News*, June 9, 2025, https://yellowhammernews.com/u-s-senate-directive-would-revive-artemis-iv-v-protect-huntsvilles-nasa-jobs-and-ensure-american-dominance-in-space/.

want to win this new race to the moon? The current administration owes us an answer."[117]

U.S. Space Force: Ready and Able

While corporations scheme to gain riches, the Pentagon's militarization of space is intensifying to protect capitalist interests and uphold U.S. domination, as discussed in the *Workers World* article "Astronomical imperialism!" in 2019.[118] That year, the U.S. Department of Defense established a sixth branch of the military, the U.S. Space Force.

The establishment of the Space Force sent a clear warning to Russia, China, Iran and any other countries that the U.S. views as global competitors, informing them that the imperialist U.S. is staking its claim to supremacy over space technology—and over outer space itself!

Billions of taxpayers' dollars, sorely needed for the health and welfare of human beings worldwide, are funneled into these corporate or militarized space programs instead. As usual, as exciting and as visionary the exploration of space appears to be, capitalists manipulate scientific curiosity and discovery into profit-making ventures.

* * *

---

117 Matthew Beddingfield, "Strong Support for NASA and Project Artemis Will Advance the U.S.," *Scientific American*, August 2, 2025, https://www.scientificamerican.com/article/strong-support-for-nasa-and-project-artemis-will-advance-the-u-s/.

118 Janet Mayes, "Astronomical Imperialism!," *Workers World*, October 1, 2019, workers.org/2019/10/43849.

Janet Mayes

Janet Mayes is an amateur astronomer and the author of Beyond the Horse's Eye, a Fantasy Out of Time, *a science fiction novel about U.S. hegemony in space, under the pen name Janet Rose. A review can be found at tinyurl.com/y6fzefun. She is also the web manager for the International Action Center website.*

Science Fiction or Science Reality? Socialism Leads Humanity out of Artificial Scarcity

by JR Hagler

"The acquisition of wealth is no longer the driving force in our lives. We work to better ourselves and the rest of humanity," said fictional Captain Jean-Luc Picard of Star Trek: The Next Generation.

Humanity is standing on the cusp. Climate change is presenting the U.S. with the same choice nature has gifted all its species: evolve or die. Change is the only constant.

As the cost of basic goods and, more importantly, energy continues to rise across the capitalist economies of Japan, Western Europe and North America, others have decided to utilize their economy to actually innovate. Instead of phallic vanity projects of the impotent super-wealthy, presented by SpaceX and Blue Origin, the Chinese Academy of Space Technology (CAST) has shown humanity a different way forward into the stars.

The construction of a "Space Solar Power Station" (SSPS) has already begun and is expected to launch into low orbit by 2028. Over 100 researchers and students across a multitude of disciplines are collectively leading the project for the SSPS at Xidian University.

An article from the Chinese Global Television Network (CGTN), published in June of 2022, reads: "SSPS is a space-based power generation system used to collect solar energy before converting it to electricity and then microwaves. Next, the energy in microwaves is to be transmitted and harvested by the receiving antenna either in space or on the Earth's surface, which converts microwaves back into electricity."

The project illustrates socialist China's ability to do long-term planning. The same article says: "By 2035, the microwave transmitting antenna is expected to be enlarged to about 100 meters plus power generation of 10 megawatts. The goal in 2050 is to build a commercially operated solar plant that generates electricity of two gigawatts with an antenna that would be around one-kilometer and a complex solar cell array to be assembled in space."[119] This monumental undertaking has the power to generate more kilowatt-hours of energy in one year than all of the oil contained within the Earth. It has been called everything from the "Manhattan Project of Energy" to the "Three Gorges Dam in Space."[120]

The potential to create free, clean energy is here, and is being led by a country with a planned economy, actively pursuing socialist development.

U.S. Scientists Knew it Since 1968

The irony of this announcement is that scientists in the capitalist-led United States have known about this technology since 1968, when

---

119 CGTN, "China Aims to Construct First Space Solar Power Station in 2028," *China Global Television Network*, June 22, 2022, https://news.cgtn.com/news/2022-06-22/China-aims-to-construct-first-Space-Solar-Power-Station-in-2028-1b49ktMx5W8/index.html.

120 Zhang Tong, "China Plans to Build 'Three Gorges Dam in Space' to Harness Solar Power," *South China Morning Post* (Beijing), January 9, 2025, https://www.scmp.com/news/china/science/article/3294091/china-plans-build-three-gorges-dam-space-harness-solar-power.

scientist and aerospace engineer Peter Glaser conceptualized the idea. U.S. corporations could have spearheaded the development of this technology decades ago. Instead, the government invested a measly $17.5 million into Northrop Grumman in 2013 so the weapons manufacturer could "research" the development of an SSPS.

Similar investment is also going into other weapons companies like Lockheed Martin. Imagine, instead of spending 1.5 trillion U.S. tax dollars on the boondoggle of all weapons systems, the F-35, the U.S. had spent that money building the groundwork of an SSPS. If the U.S. government had something akin to a "five year plan," it could have made progress in developing this energy source.

It's easier, however, for capitalist enterprises to make quarterly profits supplying weapons for killing women and children in Palestine than to develop an economy in a way that benefits all of society, instead of just a wealthy few.

Projects like the SSPS could not be coming at a more crucial time. Climate change is putting into question the future of humanity and, if the worst-case scenarios are to unfold, of most other species as well. The rate of CO_2 being pumped into the atmosphere is unprecedented in planetary history. Humanity is truly in uncharted waters.

Running an entire economy and society based on what is most profitable is what led the U.S. into these crises. The capitalist class cannot lead the U.S. out of them, because the gears of capitalism would grind to a halt if profits are even interrupted, never mind if they ceased entirely due to technologies capable of providing near-limitless, scarcity-free energy.

The Communist Party of China has proven that innovations capable of seeing humanity through this storm are possible with central planning and socially directed investment, if necessary over a long term. The U.S., Western Europe, Japan and world capitalism are going

Science Fiction or Science Reality?

through yet another economic crisis while engaged in yet more "forever" wars as their rates of profit continue to fall.

The working and oppressed masses of these countries do not have to continue letting their leaders take them down the primrose path to ecocide and World War III. As we near the physical limits of the planet itself, Rosa Luxemburg's challenge of "socialism or barbarism" is now being replaced by the challenge of "socialism or extinction."

* * *

> *J Hagler is an anti-war community organizer in Coeur d'Alene, Idaho, a stronghold of right-wing reaction where the youth have a very limited future. J focuses on the liberating potential of the masses and scientific social planning as a way out of capitalist dystopia.*

4.

Moving from Isolation to Prosperity

Leadership Was the Key in China's Targeted Poverty Alleviation Campaign

by Dee Knight

China's historic achievement of eliminating extreme poverty across the country can be compared with the Long March, the legendary escape from fascist repression that saved the revolution nearly a century ago. The Long March enabled the Communist Party to set up revolutionary base areas and launch the bold and massive land reform that was the first step in overcoming poverty for millions of peasants.

Much of the struggle in both the Long March and the Targeted Poverty Alleviation (TPA) campaign took place in China's remote mountain areas, far removed from the major cities located on the country's eastern and southern coasts. In these cities, large-scale socialist industrialization was the motor of China's rapid development. But the development was uneven: industrialization propelled the cities to advance ahead of the countryside, requiring a large-scale campaign to correct the imbalance. Commenting on this campaign, President Xi Jinping said:

> "China's overall productive forces have significantly improved and in many areas our production capacity leads the world. The more prominent problem is that our development is unbalanced and inadequate. This has become the main constraining factor in meeting the people's increasing needs for a better life."

Leadership Was the Key

According to the landmark 2021 study *Serve the People: The Eradication of Extreme Poverty in China* by Tings Chak of the Tricontinental Institute for Social Research, in the TPA campaign, the Party mobilized 800,000 members to go to areas of deep poverty to visit and survey every household across the country. Then it mobilized more people to verify the data, then dispatched over three million cadres to poor villages to work directly with residents. Of that number, about half a million were carefully selected to act as village first secretaries of the Party.[121]

It was the heroism of thousands of Party leaders and organizers that led to success. "Many cadres were unable to return home to visit families for long stretches of time," the *Serve the People* study says. "Some fell ill in the harsh natural conditions of rural areas and more than 1,800 Party members and officials lost their lives in the fight against poverty."

Rugged, cave-filled mountains form the border between China's provinces of Hunan and Guizhou, where some of the earliest steps of the Long March were taken. The people there are isolated from the thriving nearby industrial cities to the north and south. Guangzhou and Shenzhen, close to bustling Hong Kong, are vibrant show-places of China's lightning-fast development in recent decades. Many poor families who lived west of the mountains sent their men, or both parents, to the factories in Guangzhou, leaving the children in the care of their grandparents. That was their way of coping with the region's deep poverty. (Guangzhou was formerly known as Canton.)

---

121 Tings Chak (翟庭君) et al., *Serve the People: The Eradication of Extreme Poverty in China*, Studies on Socialist Construction (The Tricontinental Institute for Social Research, 2021), 62, https://thetricontinental.org/studies-1-socialist-construction/.

These mountains had sheltered the beleaguered Chinese Red Army in the Long March. The TPA campaign can be considered a return of the revolution to the isolated mountain people. As part of launching the campaign, in November 2013, Communist Party General Secretary Xi Jinping made his way along an unpaved dirt road to Shibadong (literally "18 Caves") Village to visit the residents there.[122] His hosts were an aging couple of the Miao ethnic minority, one of China's 55 officially recognized ethnic minorities, with a population of about 11 million. The Miao are the largest of Guizhou's 17 ethnic minority communities, which together comprise roughly 40 percent of the province's population of about 40 million. President Xi needed a language interpreter to communicate with them.

When Xi Jinping entered their house the villagers recalled that "he looked at the barn and asked if we had enough food to eat, if we planted fruit trees, and if we raised pigs. He also went to the pigpen to see if the pigs were big and fat." Speaking later with a group of villagers, President Xi gave advice for developing Shibadong Village. "We should adapt our measures to local conditions, and go for targeted poverty alleviation."

President Xi compared Shibadong Village to a famous nearby national forest park, which was featured in the movie *Avatar*, with dense forests, deep ravines, deep canyons, unusual peaks, caves, and pillar-like rock formations. He suggested rural tourism could be fostered and combined with cooperative farm industry, such as fruit plantations and cattle breeding, as well as Miao handicrafts.

---

122 The Contemporary World Press, *Leaving No One Behind: China's Stories of Poverty Alleviation*, First (The Contemporary World Press, 2020).

Leadership Was the Key

Village First Secretaries: The Strategic Core of Targeted Poverty Alleviation

The key was leadership at local, county and provincial levels: a work team composed of the natural leaders locally and young Communist Party officials in the region who were well versed in rural work, able to speak the local language, and understand local customs. The role of the Party was crucial. It dispatched a carefully selected village first secretary who was transferred to the village to work there as a resident official for poverty reduction—to "go all out in support of the village's Party branch." The first secretaries' average age was 37. Nearly half of them had master's degrees. But most important was their high social and political consciousness, to "take roots in the rural areas, brave all hardship, and lead the local people to win the fight against poverty with their wisdom, toil and sweat."

I met such a "selected leader," a government functionary in her "day job" in the southwestern province of Guizhou, who answered the call to volunteer in the TPA campaign. She told of her experience as a first secretary in a Miao village, visiting all the residents, identifying the local leaders and making inventory of strengths, needs and resources. She helped train and develop the local Party leadership, and organized work teams for each project. She was especially proud of a marketing plan for local handicrafts, which allowed the villagers to generate income from their treasure trove of products and talents.

The Party was the glue linking the village work team with support resources from across the country. Cities that were already prosperous were mobilized to send all kinds of help. Leaders there pressured private companies to "adopt" village work teams. For example, the internet giant Alibaba was "drafted" to connect the villages to the internet. Public and private sectors got involved to provide poor people with access to financing (loans, subsidies and microcredit), technical training, equipment, and markets.

It was a united front. President Xi said "We should mobilize the energies of our whole Party, our whole country, and our whole society... We will pay particular attention to helping people increase confidence in their own ability to lift themselves out of poverty."

The "Foolishness" of Moving Mountains

The ancient fable of the Foolish Old Man Who Dared to Move Mountains is a Chinese favorite. Nearly all Chinese school children know the story by heart. In the modern version, the "old man" is understood to be the Communist Party, and the mountains were feudalism, capitalism, and imperialism. But in the remote mountains of Guizhou province where ethnic minorities predominate, the famous story got a new version, with the "foolish old man" replaced by Ms. Deng Yingxiang, who led her village over many years to forge a tunnel through a cage-like mountain that had trapped them in isolation and poverty.

The village's entrapment in the mountain caused enormous hardship. Deng Yingxiang lost her first child due to the difficulty of carrying the feverish baby through a treacherous mountain path to a hospital. Cattle herded along the steep mountain path by the villagers often fell off the cliff and died. When the county government planned a rural power grid project in 1999, it wasn't possible to transport utility poles and transformers to the isolated village, so grid construction was postponed. That was the last straw.

The villagers decided to dig a primitive tunnel, at least large enough to get utility poles and transformers through, so the village could be electrified. Deng Yingxiang led a work group digging through the mountain with hand tools ten hours a day for several years. The villagers recognized her tough tenacity, encouraged her to become a Party member and elected her to the village branch committee. In that role, she was determined to speed up the tunnel project, calling on the township and county governments to help her buy an old tractor, rent an air compressor, and buy some explosives. Ten years after the first tunneling began, in December 2010, Deng Yingxiang spoke at a groundbreaking ceremony saying "We have been trapped here in the mountains for generations and we have suffered a lot. Today I swear that even if I have to dig with my hands and bite with my teeth, we will have a road connecting to the outside world."

Yingxiang and her husband organized drilling teams with the other villagers, and mobilized at every level possible—county government, urban construction bureaus, forestry and water conservancy bureaus, and much more. After 270 days of hard work, a tunnel 216 meters long, five meters high and four meters wide was completed. People could drive cars through the tunnel to the village for the first time ever. Village life changed dramatically. Villagers built brick houses, bought motorcycles and even cars. Children could walk to school in thirty minutes.

As leader of the villagers' committee, Deng Yingxiang mobilized funds from county and provincial levels to build an activity center and a cultural plaza. She helped renovate more than 200 houses, installed a 4G mobile base station and upgraded the power grid, rebuilt and expanded access roads, and secured safe drinking water in the village. She also established "joyful farmhouse" diners, small supermarkets, and an e-commerce platform. Villagers who had been migrant workers were able to return home and help form growers' cooperatives and industrial development projects—"planting fruit trees and herbal medicine in the mountain, growing rice and vegetables in the field, raising chickens and ducks at the waterside, raising black pigs at home."

Deng Yingxiang's leadership was the key to success. She was able to galvanize the villagers to continue with many more improvements. Through joining the three forces of the village Party branch committee, the villagers' committee, and a new ecological agriculture development cooperative, they transformed their lives.

A "Workaholic" Village First Secretary

Gao Shanshan was a notable village first secretary. She was nicknamed a "workaholic" by the villagers she led in the old revolutionary base area of northern Shanxi province, near the border with Mongolia. When she won an award for outstanding performance working with the villagers, Gao said "I think the remoter and poorer a mountainous village one works in, the more one can hone her ability and temperament; and the more difficult the environment is, the more one can grow and be enlightened…"

As village first secretary, Gao used the Party's "seven-in-one" toolkit of poverty alleviation measures: industrial development, Party building, social welfare, remolding people's thinking, sharing culture and knowledge, improving infrastructure, and starting local businesses. She made a study tour of cities outside her assigned areas, then held meetings with villagers on her return to share advanced thinking and methods. With help from the Communist Youth League's Central Committee, she launched a "dream-assistance" project called "constant self-exertion and high and grand aspiration." She won support from private companies and foundations, as well as educational institutions in Beijing, for village education initiatives, and inspired the villagers she worked with, arousing their enthusiasm to escape poverty. They told her "We will follow in whatever you do!"

Leadership Was the Key

The Campaign's Impact

In February 2021, the Chinese government announced that extreme poverty had been abolished in China. It was the culmination of decades of revolution, beginning even before the triumph in 1949. The early decades of socialist construction laid the foundation that was enriched and deepened during the Reform and Opening Up period. In the "targeted" phase that began in 2013, the Chinese government built more than a million kilometers of rural roads, brought internet access to 98 percent of the country's poor villages, renovated homes for millions of people and built new ones for millions more.

The Communist Party leadership mobilized broad sectors of the society—millions of people, state-owned and private enterprises, educational institutions, and the military, which assisted nearly a million people in more than 4,000 villages, contributing infrastructure and health projects. This was socialist leadership at its best. A participant in a recent Friends of Socialist China visit said that socialism is "doing the most important work there is, which is lifting up people's lives and solving huge complicated problems like poverty, climate change, and attacks on sovereignty and threats of war."

The poverty alleviation program assures a minimum income and "two assurances" of food and clothing, plus "three guarantees" of basic medical services, safe housing with drinking water and electricity, and free and compulsory education. Life expectancy in China was just over 30 in 1949. Now it is 78—higher than in the United States. Illiteracy has been largely eliminated across the country.

The *Serve the People* study by Tings Chak summed up the success of the Targeted Poverty Alleviation program this way: "TPA's industrial poverty alleviation policies impacted 98 percent of poor households and established 300,000 industrial bases for agricultural production as well as animal breeding and processing across each of 832 poor counties. Millions of poor people are employed in these bases, plus millions more in rural enterprises. Poverty alleviation workshops (small-scale centers of production organized on idle land or in people's homes) contributed to nearly tripling the per capita income of poor households from 2015 to 2019…"

In the cases of people living in extremely remote areas or exposed to frequent natural disasters, the TPA helped people move from rural to newly built urban or suburban communities. New housing was constructed, along with thousands of schools and kindergartens, hospitals, community health centers, elder-care facilities and cultural centers.

Ecological conservation and restoration have been key methods to address poverty. Afforestation in desert areas has mobilized thousands of poverty alleviation cooperatives. The UN's Food and Agriculture Organization (FAO) has ranked China as a global leader in reforestation, accounting for 25 percent of the world's total growth in "leaf area" between 1990 and 2020.

Infrastructure Development as Economic Motor

Alongside the giant Targeted Poverty Alleviation campaign, China has implemented the most ambitious infrastructure development in human history. Trains, highways, bridges, seaports and airports, together with internet and telephone connectivity, have transformed the country's infrastructure, employing millions of workers, while dynamizing economic linkage between the cities and countryside. Health and education is now within reach for China's entire population.

For the people of Guizhou, the poverty alleviation campaign ran parallel with massive infrastructure projects—building many bridges and high-speed highways, and making Guiyang, Guizhou's capital, a hub for bullet trains running north to south and southeast to northwest, criss-crossing in Guiyang. This surge of development has been the hallmark of the policy of Common Prosperity—a way of "leveling" the country's new-found wealth.

There are pundits in the West who say China's momentum of success can't last, that it "can't afford" to spend billions on poverty alleviation, and infrastructure that may not be immediately profitable. These calculations fail to grasp that China's socialist path has laid the basis for long-term viability, based on Common Prosperity. It has unleashed the economic capacity of half the population who previously were isolated. In fact, this new path is inspiring leaders across the globe to emulate China's success, leading to a shared future of common prosperity for the entire world.

* * *

Dee Knight is the author of Befriending China: People-to-People Peacemaking, *and* A Realistic Path to Peace: From Genocide to Global War… And How We Can Stop It. *He serves on the Advisory Council of the Friends of Socialist China, and on the China Working Group of the Democratic Socialists of America's International Committee.*

Dismantling Western Hypocrisy on Xinjiang and Gaza

by Arjae Red

The movement in the U.S. supporting Palestinian national liberation has drawn truly massive numbers of people in action. On January 13, 2024, for example, a reported 400,000 people marched on the White House, marking the largest pro-Palestine demonstration in U.S. history.

To counter this growing outpouring of support for Palestine in the center of world imperialism, Western propagandists are trying to misdirect the popular outrage towards the People's Republic of China. They are trying to revive the discredited "Uyghur genocide" narrative, making bogus comparisons between the Israeli settler regime's treatment of Palestinians and the treatment of Uyghur people by the Chinese government and the Communist Party. A closer look at each situation reveals enormous differences.

Whom Do We Believe?

The intense propaganda alleging the "Uyghur genocide" started in 2016 and grew to saturate the U.S. corporate media, relying on statements from U.S.-funded NGOs and U.S. politicians. These statements were used as a justification for heavy sanctions against China.

Following a fact-finding trip to the region, however, a 2019 delegation from the Council of Foreign Ministers—a key decision-making body of the Organization of Islamic Cooperation (OIC)—endorsed and commended China's treatment of its Muslim citizens.[123] With 57 member states, the OIC is one of the largest intergovernmental bodies in the world.

A week after our trip to Xinjiang last year, a large delegation from the League of Arab States, including top official representatives from more than 16 majority-Muslim countries, also visited Xinjiang. In a June 2023 press statement, the delegation praised "the social harmony, economic development, people of all ethnic groups living in harmony in Xinjiang and accelerated progress." They urged caution toward "international forces who smear and even demonize Xinjiang."

No governments in majority-Muslim countries support the U.S. charge of "genocide" of a Muslim minority population in Xinjiang. Meanwhile, these governments publicly criticize U.S.-supported Israeli genocide in Gaza.

Multinational Workers' State Versus Zionist Settler Colony

Central to the comparison is a class analysis of the social foundation of the states of Israel and the People's Republic of China. Like the United States, Israel was founded as a settler colony, built upon the slaughter and forced removal of Indigenous peoples, the theft of their lands, and the settlement of a majority-European population.

U.S. strategists viewed the Israeli state on Palestine's land mainly as a staging ground for U.S. military and economic domination of

---

[123] Holmes Chan, "Organisation of Islamic Cooperation 'Commends' China for Its Treatment of Muslims," *Hong Kong Free Press*, March 14, 2019, https://hongkongfp.com/2019/03/14/organisation-islamic-cooperation-commends-china-treatment-muslims/.

West Asia, and thus as a major contributor to the profits of the world imperialist ruling class. They saw Palestinians as an obstacle in the way of their accumulation of these superprofits. To accomplish this conquest, the Israeli state has threatened to appropriate or erase every vestige of Palestinian culture, including Palestine's history and cuisine.

Israel as a state is exploitative, extractive, and oppressive to the core. The state and the settler population, if it subscribes to the Zionist ideology, serve the ends of the global imperialist ruling class.

The People's Republic of China, on the other hand, was founded as a multinational workers' state, forged by overthrowing feudal and capitalist ruling classes and by ousting parasitic foreign forces, such as Japanese and British imperialism. The Chinese Revolution established a state based on the political rule of an alliance between the workers, peasants and other progressive classes, led by the Communist Party.

The People's Republic of China inscribed regional autonomy for formerly oppressed nationalities—like the Uyghurs in Xinjiang—into its political framework. Historic Uyghur cities, such as Ürümqi, which had been renamed "Dihua" (meaning "to civilize") following a 1755 Qing Dynasty invasion, regained their original Uyghur names.

Uyghur culture is widespread and celebrated in today's China, which includes teaching the Uyghur language, as well as the languages of other ethnic populations in the region, in public schools. Before the Chinese Revolution, these languages were suppressed.

The People's Republic is thoroughly multinational, based on the political rule of the working class and guided by the Communist Party. Its public goals involve developing a socialist economy and maintaining social harmony between ethnicities.

Israel Destroys, China Builds

Videos abound of the unmitigated destruction of Gaza by Israeli Occupation Forces. The IOF have bombed and bulldozed entire city blocks to dirt and rubble, razing homes, hospitals and schools.

Over decades, Israel has kept Gaza under a brutal blockade and crushed Palestinian businesses. Now the attacks have left the population without food, water, medicine or electricity.

Rather than destruction and extraction in Xinjiang, Beijing's policies promote development. Major infrastructure initiatives have built new housing, schools, hospitals and high-speed public transport. These projects outdo anything U.S. business or government projects have done on U.S. territory.

Uyghur and other ethnic minorities enjoy government grants and other affirmative action programs in education and job opportunities, which enable them to establish their own thriving businesses and fully participate in the vibrant Chinese economy. All of this has gradually reduced the wealth and development gap between the western Xinjiang region and the eastern coastal region of China, where, historically, all of the country's heavy industry was concentrated.

Xinjiang experiences no economic blockade except what U.S. policies impose. The Chinese government ensures that the basic needs of the people are met. During the COVID-19 outbreak, for example, Communist Party organizations delivered food and other supplies to Uyghur communities.

BDS Against Israel Versus U.S. Sanctions on Xinjiang

A global movement calling for boycotts, divestments, and sanctions (BDS) against Israeli businesses complicit in the genocide of Palestinians emerged as a way to pressure Israel to stop its genocidal policies. The BDS movement appeals to progressives around the world to cease financial support for the Zionist colonial project.

Washington has appropriated some of the progressive rhetoric used by the BDS campaign and weaponized it against China. U.S. officials claim its sanctions against Xinjiang punish China for the alleged genocide of the Uyghur people. Yet the U.S. sanctions are based on the false assumption that all products exported from Xinjiang are made with slave labor. This means that in order to access the international market, businesses in Xinjiang must go to extraordinary lengths to prove they aren't using slave labor. The U.S. sanctions thus harm Xinjiang's local economy, of which a large portion is Uyghur-owned businesses and farms, and many of those small family businesses.

BDS targets the oppressor nation's corporations. U.S. sanctions harm the Uyghur people themselves, with a twofold intent:

1. Disrupt the development of China's Belt and Road Initiative. The BRI would integrate Xinjiang's economy as a key region into the national and international market;
2. Cause economic hardship for the local population, which would further exacerbate inequality, ethnic and cultural divisions, and create political instability and lack of trust in the Chinese government to effectively develop the region.

Palestinian Self-Determination Versus U.S.-Promoted Uyghur Separatism

The Palestinian movement for self-determination is a mass movement with broad support from both people within historic Palestine and in the diaspora, originating organically as a response to Israeli colonial occupation.

The Uyghur separatist movement, on the other hand, is primarily pushed by U.S.-based anti-China think tanks and NGOs, usually with millions of dollars of U.S. government funding and full support from the State Department and corporate media.

There is no evidence that the Uyghur separatist forces, represented mostly in the diaspora and many based in Washington D.C., represent the views of the millions of Uyghurs living in Xinjiang. Only a small minority of Uyghur people in Xinjiang have fought for separatism, and this has often manifested as reactionary religious sects that utilize tactics such as bombings in crowded public places and machete attacks at bus stops, marketplaces and airports.

Anti-imperialist forces can be in solidarity with the Palestinian struggle for sovereignty, while at the same time remaining skeptical of U.S. attempts to portray its efforts to destabilize China as a popular movement for self-determination. Anyone who still has questions, however, can compare the contrasting responses of the Israeli and Chinese governments to their respective situations.

Israel's Anti-Popular Response

In its announced efforts to destroy Hamas, Israel has made no attempt to differentiate between combatants and civilians. Every adult and child in Gaza is a target of Israel's so-called "anti-terror" massacres. Israel's disregard for all Palestinian life is well known worldwide and deeply understood by Palestinians.

China's approach to eliminating attacks by separatist forces that harm (mostly Uyghur) civilians has been different. It's true that, during a period of time, increased police presence was necessary to prevent unpredictable public attacks. However, the Chinese government believes that people who have access to good education, job opportunities and have their basic needs met are less likely to commit crimes and less susceptible to being recruited by separatist extremist organizations.

Thus, the Chinese government took steps to build schools, create jobs and vocational training centers, and to develop the region through infrastructure projects and assistance for small businesses. Poverty alleviation is the primary method for solving violence in Xinjiang—and it has worked. Over the last two decades, political and religious violence in Xinjiang has now been nearly eliminated, and Xinjiang is quickly catching up with the rest of the country economically.

What We Saw in Xinjiang

Today, both Uyghur culture and a vibrant economy are thriving in Xinjiang. Although China is still a developing economy, its citizens enjoy more benefits and protections within the framework of their socialist market economy than many of us who live inside the core of global capitalism.

For example, during our visit to Xinjiang's rural regions outside of the city of Kashgar, we visited a small farming village of around 600 residents which mainly produced livestock. It was explained to us that the Communist Party had an officer assigned to each village to attend to the needs of the people there and convey feedback to the government on how their lives could be improved.

We were told that one of the largest challenges faced by that particular village was that they needed a veterinarian to tend to the animals, as there were none nearby. The government's solution was to send one of the local sheep farmers to school to train as a veterinarian, and then provide him with funding to open his own veterinarian practice. Now, he is able to meet the needs of his community as well as train other students who study under him.

When I asked what options farmers who could not afford to bring their animals in for treatment had, I was told that the government would cover the cost. As someone from a country where even the humans are still fighting for free healthcare, this was amazing to me.

We also spoke with other workers of different ethnicities in Xinjiang—Uyghur, Kazakh, Tajik, etc. One man was a carpenter who faced wage theft from his boss, and he shared the story of how the government forced his boss to pay him what he was owed. In the U.S, wage theft is one of the largest forms of theft, and there are no ways to compel your boss to pay you what you are owed, even in cases where the court finds them guilty.

We spoke with another family who just a generation or two ago were nomadic farmers. Now, with the help of the government, the family has received grants to open a dairy production facility and storefront. Instead of merely raising animals, they now produce yogurt, ice cream, and various cheeses. Their daughter was the first in her family to go to college, utilizing the affirmative-action-style education programs the government provides to ethnic minority groups in Xinjiang.

Although these are merely anecdotes, this is the true Xinjiang I saw with my own eyes. Not the "police state" totalitarian narrative peddled by Western propagandists.

Drawing a Line for the Anti-Imperialist Movement

It is critical that organizers against imperialism and supporters of decolonial movements around the world have a clear and sober assessment of developments in each country and the forces behind them. We have a responsibility to engage with these struggles in a deeper way and not just take the narratives at face value.

The forces that accuse China of genocide against Uyghur people are the same that arm, fund, and profit from Israel's actual genocide of the Palestinian people. We cannot separate this fact from reality, no matter how the corporate media and U.S. government-funded "human rights" groups try to conflate the two situations.

The U.S. empire, which, during its development, massacred and forcibly removed Indigenous peoples and enslaved Africans, and currently arms the Israeli genocide of Palestine, has absolutely no credibility to charge China with human rights abuses against the Uyghurs. Washington has never been on the right side of history in an anti-colonial struggle.

We must continue to say: Free Palestine from the river to the sea! U.S. hands off China!

* * *

Arjae Red is a union activist and Workers World Party leader who traveled in May 2023 to the Xinjiang Uyghur Autonomous Region (XUAR) in China's far northwest as part of a WWP delegation along with Workers World *contributing editor Sara Flounders, organized by the China–U.S. Solidarity Network.*

Xizang's Leap from Serfdom to Socialism with Chinese Characteristics

by Arnold August

My seven-day visit to Xizang (better known in the West as "Tibet") in 2023 provided the foundation for this chapter. I expand here on three articles and one video, first published in Global Times *and China Global Television Network (CGTN),*[124] *which were widely reprinted in the West.*

From Serfs to Architects of Their Own Destiny

As a participant in the 2023 trip, I viewed Xizang's historical film footage. The images and video show life under serfdom before 1951. These visuals were reinforced by conversations with people in Xizang, which further solidified our understanding during the tour.

---

124 Arnold August, "Witnessing Xizang: Serfdom to Socialism with Chinese Characteristics," *CGTN*, May 23, 2024, https://news.cgtn.com/news/2024-05-23/Witnessing-Xizang-Serfdom-to-socialism-with-Chinese-characteristics-1tPXIWdtBHq/p.html; Arnold August, "Xizang at 60: How the region Balances Tradition, Nature, and Progress," *Global Times*, August 31, 2025, https://www.globaltimes.cn/page/202508/1342195.shtml; Arnold August, "What I Saw in Xizang Was a Proactive, Well-Funded and Systematic Commitment to Heritage Preservation," *Global Times*, July 29, 2025, https://www.globaltimes.cn/page/202507/1339572.shtml; Arnold August, "Truth Seen in Xizang: Xizang's Infrastructures Links Tradition with Modernity, Says a Canadian Journalist," *Global Times*, September 9, 2025, https://www.globaltimes.cn/page/202509/1343040.shtml.

Xizang's Leap from Serfdom to Socialism

"Tibet" has long been shrouded in mystery and misinformation. But in old Tibet, the reality was stark. Under a feudal theocracy, about 5% of the population were serf-owners, while at least 95% were serfs. I will never forget the film about a mother, a grandmother, and a small child, all born in the same cowshed of a serf-owner. They lived there under such conditions for four generations.

On May 23, 1951, the Agreement of the Central People's Government and the Local Government of Tibet on Measures for the Peaceful Liberation of Tibet (the 17-Article Agreement) was signed. Yet this outcome did not come without conflict. In December 1949, Mao Zedong wrote to the CPC Central Committee, stressing the strategic need for the PLA to enter Tibet "sooner rather than later." The PLA's victory in the Qamdo Battle paved the way for the peaceful liberation of Tibet.[125]

After 1951, parts of the old ruling class resisted change to maintain the serf system. On March 10, 1959, the deposed elites who opposed democratic reforms, along with the Dalai Lama and with the help of the U.S., organized an armed revolt. The insurrection was defeated, and the Dalai Lama fled to India with his close followers.

The event that remains most vivid for the people we spoke to is the abolition of serfdom on March 28, 1959. While most serf-owners and theocrats abandoned Xizang in 1959, the People's Republic of China (PRC) and the Communist Party of China (CPC) has pressed ahead in cooperation with the Tibetans. According to the people we met during the visit, Beijing created around ten activist-advisor committees, which were dispatched to grassroots areas more than 190,000 times between 2012 and 2020. Their task was to achieve the goal of

---

[125] Xinhua, "Full Text: Tibet Since 1951: Liberation, Development and Prosperity," *Global Times*, May 21, 2021, https://www.globaltimes.cn/page/202105/1224100.shtml.

eliminating extreme poverty. This project, led by and for Tibetans, was completed in 2020—a remarkable milestone for Xizang.

Since the founding of the Xizang Autonomous Region in 1965, progress has been striking. From 1965 to 2024, the most recent period for which figures are available, Xizang saw dramatic improvements—progress that Nepal and the Himachal Pradesh state in India, where most of the Tibetan diaspora has lived since then, have seen very little of:

- **Per capita disposable income of rural residents** rose from 108 to 21,578 yuan.
- **Life expectancy** climbed from 35.5 to 72.5 years.
- **Road network length** expanded from 14,000 km to 124,900 km.
- **Number of schools** grew from 1,828 to 3,618.
- **Rail network operation** increased from zero to 1,359 km.[126]

And I discovered even more advances, as discussed below.

Infrastructure as a Unifying Force: From the Qin Dynasty to the Present

My interest in Xizang's infrastructure began with the Qin Dynasty, which flourished more than 2,000 years ago, and its vision of unification. I first encountered this history during my three-week trip across much of China in 2006. During this tour I learned that the Qin Dynasty established a uniform axle width for its dirt roads. This

---

126 GT Graphic, "60 Years of Xizang Autonomous Region's Development in Numbers," *Global Times*, August 19, 2025, https://www.globaltimes.cn/page/202508/1341207.shtml.

standard ensured that all animal-drawn carts could follow the same ruts without damaging roads or creating confusion.

It may sound banal, but the problem was serious. Rain could worsen the road conditions. The Qin axle width norm reminded me of driving in Canada in ice and snow, where cars leave separate furrows. Drivers must sometimes slide sideways from one rut to another, an exhausting and unsafe experience.

In the Qin period, the uniform axle width was revolutionary. It showed the dynasty's dedication to unity. First, the Qin recognized a widespread problem. Then they devised an engineering solution suited to their time, highlighting an early concern for the population's well-being that has endured for generations of Chinese. That consideration, rooted in governance 2,000 years ago, remains a feature of political rule in China today.

The Qin connection came to mind again during my 2023 train trip on the "Roof of the World" to Lhasa. The journey began in Qinghai Province, Xizang's neighbor, where one-fifth of the population is of Tibetan descent. Its capital, Xining, has a modern railway station. From there, we traveled close to 2,000 km over 22 hours, often at altitudes near 5,000 meters. This is equivalent to half the height of Mount Everest (known in Tibetan as Qomolangma). We passed through breathtaking mountains and herds of yak. The long climb also allowed us to acclimatize gradually to the thin air before reaching Lhasa, and it proved ideal for meditating on China's long tradition of unifying infrastructure—stretching back centuries—now contributing to the integration of Xizang with the rest of China.

This railroad itself is an engineering marvel, recognized even by many Western experts. It is also a medical milestone. More than 2,000 medical staff accompanied the workers who built it under harsh conditions—low oxygen, extreme cold, heavy snow, and unstable permafrost. The railway, along with other transport projects in Xizang, shows that development in the PRC is not just a modern feat. It continues China's historical tradition of unification through standardization and connectivity.

The Individual and the Collective in Xizang: The Story of a Drone Invention

Beyond the railroad, I was struck by another kind of infrastructure in Xizang. I discovered it in a newly built town near Lhasa, at the High-Tech Zone Innovation and Entrepreneurship Service Platform.

Here, individual initiative is encouraged. One example stood out: a specialized drone designed to help farmers in mountainous areas. Developed by small start-up companies housed in the High-Tech Zone, these drones operate at high altitudes, where it is difficult for people to work. The drones spray pesticides and fertilizers, saving time and lowering costs compared with traditional methods. They also provide advanced field mapping, which supports more substantial harvests and stability in rugged terrain.

But how did such a drone emerge in Lhasa?

At the High-Tech Zone, anyone with a computer and internet access can apply. The appeal is simple: "Bring your ideas." Yet there are conditions. Applicants must agree to work toward the goals of socialism and modernization set by the government. Membership in the CPC is not required, but anyone who has been expelled from the Party cannot apply. This political orientation is clear even in the murals inside the tech center, which display portraits of Chinese leaders from Chairman Mao to President Xi, alongside milestones of the PRC's development, including those in Xizang.

Does this political framework stifle individual initiative? Some in the West, their opinion shaped by the U.S.-centric notion of the sacred "individual," may think so. But what I observed suggested otherwise. The tech center represents a balance between collective purpose and individual creativity, a hallmark of socialism with Chinese characteristics. Innovators there integrate social responsibility with personal ambition. They are rewarded not only with the satisfaction of turning their ideas into reality, but also with solid income from marketing their products.

For me, the drone stood as proof that the market and state-led socialism fully complement each other. Alongside the drive to eradicate extreme poverty and the marvel of the railway, it shows once more how China succeeds through a dynamic blend of bottom-up and top-down efforts, where everyone has a role.

Boarding Schools

As part of Western disinformation campaigns against China, authorities in Canada, the U.S., and Europe, along with some of the corporate press, claim that Tibetans face "suppression." They point to boarding schools in Xizang and neighboring Qinghai Province, where about one-fifth of the population is Tibetan. The PRC is accused of carrying out "cultural genocide" against Tibetans.

But consider this testimony from a youth in a boarding school, also called a residential school. Authorities berated him constantly, beat him, forbade him from speaking his language or practicing his culture, and sexually assaulted him. Did this incident occur in China? No. It happened in Canada, as documented by one of the foremost historians of Canada's Indigenous peoples and residential schools, Professor Sean Carleton of the University of Manitoba.[127]

And this was not an isolated case. Multiply it by hundreds of thousands—even Canada's own records show that more than 150,000 Indigenous children were forced into residential schools, and an estimated 6,000 of them died there.[128]

In 2024, I conducted an exclusive interview with Mohawk Nation representative Katsi'tsakwas Ellen Gabriel, whose insights carry deep weight for this discussion. In the northern portion of Turtle Island,[129] she first rose to prominence in 1990 as the spokesperson for the Mohawk Nation during the 78-day siege known as the so-called "Oka Crisis." At that time, fully armed Canadian soldiers encircled her community with armored vehicles, supported by local police.[130] The struggle was over the defense of traditional Mohawk land.

Katsi'tsakwas Ellen Gabriel's lifelong advocacy has since earned wide recognition. In 2024, she became the first Indigenous person to receive the 38th Grand Prix du Conseil des arts de Montréal, awarded for her decades of work and for a documentary highlighting the pivotal

---

127 Alessia Passafiume, "Manitoba Historian Concerned Residential School Denialism Will Rise After Biden's Apology in U.S.," *CBC News*, October 27, 2024. https://www.cbc.ca/news/canada/manitoba/canada-indigenous-residential-school-denialism-1.7364980.

128 USW union directors, "There's No Denying It: Indigenous Children Suffered and Died at Residential Schools," United Steelworkers (USW), September 22, 2023, https://usw.ca/theres-no-denying-it-indigenous-children-suffered-and-died-at-residential-schools/.

129 A common Indigenous term for the North American continent.

130 Katsi'tsakwas Ellen Gabriel, "Kanehsatake 35 Years Later: Remembering the Day Canada Sent in the Military to Violently Clear Mohawk Land for a Golf Course," *Ricochet Media*, July 11, 2025, https://ricochet.media/indigenous/landback/kanehsatake-35-years-later-remembering-the-day-canada-sent-in-the-military-to-violently-clear-mohawk-land-for-a-golf-course/.

role of Mohawk women in the 1990 land defense.[131] That same year, she published a book on the same subject with Professor Carleton. It quickly became a bestseller and has already reached its fourth printing.[132]

In my interview, Katsi'tsakwas Ellen Gabriel explained that Canada's "boarding schools" were designed to "get rid of the Indian problem." This goal should not come as a surprise. As she pointed out, the Canadian Indian Act created a colonial settler state and provided the legal foundation for cultural genocide through the residential school system. That same legislation was even studied and copied by South Africa as a blueprint for Apartheid.

Katsi'tsakwas Ellen spoke candidly about her own childhood. She and her siblings were raised to "feel ashamed of the Mohawk language; my parents whispered it when speaking." Canada's aim, she said, was to instill "cultural self-hatred and the erasure of self-esteem." Despite this, her parents tried to shield their children from racism. "Some teachers and students called us savages and unruly," she recalled, but "my parents taught us: you are not a savage, not stupid, you can go to school."[133]

Even before the recent discovery of unmarked graves at former residential school sites, the government-appointed Canadian Truth

---

131 Conseil des arts de Montréal, "Katsi'tsakwas Ellen Gabriel Wins the 38th Grand Prix du Conseil des arts de Montréal," press release, April 11, 2024, https://www.artsmontreal.org/en/news/katsitsakwas-ellen-gabriel-wins-the-38th-grand-prix-du-conseil-des-arts-de-montreal/.

132 Katsi'tsakwas Ellen Gabriel, with Sean Carleton, *When the Pine Needles Fall: Indigenous Acts of Resistance* (Between the Lines, 2024), https://btlbooks.com/book/when-the-pine-needles-fall.

133 Arnold August, *Interview: Katsi'tsakwas Ellen Gabriel, Grand Prix, Conseil des arts de Montréal by Arnold August,* YouTube video, uploaded May 22, 2024, https://www.youtube.com/watch?v=bJ5b3rVDwZA.

and Reconciliation Commission (TRC) had already exposed the scale of the crimes. In 2015, its final report concluded that the residential schools had been a "central element" of the Canadian government's policy of cultural genocide."[134] The government formally accepted the TRC report but has become notorious for failing to implement most of its key recommendations. This ongoing inaction and ambiguity have fueled what some now call "residential school denial."[135] Canada, in denial mode, also denies the view that China's "Tibet" policy demonstrates how modernization can be pursued alongside cultural preservation and promotion. Furthermore, even as Canada levels unfounded accusations of cultural genocide against China in Xizang and Tibetan regions of Qinghai, it has yet to confront its own human rights violations, including the genocide of Indigenous peoples.

During my 2023 trip, I visited a boarding school in a Tibetan minority area of Qinghai Province, near the Xizang border. In contrast to the genocidal Canadian residential school system, students there are taught primarily the Tibetan language, as well as Chinese and English, to facilitate communication throughout the country. The curriculum also includes Chemistry, History, Psychology, Biology, Physics, Politics, Morality, Geography, Sports, and Health. The cafeteria serves a wide variety of high-quality food and beverages, likely to be the envy of many Western students from working-class families. Up to 1,200 students can dine together across two floors. Modern dormitories are heated with underfloor heating, with separate floors for boys and girls.

---

134 CBC News, "Truth and Reconciliation Commission Urges Canada to Confront 'Cultural Genocide' of Residential Schools," *CBS News*, June 2, 2015, https://www.cbc.ca/news/politics/truth-and-reconciliation-commission-urges-canada-to-confront-cultural-genocide-of-residential-schools-1.3096229.

135 Niigaan Sinclair and Sean Carleton, "Residential School Denialism Is on the Rise. What to Know," *The Tyee*, June 20, 2023, https://thetyee.ca/Opinion/2023/06/20/Residential-School-Denialism-On-Rise/.

While the Tibetan language is flourishing at that boarding school, the proportion of Indigenous people in Canada who can speak an Indigenous language has steadily declined. In 2021, only 13.1% of the Indigenous population reported being able to hold a conversation in an Indigenous language.[136] In the United States, official figures suggest that only about 5% of Indigenous people can do so.[137] In contrast, in Xizang and the Tibetan areas of Qinghai Province, close to 100% of the population speaks their ancestral language. In a 2025 documentary reflecting on his visit to Xizang, Andy Boreham, a Shanghai-based New Zealander, examines Western biases regarding the region's language.[138] The Tibetan language is used in publishing, media, and everyday life. By the end of 2024, Xizang had seventeen periodicals and eleven newspapers in Tibetan, and had printed 46.85 million copies of 8,794 Tibetan-language books. Primary and secondary schools in Xizang offer courses in both standard Chinese and Tibetan.[139] Today, fifteen years of publicly funded education are

---

136 Statistics Canada, *Indigenous Languages across Canada, Census in Brief, 2021 Census of Population: Analytical Products,* 98-200-X2021012 (Ottawa, released March 29, 2023), https://www12.statcan.gc.ca/census-recensement/2021/as-sa/98-200-x/2021012/98-200-x2021012-eng.cfm.

137 Julie Siebens and Tiffany Julian, *Native North American Languages Spoken at Home in the United States and Puerto Rico: 2006–2010, American Community Survey Briefs* ACSBR/10-10 (Washington, DC: U.S. Census Bureau, December 2011), https://www2.census.gov/library/publications/2011/acs/acsbr10-10.pdf.

138 Andy Boreham, "The West constantly Says 'Forcing' Tibetan Kids to Learn Mandarin Is 'Erasing' Their Culture," X, July 10, 2025, https://x.com/Andy-Bxxx/status/1943309324606230692.

139 Xinhua, "Full text: Human Rights in Xizang in the New Era," *Global Times*, March 28, 2025, https://www.globaltimes.cn/page/202503/1331090.shtml.

available, from kindergarten through high school,[140] and the region's primary and secondary school enrollment rate is nearly 100 percent.[141]

"But at What Cost"?

When we challenge the mainstream media narrative about China's success in building socialism with Chinese characteristics, the response from Westerners is often: "What about Tibet?" The insinuation is that, while grudgingly acknowledging China's progress, this advance supposedly comes at the expense of Tibetan language and culture, broadly defined to include religion. As discussed earlier, this is not the case. Yet the accusation is so pervasive that it is worth examining from another angle.

During my visit to Xizang, I viewed the region through the lens of my upbringing in Montreal, Quebec, a primarily French-speaking province with a heritage dating back to France since 1618. Yet in Quebec, our music, cinema, journalism, fiction, non-fiction, and poetry remain entirely marginal under the dominance of Anglo-American culture. Despite government protection efforts, Quebec is constantly inundated with the most superficial American and British cultural icons, and U.S. television dominates our homes. This infiltration occurs either directly, through outlets such as CNN or American culture-focused TV channels, or indirectly, such as through the Canadian media. This personal background has given me a deep appreciation

---

140 GT Staff Reporters, "Feast on Plateau: Images, Data Reveal Xizang's Modernization Miracle on Autonomous Region's 60th Anniversary," *Global Times*, August 22, 2025, https://www.globaltimes.cn/page/202508/1341521.shtml.

141 Shan Jie, Cao Siqi and Li Jieyi in Lhasa, "In Xizang, Tibetan Language, Traditional Culture Passed on Well to Children in Kindergartens, Schools," *Global Times*, March 30, 2023, https://www.globaltimes.cn/page/202303/1288302.shtml.

for issues of language, identity, and cultural preservation, making me particularly sensitive to what I observed in Xizang.

My visit to Lhasa's Old Town was a powerful reminder of China's unique approach to integrating language and culture—including religion—with modernity, while fully safeguarding traditional practices. As I walked through Lhasa, I saw people dressed in traditional garments, hundreds of Buddhist monks in religious attire, and traditional architecture alongside modern malls. Children were rollerblading, families were enjoying amusement parks, and curious local people approached our group to practice their English.

At Jokhang Temple, in the heart of Old Town, I observed traditional Tibetan architecture housing a monastery featuring the Gelug school of Tibetan Buddhism, established in the 7th century (AD 647). The teaching language is, of course, Tibetan.

A visit to the imposing Potala Palace, overlooking Lhasa, also offered another perspective. The Palace plays a central role not only in religion but also in Xizang's traditional politics and thought. It contains nearly 700 murals, 10,000 painted scrolls, and an extensive collection of historical documents. If the Western-driven narrative of Tibetan "suppression" were true, China's commitment to preserving and promoting Xizang's history would be inexplicable.

The preservation of the Tibetan language is equally evident. At Xizang University, established in 1985 in Lhasa, courses are taught in Tibetan and Mandarin. The university enrolls more than 20,000 students and maintains an internationally renowned Tibetan studies department, along with a majority-Tibetan student body.

The special visit to the Tibetan Ancient Documents Research Center on its Lhasa campus, which focuses on the Phuri Manuscripts, was impressive. These manuscripts constitute China's most ancient and extensive collection of ancient Tibetan literature. They offer insights into a kingdom established around the 13th and 14th centuries, and portray its natural environment, traditional customs, social structures, and history.

If there were any truth to the Western anti-China narrative of "cultural genocide" in Xizang, China would need to "root out" these seeds of the Tibetan people to erase their collective memory, as is being attempted in Canada and the U.S. against Indigenous peoples. However, on the ground in Xizang, we witnessed the opposite.

The Xizang Museum, completed in 1999, is the first large, modern museum in Xizang. It features a collection of more than 520,000 artifacts, focusing on the various dynastic periods of Tibetan history. It is widely accepted that, to commit genocide against a people, the very roots of their civilization and history must be eradicated. Yet, on the ground, we observed the opposite.

We also visited the Tibetan Autonomous Region Intangible Cultural Heritage Preservation Center. Since 2012, the central and local governments have invested more than 400 million yuan (USD 55.7 million) in protecting intangible Tibetan cultural heritage through this center. We saw seniors playing Tibetan musical instruments, and youth performing traditional Tibetan opera. The unfortunate situation in Quebec stands in sharp contrast to the flourishing Tibetan culture. What I saw in Xizang was a proactive, well-funded, and systematic commitment to the preservation of Tibetan heritage. The government has helped the region develop through the creative application of socialism with Chinese characteristics, while promoting its language, culture, and religion.

* * *

Arnold August is a Montreal-based author and journalist specializing in geopolitics, China, First Peoples, and many other international issues. He has written four books and contributed a chapter to a fifth. He holds an M.A. in political science from McGill University, where he also completed two years of Ph.D. studies, and he is a member of the editorial board of the International Manifesto Group. As a journalist, he is published in Global Times, Black Agenda Report, Orinoco Tribune, Global Research, Al Mayadeen, teleSUR, Friends of Socialist China, Venezuela Analysis, CGTN, *and is a frequent guest on* Press TV *and* teleSUR TV. *His website is www.arnoldaugust.com.*

5.

The U.S. War Drive Against China Intensifies

The U.S. Advances Its Dystopian Plan to Destroy China

by Megan Russell

Imagine: it's the summer of 2025, and the United States has been surrounded by foreign military bases. The bases have been built by some antagonistic country on the other side of the world that drones on about the inevitability of war. Leaders of this country pump billions into their military, drumming up advanced AI weaponry, building long-range ballistic missile systems targeting the most populated U.S. cities, and sending thousands of troops to the Caribbean in preparation. Large-scale war games are held throughout the region, including drills that simulate nuclear war on the U.S. *In the next two years,* they say. *War is coming, and we need to be ready.* Meanwhile, back on domestic soil, the nation's top thinkers gather to plan the collapse of the U.S. government, releasing a 120-page document outlining the steps to take after the war leaves nothing but dust and instability behind.

But wait. You don't need to imagine. That *is* happening, just not to the United States. No, the U.S. is not the victim at all—the U.S. is the antagonistic country on the other side of the world, bloating its military, prepping for war, and outlining the collapse of another nation's government.

The U.S. has built over 300 military bases in the Asia Pacific region alone, installed long-range missile systems pointed at China's largest cities, and held joint war exercises with regional allies simulat-

The U.S. Advances Plans to Destroy China

ing nuclear war with China. And just last week, the federally funded Hudson Institute released its 128-page plan for the collapse of China's government.

Western media tells you that China is the most aggressive nation on earth, but China has shown extreme restraint in the face of U.S. military buildup and hostile rhetoric calling for war. If the opposite were true—if China had surrounded the U.S. with missiles, troops, and bases—the U.S. would have already considered that an act of war. Just think back to the 1962 Cuban Missile Crisis, when the installation of Soviet nuclear missiles in Cuba almost led to the U.S. declaring full-scale nuclear war.

Luckily, the facts speak louder than U.S. war propaganda, and these are the facts: the U.S. has over 900 foreign military bases, while China has just one. The U.S. has surrounded China with over 300 military bases, while China has zero in the entire Western Hemisphere. The U.S. has launched 251 military interventions since just 1991, while China hasn't intervened in any country for 50 years.

And as the newly deemed "Department of War" marches rapidly toward a $1 trillion dollar war budget, consider the deep emphasis China has placed on maintaining a "peaceful coexistence" with other nations, with strict guidelines of non-interventionism and mutual respect.

The truth is, you can't understand China from a Western perspective. The U.S. is a relatively young nation born out of settler colonization and genocide of the native people. Our wealth was amassed through resource extraction, exploitation, and slavery. In comparison, China has undergone thousands of years of dynastic empires rising and falling. It has a strong cultural continuity and shared historical experience that informs how it conducts itself in the global theater. Its wealth was amassed internally, not through imperialist behavior or exploitation of another. It's an ancient civilization with deep roots, and a unique vision of the world shaped by a long philosophical tradition and an anti-capitalist, anti-imperialist framework.

Additionally, China was one of the world's largest economies for over 2,000 years, accounting for around 25-30% of global GDP. It wasn't until the 1800s that colonial violence and occupation by the British Empire, and later Japan, drove China into poverty. In the 1970s, it was one of the world's poorest nations. The fact that China was able to return to its former prosperity despite decades of foreign intervention is nothing less than a miracle.

So why is the U.S. so set on war? It's simple. China's economic prosperity threatens the current global order that positions the U.S. at the top, and forces all other countries to bend to its will. It's a war that will be waged to protect U.S. global hegemony and the monetary interests of the Western elite. The only threat here is the United States preserving its interests through bombs and bloodshed.

On July 10, 2025, the U.S. and its allies began conducting the largest military exercises in the Pacific since World War II. Nicknamed Resolute Force Pacific, or REFORPAC 2025, the exercise involved over 350 aircraft, more than 12,000 service members, and took place at more than 50 locations across 3,000 miles in the Pacific, including Hawaii, Guam, Japan, and international airspace. The U.S. Air Force says these exercises will "prove how we'll fight and win" a war against China.

Modern U.S. war-waging often occurs through the use of proxies and funding the troops of another country, as long as they act in U.S. interests. They'll call it military strategy, but at the very root of it, you'll find a dark feeling of indifference towards the citizens of other nations. Our government couldn't care less what happens to innocent people in Japan, South Korea, or the Philippines. As long as

The U.S. Advances Plans to Destroy China

U.S. global hegemony is preserved, death, human rights abuses, and planetary destruction will go unconsidered.

China's "acts of aggression," as labeled by mainstream Western media, are often just its own defensive military exercises that it conducts in response to the constant war games off its shores. But please, let's be honest with ourselves—what country *wouldn't* respond that way? If anything, it's an *act of restraint* in response to blatant preparations for war.

Just last week, the Hudson Institute (which has received *millions* from the U.S. Department of Defense) held a conference to discuss the collapse of China's government and released a 128-page document outlining the plan. The document is heinous and dystopian, outlining a gradual invasion of China through clandestine disinformation campaigns, cultural and psychological restructuring, military intervention, and an overall manipulation of the soul of China from the shadows.

Phase 0 will begin before the collapse. U.S. Special Operations Forces will use psychological and political warfare to sow division between the government, the military, and the people—and the government has already funded billions of U.S. tax dollars to do just that. They plan to twist narratives to undermine China's history, exploit trauma, and mock the CPC through disinformation campaigns. Phase 1 will go into play after China's collapse, which is U.S. occupation in everything but name. U.S. forces will be deployed to China's cities and embedded into China's military. A new puppet government will adhere to the whims of U.S. leaders. Anyone sympathetic to the CPC will be "controlled" while U.S. forces conduct action raids to secure nuclear weapons. And finally, Phase 2 will attempt to rewrite national consciousness by installing a U.S.-approved version of history. They will create a "Voice of China" modeled after the "Voice of America," the people will be re-educated about the evils of communism, and a "sad but transparent" period of national mourning will pave the way to a new China shaped entirely by the United States.

The rest of the document outlines how to precisely target China's facilities, restructure China's financial system to suit U.S. interests, secure assets, restructure the military, and conduct a "reconciliation" campaign. At the end, the document mentions an imaginary, arbitrarily drawn line across China separating east from west, and discusses potentially splitting or partitioning territories. It also considers name changes for China, such as Taiwan or the Chinese Federal Republic.

The document is as Orwellian as it sounds, written by "experts" such as Miles Yu, Ryan Clarke, and Gordon G. Chang. Chang is one of the most frequently cited "China experts" in the U.S., but he's not an expert so much as a propaganda mouthpiece. He has built an entire career out of making bold, spectacularly wrong predictions about China's collapse, all while reinforcing U.S. imperial talking points.

His most infamous claim came in his 2001 book, *The Coming Collapse of China*, in which he confidently declared that the Communist Party of China would fall by 2011 at the latest. When that didn't happen, he extended the deadline... and extended it again. He even made *Foreign Policy*'s "10 Worst Predictions of the Year" list *twice*. Over two decades later, not only has China not collapsed, but it has grown into one of the world's most powerful economies and a leading force in global diplomacy and development.

Despite his long track record of failure, Chang remains a regular on Fox News, a speaker at military think tanks like the Hudson Institute, and a go-to figure for anti-China hardliners in Washington. Why? Because he tells them exactly what they want to hear. His role is simply to justify aggression, stir up fear, and promote regime change narratives under the cover of "expertise." In truth, Chang is no more than a state-aligned propagandist, useful only because he reinforces the

U.S. imperial worldview so Congress can use more of your tax dollars to go to war on China.

People like Chang will keep returning to live Congressional hearings and federally funded organizations like the Hudson Institute to justify U.S. war and domination abroad. It is intentional *information warfare* being waged by the U.S. government, and it is the first step to manufacturing consent for military action abroad. It's time to demand that lying imperial mouthpieces like Chang no longer get uplifted to be used as a means for global death and destruction—not in Congress, in academia, or anywhere. We must reject the path of endless war and build a world based on mutual respect, not militarism. But that future requires us to stop imagining that we are always the victims and start recognizing when we are the aggressors.

* * *

Megan Russell is CODEPINK's China is Not Our Enemy Campaign Coordinator. She graduated from the London School of Economics with a Master's Degree in Conflict Studies. Prior to that, she spent one year studying in Shanghai and over eight years studying Chinese Mandarin. Her research focuses on the intersection between U.S.-China affairs, peacebuilding, and international development.

China Cannot Be Contained

by Margaret Kimberley

"It's pretty ironic that we've gone within the space of 3 years from the US banning chip exports to China to slow their tech development, to China now telling its companies to avoid those same US chips in favor of domestic alternatives – which now exist because of those US export controls."

—Arnaud Bertrand[142]

In July of 2025, *Black Agenda Report* was invited to join media outlets from around the world to participate in the 2025 Belt and Road Journalists Forum which was held in the city of Ganzhou, located in Jiangxi province, China. As executive editor, I traveled to Jiangxi and experienced China's world-famous high-speed rail as I traveled from Jingdezhen to Ganzhou. At one point, a video screen on the train reported that it reached a speed of 300 kilometers per hour, the equivalent of 186 miles per hour.

The United States Amtrak rail service recently added five upgraded trains to its high-speed Acela service between Boston, Massachusetts and the nation's capital city of Washington. Press announcements reported that among other improvements, these new Acela trains,

---

142 Arnaud Bertrand (@RnaudBertrand), x.com, August 12, 2025, https://x.com/RnaudBertrand/status/1955286249029202411.

known as NextGen, can reach a speed of 160 miles per hour. However, because tracks along the route have not been upgraded,[143] they will rarely reach this top speed, which is already low in comparison to China's high-speed rail service. While the U.S. introduced new, faster trains along what is known as the Northeast Corridor with great fanfare, the People's Republic of China has the world's largest high-speed rail system, which covers more than 25,000 miles.

This anecdote about train travel explains why any idea of the United States being able to restrict China's growth as an economic and political power is a non-starter. The United States spends more money on its military—over $994 billion in Fiscal Year 2024—than the next nine countries combined,[144] but is behind the rest of the world in spending its resources to help its people. Train travel from its capital to major cities such as Philadelphia, New York, and Boston is hobbled by a lack of the kind of infrastructure that China excels in producing and maintaining.

While the military budget grows, it cannot account for the huge expenditures approved by presidents and members of Congress of both major parties. In fact, the Department of Defense has failed every annual audit it has been required to carry out since that process became required in 2018, and is the only federal agency that

---

143 Tom Sanders, "Amtrak Rolls Out New High-Speed Trains Running Slower Than the Old Ones," *The Daily Beast*, August 28, 2025, https://www.thedailybeast.com/amtrak-rolls-out-new-high-speed-trains-running-slower-than-the-old-ones/.

144 Peter G. Peterson Foundation, *The United States Spends More on Defense than the Next 9 Countries Combined* (Peter G. Peterson Foundation, 2025), https://www.pgpf.org/article/the-united-states-spends-more-on-defense-than-the-next-9-countries-combined/.

is still unable to pass an audit.[145] Democrats and Republicans alike are committed to throwing away public funds on a military-industrial complex which does nothing to improve the lives of the people. On the other hand, a true high-speed rail system would benefit millions.

For years, United States politicians, from presidents to members of Congress, have insisted that China can and must be "contained". The cry for this impossible dream is completely bipartisan; there is no daylight between Republicans and Democrats when Sinophobia is on the political agenda. China's economic strength is labeled as "overcapacity" as it continues in its role as the manufacturing juggernaut of the world and now as the leader in technology.

Yes, China's Reform and Opening Up and years of planning have made it so, but the West, especially the U.S., played a role in its own demise as finance capital deindustrialized its nations, creating economic dislocation and even coining the new phrase "Rust Belt" to describe the regions decimated by greed and short-sighted thinking. These ill-fated decisions coincided with Deng Xiaoping's reforms, and the rest, as the expression goes, is history.

It doesn't matter whether a Republican or a Democrat is the president of the United States, or which party controls Congress. The obsessive belief that the U.S. should control or contain China is constant. This mania manifests in different ways. For example, Joe Biden may call China's President Xi Jinping a dictator, or former Speaker of the House of Representatives Nancy Pelosi may tell silly stories about digging a hole to China when she defied Beijing's wishes and paid

---

145 Lindsay Koshgarian, "Take 7: The Pentagon Fails Another Audit," *National Priorities Project*, November 25, 2024, https://www.nationalpriorities.org/blog/2024/11/25/take-7-pentagon-fails-another-audit/.

a visit to Taiwan.[146] U.S. officials cannot accept that their country is outmatched and that any thought of dominating China, a major world power, is absurd on its face. This absurdity is the rule, not the exception, when China becomes an issue in U.S. politics.

The Biden Administration was the first to enact restrictions on sales of advanced computer chips to China. Yet even think tanks such as the Brookings Institution, an important part of the U.S. foreign policy apparatus, acknowledge the folly of such an effort, writing that "starving China's supply of U.S.-designed AI chips will have the opposite effect, as it will push China to more effectively develop and deploy its own AI chip capacity and ecosystem."[147]

In fact, China has moved ahead not just in artificial intelligence chip production but in building the grid needed to make AI possible. China has an oversupply of electricity while the U.S. grid is so weak that the race may be over[148] as it struggles to build AI data centers that the public oppose because of stresses on the already underdeveloped infrastructure.[149] The announcement of DeepSeek revealed that a Chinese company had created an open-source Artificial Intelligence platform at a fraction of the cost of the much-vaunted ChatGPT.

---

146 Margaret Kimberley, "Nancy Pelosi, White Supremacy, and China," *Black Agenda Report*, August 10, 2022, https://blackagendareport.com/nancy-pelosi-white-supremacy-and-china.

147 John Villasenor, "How Overly Aggressive Bans on AI Chip Exports to China Can Backfire," *The Brookings Institution*, August 15, 2025, https://www.brookings.edu/articles/how-overly-aggressive-bans-on-ai-chip-exports-to-china-can-backfire/.

148 Eva Roytburg, "AI Experts Return from China Stunned: The U.S. Grid Is so Weak, the Race May Already Be Over," *Fortune*, August 14, 2025, https://fortune.com/2025/08/14/data-centers-china-grid-us-infrastructure/.

149 Brad Reed, "Cheers Erupt as Tucson City Council Unanimously Kills Massive Amazon-Linked Data Centers," *Common Dreams*, August 7, 2025, https://www.commondreams.org/news/tucson-arizona-data-center.

There can be no containment of China; Biden's efforts to restrict chip production in China resulted in more and better chip production instead.

The Huawei telecom giant provides another example of foolish decisions which may inconvenience China temporarily, but hurt the U.S. more. In 2019, the Biden Administration passed the National Defense Authorization Act which included provisions forbidding U.S. government agencies from contracting with entities that use Huawei components, only for the Defense Department to request exemptions from the ban. According to *Bloomberg*, Huawei was "so firmly entrenched" in the telecommunications systems of the countries where it does business that finding a replacement would be "impossible."[150]

Today, the Trump Administration is attempting more of the same. While Donald Trump is ending green energy projects, recently cancelling $679 million in funding for offshore wind projects[151] and bragging about prioritizing fossil fuel production, China is marching ahead, and is now the world leader in clean energy, installing more wind and solar capacity in one year than exists in the entire United States.[152]

---

150 Global Times, "US' Ban on Huawei Eventually Boomerangs on Itself," *Global Times*, July 4, 2024, https://www.globaltimes.cn/page/202407/1315441.shtml.

151 Lauren Sommer, "Trump Administration Cancels $679 Million for Offshore Wind Projects at Ports," *National Public Radio*, August 31, 2025, https://www.npr.org/2025/08/31/nx-s1-5522943/trump-offshore-wind-energy-ports.

152 Ella Nilsen, "America Was Already Losing to China on Clean Energy. Trump Just Sealed Its Fate," *CNN*, July 16, 2025, https://www.cnn.com/2025/07/16/climate/china-us-wind-solar-energy-trump.

China Cannot Be Contained

Trump believed that he could bully China into submission with an announcement of tariffs that eventually reached the 145% mark.[153] He made the bizarre announcement on what he called Liberation Day, which amounted to the declaration of a trade war against the rest of the world, and then seemed to be surprised when China would not agree to his demands. He sought to save face by announcing a 90-day pause before enacting the tariffs, but China was not swayed, and refused his demands, which would ultimately have only succeeded in raising prices for U.S. consumers.

While USians run from one foolish accusation to another—that China is buying up farmland, depriving U.S. students of college enrollment, sending spy balloons that can be seen with the naked eye, or stealing technology—it is rare that socialism is acknowledged as being the foundation of China's success. Doing so would mean that the capitalist West would have to examine itself and find itself lacking.

China's planned economy and emphasis on people-centered decision-making inevitably resulted in a country which does a better job of meeting its people's needs. A country which spends billions of dollars on the military—or rather, feeds that money to military contractors—will inevitably fail at meeting the needs of its population. To the U.S. government, the needs of the people are not only of no consequence, but meeting those needs would damage a system which is meant to be a money laundering scheme for capitalists. Why would such a state feel the need to improve transportation when its true goal is to enrich the already rich and to protect their interests? The people are in fact

---

153 Lionel Lim, "Trump's 'Done' Deal with China Just Brings Tariffs Back to Liberation Day Levels," *Fortune*, June 12, 2025, https://fortune.com/asia/2025/06/12/trumps-done-deal-china-brings-tariffs-back-to-liberation-day-levels/.

seen as a hindrance who, if given the opportunity, might obstruct the corruption that has become normalized.

The U.S. political economic system is based on the drive for what is known as primacy, the belief that no other country should move ahead of it economically or politically. Even allies of the U.S. aren't truly allies but vassals, and any country that is not a vassal is considered an enemy. While the U.S. finds new ways to wage a trade war against the rest of the world, China announced that it would conduct tariff-free trade with 53 of 54 African nations.[154] The people-centered philosophy extends to other nations too.

One country produces clean energy because it meets the people's needs, while another promotes fossil fuels because the fossil fuel industry dictates policy. Capitalism controls the United States. The word "democracy" is thrown about quite frequently, but it is little more than a marketing ploy, a ruse meant to quiet the population and convince them that periodically changing from one wing of the duopoly to the other will solve their problems. The truth can no longer be denied. The country emerging as the preeminent economy in the world has done so because it is socialist, and that is why it cannot be contained.

* * *

---

154 Liao Ruiling, "China Implements Zero-Tariff Policy for 53 African Countries," *People's Daily Online*, August 13, 2025, https://en.people.cn/n3/2025/0813/c90000-20352561.html.

Margaret Kimberley is a co-founder, executive editor and senior columnist at Black Agenda Report. *She has twice participated in delegations traveling to China. Her work as an activist includes leadership roles in the Black Alliance for Peace (BAP) and the United National Antiwar Coalition (UNAC). Ms. Kimberley is the author of* Prejudential: Black America and the Presidents. *She has also contributed to the anthologies* Killing Trayvons: An Anthology of American Violence, In Defense of Julian Assange, Capitalism on a Ventilator: the Impact of COVID-19 in China and the U.S., From the Flag to the Cross: Fascism American Style, *and* Confronting Counterinsurgency: Cop Cities and Democracy's Terrors. *In 2024 she briefed the United Nations Security Council as a civil society representative.*

The U.S. Wants War with China

by Joe Lombardo

The United States is preparing for a war with China. U.S. Secretary of Defense Pete Hegseth and many other US officials have stated that they expect to be at war with China by 2027. They claim this is in response to China's aggression, especially towards Taiwan. But China, the UN, and most of the rest of the world, including the U.S., recognize Taiwan as a province of China, and China has not threatened their own island province. Additionally, the U.S. claims of Chinese aggression are at odds with reality. In the past fifty years, China has not attacked another country or dropped bombs on anyone; yet the U.S. has had military operations against seventy-two countries in the past twenty-five years alone. In the past twenty years, the U.S. has dropped 337,000 bombs on various countries for an average of around forty-six per day. China has not dropped a single bomb on another country during this period. It is the U.S., not China, who is aggressive.

The U.S. military budget has recently grown to more than one trillion dollars, about 40% of the total military budgets of all countries combined. The U.S. has surrounded China with military bases and Navy vessels. The U.S. has eighty military bases in Japan, around 28,000 troops in South Korea, and a large and growing presence in the Philippines, which includes the recent introduction of Typhon missiles that can hit most Chinese cities and can carry nuclear warheads.

The U.S. has framed its aggression towards China in what it calls its "Pivot to Asia." This policy, announced by President Obama, shifted U.S. military resources from Europe and Western Asia to the so-called "Indo-Pacific region" with the goal of militarily surrounding China. In 2021, under the Biden administration, the U.S., the UK and Australia formed the AUKUS security partnership, an agreement focused on Australia acquiring nuclear-powered attack submarines, stationing U.S. and UK attack submarines in Australia, and the development of electronic warfare capabilities. The Chinese government stated at the time that AUKUS is "severely damaging regional peace" and that it showed a "cold-war mentality."

After World War II, the U.S. was the undisputed power in the world, both militarily and economically. Countries in Europe and Asia had been destroyed by the war and needed to be rebuilt. The U.S. used its position to create political, economic and military institutions that placed it in a privileged position at the center of world capitalism. It was the "American Century."

But the world has now moved on. The capitalist need for an ever-increasing rate of profit led the U.S., and its European allies, to increasingly move their industry out of their own countries to areas of the world where they could get cheaper labor and more favorable conditions for their manufacturing to make higher profits. During this period, they changed from an industrial capitalist model to a financial capitalist model, while China increased its industrial production by leaps and bounds. The U.S. has lost its monopoly over production. Today, the country with the most manufacturing in the world, by far, is China. It had around 31.2% of the global manufacturing output as of 2024, and the U.S. came in second, with 15.9% of the global manufacturing output. Most of the European capitalist countries have also deindustrialized.

The Ukraine war has laid bare a remarkable reality: Russia has been able to outproduce all of Europe and the U.S. in manufacturing shells, missiles, and other weapons, and is therefore winning the war.

Unlike in the U.S., where increased profits mean more billions for the billionaire class and nothing for the working class, China used its growing economy to build advanced infrastructure, housing for the people, and virtually eliminated poverty in the country while building a massive middle class. China has now surpassed the U.S. in GDP at purchasing power parity.

The U.S. has used its vast economic power to bully the world into supporting its political and economic policies, and has backed up its bullying with a vast military network that includes around 1,000 foreign military bases, about twenty times the number of foreign bases of all other countries combined. Today, the sun never sets on the U.S. military. The U.S. has also weaponized its economic might through sanctions and tariffs. It has sanctioned over forty other countries simply for seeking sovereignty and independence from U.S. imperialism and its economic institutions. To survive and prosper, many of these countries have come together to build new economic institutions such as the BRICS that will allow them their sovereignty, and allow them to develop and advance economically. In addition to China being a founding member of BRICS, China has moved ahead with its Belt and Road Initiative to build infrastructure and trade agreements with countries around the world, which can greatly benefit them as well as China. The U.S., however, sees this as a threat to its hegemony that it is preparing to go to war to preserve.

The U.S. empire is ending. Its domination of the world is being challenged, and rather than peacefully accepting the loss of its hegemonic privilege and power, it intends to bring the world to the brink of annihilation.

As always, as the U.S. moves towards war, propaganda by the U.S.

media is playing a big role. The U.S. media falsely portrays China as an oppressor of its people domestically, especially minorities, and a security threat to the U.S. and to China's neighbors. We have also heard the false narrative that China's trade practices are "unfair"—that they have stolen trade secrets and intellectual property, and that they have been involved in currency manipulation to make Chinese goods more competitive. Donald Trump has imposed high tariffs on China based on such claims. The most recent tariffs were initially set at 145%, much higher than on any other country in the world. They were only lowered when China retaliated with similar tariffs on the U.S. that caused financial chaos in U.S. markets. As of this writing, the harsh tariffs have been delayed for an additional ninety days until November 2025 while Trump tries to figure out what to do.

Although the narrative from the U.S. government has varied in its policy towards China—between pro-engagement and outright hostility—it seems that the U.S. media is always in lockstep with the U.S. administration. This is because the U.S. media is tightly controlled. When the Clinton Administration passed the Telecommunications Act of 1996, it resulted in a massive deregulation of the telecommunications industry. This caused a tremendous consolidation of the media in the hands of a few major corporations that control the narrative we hear. This process led to fewer alternative views in the corporate media and tighter control over social media.

It is also important to note that the U.S./Israeli genocide against the Palestinian people has shown the world what horrors imperialism and Zionism are capable of. These genocidal policies are an implied threat to all other countries: if they oppose the U.S. or Israel, they may suffer the same fate. As people around the world see the reality of Gaza, and as they protest in the streets in numbers that we have not seen in decades, the Western imperialist countries are cracking down on domestic civil liberties, making it more dangerous for their people to protest against U.S. and European government policies, as well as against all wars—not just the war in Palestine, but NATO's proxy war in Ukraine, and the aggressive moves towards China by the U.S. and its allies.

It is clear that there is a widening gulf between the positions of the Western governments and their people, which allows us the possibility to build a movement against war today as we have not been able to do in many years. As the U.S. moves towards war with China, we must prepare to fight to stop them, by demanding that the U.S. bring its troops home, close its foreign military bases, end all sanctions, and cut the military budget and use the money for human needs.

* * *

Joe Lombardo is a long-time peace and labor activist, and the coordinator of the United National Antiwar Coalition (UNAC).

The Greatest People's Success Story in Human History

by K.J. Noh

This chapter was originally a speech delivered at the celebration of the 75th Anniversary of the founding of the People's Republic of China (PRC).

Friends, colleagues, comrades, it's a great honor for me to join you in this extraordinary, historical moment of celebration and reflection on the 75th anniversary of the founding of the PRC.

As it has been said many times before, in the current historical moment, we are seeing changes unseen in a century—changes both great and terrible. We are currently seeing the unravelling of the Empire—and its last desperate, violent, hideous death rattle.

We are seeing the unmasking of 500 years of Western "civilization" and the laying bare of its hypocrisy and unspeakable brutality. We are seeing the true face of capitalist imperialism, not its made-up public relations face, but its *resting* capitalist face. And it's not pretty.

One of the precipitating factors of the end of the Empire—not the only factor, but a very important one, because it allows countries to resist hegemony together—is the rise of China. The rise of China is one of the greatest success stories in the history of human civilization.

We could talk about China's accomplishments all day. There are too many to list, but we can highlight three.

The Greatest People's Success Story

We all know in 1949 when China stood up, liberating half a billion people, 10-20% of China's population was still addicted to opium. In four years, the CPC eradicated opium addiction, liberating 90 million people from this colonial scourge. It's also one of the greatest public health accomplishments of the twentieth century, and chances are good that you've never heard of it. But by giving everyone the means of production—at the time, by redistributing land—and by offering everybody education, community, meaning, hope, purpose, and doing so at scale—because it has to be done at scale—the Party was successful. You can't do this in dribs and drabs, tinkering at the edges; you have to do it all at once for everyone.

We all know and understand that *we can't liberate anyone until everyone is liberated.* We must liberate each other because we are fundamentally socially interconnected, and therefore we are all a part of each other's futures.

We saw the same thing with extreme poverty alleviation. In China, poverty is not seen as an individual failing, as it is in the capitalist West. It is a whole-of-society responsibility requiring a whole-of-society response. It focused on everyone.

And so, 850 million people were brought out of extreme poverty. *"The poor will always be with us,"* says the West; but China's accomplishment in eliminating poverty lets the world know that *poverty is not an immutable, social, historical fact—it is a policy choice.* We can raise everyone up if we all work together. That's the way it works, and it works that way for everything. If we start from this principle, we can succeed, no matter how vast and immense the challenge is.

China is therefore proof positive of the power of people's solidarity, the power of a people's leadership, and the power of scientific planning according to socialist principles to overcome unthinkable challenges. This is how China accomplishes things, and it accomplishes them at scale—at a scale so vast that *nothing under heaven*, as it is said, is left behind.

Now, there is another achievement that China is working on. Yes, a socialist society is its ultimate goal, but this is an important stepping stone on the way to it. And it is a big one—it is the creation of an ecological civilization. China is literally greening the planet, creating single-handedly the conditions, the means, and the material tools to transition to a sustainable energy regime, to enable sustainable development, and turn back the tide of global warming.

And it is doing it at a scale that is truly inconceivable—but necessary. A challenge of this magnitude means you have to do this at that scale, and China knows how to accomplish things at scale. It knows how to solve problems even when the problems are unthinkably immense. And the leadership and the people do not flinch at the immensity of the challenge.

China is concretely showing us the pathway out of global climate catastrophe. As I said before, none of us are safe, good, or well until all of us are. That's true for poverty alleviation, it's true for drug eradication, and it's especially true for fighting global climate change. Until all of us are safe from the effects of the climate crisis, none of us are.

All the West needs to do on this issue is work together with China. China has provided the tools and the map showing the path out. To reduce it to its simplest terms, *going green means going red*. However, from the U.S. standpoint, they don't want that. They do not want an energy transition if it means the Chinese are going to be leading it. *They would rather be dead than red. The U.S. would rather burn up the planet than give China its place in the sun.* If China is on the side of renewable energy, then the U.S. has to be firmly on the side of global warming, because it's more important to the U.S. to beat China than to beat global warming.

The Greatest People's Success Story

We can see that right now, in the massive sanctioning of Chinese sustainable technologies that could shift the balance. If the planet heats up, we're all dead, but if *China cools the planet and saves the world, then we are no longer the coolest, and that's worse than death.* That's how the leaders of the U.S. think.

So, we can't talk about China's successes without talking about the U.S. hostility towards China. The U.S. sees China as its enemy, and is determined to take down China and all its accomplishments. Therefore the U.S. is preparing war—kinetic war—against China.

Washington is abuzz with talk of war with China. It's seen as necessary, inevitable, and—incredibly—winnable. "Winnable" means they are planning to use nuclear weapons. We have seen from Palestine and Lebanon that there are no limits to the depravity of what the Imperial ruling class will do to stay in power. Nothing is off the table. Nothing is too inhumane, too brutal, too illegal, or too dangerous. Nothing shocks their conscience. Nuclear war is definitely on the table, in the policy papers being distributed, in the military table-top exercises they conduct, and in the field training and air exercises that are now being conducted with the greatest intensity since World War II. To put it bluntly, the U.S. ruling class would rather see the end of the world than the end of their power and privilege.

So we are at a turning point in history; a crisis that is both opportunity and danger, hope and terror, unseen possibility and unthinkable tragedy. It's not if, but when.

Now, there are three distinguishable steps on the way to war. The first is information war: inventing the enemy and then demonizing them. They are manufacturing consent and shutting down opposition, like shutting down the skies before bombing. We're being fire-hosed and carpet-bombed with lies about China. The second is shaping the theater logistically for war, with arms, alliance, exercises, prepositioned stocks of fuel and material, and troops.

The third is provocation. There is non-stop provocation by the U.S.—in the Taiwan Strait, in the East China Sea, in the South China Sea, on the Korean peninsula, and everywhere else in the region. This follows the increasing, expanding ambit and intensity of proxy war in Europe and the genocidal terror in the Middle East. Kurt Campbell, Biden's "Asia Czar" and the architect of the Pivot to Asia, has threatened to unleash *"a magnificent symphony of death"* across a *"unified field [of war]"*.

We can all see and feel the shutting down of anti-war dissent, of opposing voices and alternative media. That's a key characteristic of the information war—silencing opposition, silencing voices of peace. It's like deploying anti-aircraft batteries and imposing a no-fly zone. You shut down the skies before you drop the bombs; and you shut down the opposition before you drop the narrative bombs. You attack opposition to war, attack those who want good relations or negotiations with China. You attack divergent voices and platforms in order to create a *no-think zone*. No thinking, no dialogue, no peace.

The U.S. literally seeks full spectrum dominance in all domains of war, but especially in the space domain: outerspace, cyber space, and *information space, mental space;* it literally seeks to occupy your mind.

So, resistance in this critical moment begins at the most fundamental level, with first not letting your mental space be occupied, colonized, and dominated. It means *resisting the narrative dominance of the dominant narrative:* that China is threatening the world, that war is thinkable, that war is justified. It means resisting the normalization of war, of genocide, of terror, of atrocity, of lies and propaganda. We can be vectors of this transmission of lies of propaganda, or we can impede its transmission.

It is therefore incumbent on all of us to re-engage in the mental martial art of critical thinking. We must strengthen our psychic immune system against this type of mental violence, this mental virus, this colonization of our mental spaces. We must re-orient and de-occupy ourselves, kick out the colonizing narratives, and recommit to "seeking truth from facts". What we need to do is tune up our critical thinking engines constantly, with the precision tools of wit, humor, parody, perspective, context—and facts.

Share the truth: the rise of China and the liberation of the Global South is not a threat to the peoples of the world. Instead, *it is a transformative moment of hope for human history.*

The stakes are immense. The future of the planet is at stake. As Brian Berletic said, "A war against China is a war against the world." We have already been inducted, and we all have a part to play.

Where do we start? We start with clear minds and courageous hearts.

Decolonize and de-propagandize your minds and resist together! The future of China, the future of the Global South, and the future of the world depend on it!

* * *

K.J. Noh is an award-winning journalist, political analyst, and educator focusing on the geopolitics and political economy of the Asia Pacific region. Originally from South Korea, he writes for Counterpunch, Dissident Voice, Black Agenda Report, Asia Times, Popular Resistance, Monthly Review, Pressian, Marxische Blatte, People's Daily, *and* Global Times. *He also does frequent com-*

mentary and analysis on various news programs and is the co-host of The China Report *on the Breakthrough News Network. He recently co-authored a study on the military transmission of infectious diseases by U.S. troops and its implications for the Covid epidemic.*

Taiwan's Residents Reject Being Washington's Proxy

by Chris Fry

Material for this chapter was taken from the article "Taiwan's residents reject being Washington's proxy in its war against Socialist China" published in Fighting-Words.net *on August 13, 2025.*

As of summer 2025, the Pentagon's plans for war against the People's Republic of China (PRC) have hit a snag. On July 27, Taiwan's residents voted to reject the ruling secessionist Democratic Progressive Party's (DPP) bid to recall twenty-four opposition Kuomintang (KMT) legislators. The KMT, though just as pro-capitalist as the DPP, nevertheless favors continuing dialogue and improved relations with the PRC, and agrees with the "One China policy" accepted by the vast majority of nations around the world. KMT leaders have traveled to mainland China to hold trade and cultural talks with the PRC leadership, defying the U.S-supported DPP leadership.

Another recall election in August of seven more KMT legislators was also unsuccessful, and all legislators targeted retained their seats. However, these developments will not halt the U.S. empire from arming Taiwan with the latest missiles and other military technology in preparation to launch a full-scale war against the PRC without the consent of Taiwan's residents.

The DPP's Wave of Repression Meets Mass Resistance

The recall attempts are only one part of the DPP's campaign to serve their U.S. masters by coercing Taiwan's residents to accept becoming proxies in Washington's war against the PRC, which is now on the Pentagon's drawing board.

Ever since elections were permitted in Taiwan, parties with the name "reunification" have been under attack by the government and by both major parties. The *Focus Taiwan News Service* reported in August that the Taiwan High Court "upheld prison sentences of four years and six months for two officials of the minor Reunification Alliance Party who recruited people to travel to China for political purposes."[155]

A June 8 *Wall Street Journal* article titled "Taiwan Tries to Purge Its Ranks of China Sympathizers"[156] reported:

> "Taiwan has embarked on a mission to purge any allies of Beijing from its civil service in an escalating battle against China's influence...
>
> ...In the past few weeks, Taiwan expanded the ID-vetting process to local governments, schools and universities, telling administrators to punish employees who

---

[155] James Thompson and Hung Hsueh-kuang, "High court upholds sentences for Reunification Alliance Party figures," *Focus Taiwan: CNA English News*, August 20, 2025, https://focustaiwan.tw/politics/202508200013.

[156] Joyu Wang, "Taiwan Tries to Purge Its Ranks of China Sympathizers," *Wall Street Journal*, June 8, 2025, https://www.wsj.com/world/asia/taiwan-tries-to-purge-its-ranks-of-china-sympathizers-5caf62fa.

> hold or have applied for Chinese identity cards but failed to report doing so...
>
> ...A spokeswoman for Beijing's Taiwan Affairs Office said… that Taipei was attempting to 'undermine efforts to bring people on both sides of the strait closer together.'"

Even mainland-born spouses of Taiwan residents are being threatened, as a July 8 *Taiwan News* article reported: "1,668 spouses in Taiwan miss deadline to renounce Chinese household registration."[157]

Many of these are being told they will lose their permanent residency status. The news agency *AFP* reported in a July article titled: "Taiwan pursues homegrown Chinese spies as Beijing's influence grows," that even top officials in the DPP executive branch are being targeted: "Prosecutors last week charged four recently expelled members of the ruling Democratic Progressive Party—including a former staffer in President Lai Ching-te's office—for sharing state secrets with Beijing."[158]

All of this is bitterly ironic, since the DPP gained its popularity by being an alternative to the KMT, which imposed the "White Terror": 40 years of martial law on Taiwan's residents, jailing tens of thousands and murdering between three and four thousand residents. This occurred after Chiang Kai Shek's KMT forces were defeated in

---

157 Keoni Everington, "1,668 spouses in Taiwan miss deadline to renounce Chinese household registration," *Taiwan News,* July 8, 2025, https://www.taiwannews.com.tw/news/6150855.

158 AFP, "Taiwan pursues homegrown Chinese spies as Beijing's influence grows," *MSN,* June 18, 2025, https://www.msn.com/en-us/news/world/taiwan-pursues-homegrown-chinese-spies-as-beijing-s-influence-grows/ar-AA1GZHzj.

the wake of World War II by the Red Army, but escaped to Taiwan, ruling there with an iron fist for decades with lavish U.S. support. Taiwan has been part of China for centuries. Imperial Japan seized control of it in 1895, but China regained control of it following the surrender of Japan in World War II, in 1945.

The KMT always maintained it was the legitimate ruler of the Republic of China (ROC)—the official name of the government in Taiwan—which claimed *all of China* as its territory, so it never called for Taiwanese independence or separation from the mainland. Now the DPP itself is sparking this wave of repression to force the people of Taiwan to fight a war that only serves the interests of U.S. imperialism.

The DPP's repressive campaign has sparked mass resistance, as the Hong Kong news website *Dimsum Daily* reported on April 27:

> "In a rainy Taipei on Saturday, more than 250,000 people gathered to protest what they described as the 'dictatorship' of Taiwan's Democratic Progressive Party (DPP) authorities...
>
> The demonstration occurred amidst growing discontent over the DPP's 'mass recall' campaign, launched earlier this year, which targeted legislative representatives affiliated with the KMT. Protesters also denounced recent searches conducted against KMT offices across Taiwan, viewing these actions as part of a broader effort to suppress opposition voices."[159]

---

159 Dimsum Daily Newsroom, "Over 250,000 rally in Taiwan against DPP's 'authoritarian rule'," *Dimsum Daily*, April 27, 2025, https://www.dimsumdaily.hk/over-250000-rally-in-taiwan-against-dpps-authoritarian-rule/.

Chris Fry

Trump is Not Happy with the DPP

President Trump is a fickle master, unhappy with the DPP's failure to mobilize the residents behind the U.S. warmongering against China. He is now threatening a massive 20 percent tariff on Taiwanese imports. These tariffs are vital for Silicon Valley's accumulation of capital for its Artificial Intelligence and cryptocurrency schemes.

Trump even told President Lai Ching-te not to bother stopping in New York City to drum up support for Taiwan's "independence" during Lai's recent international diplomatic tour, in which the DPP politician also visited the few remaining small countries left in the world that still recognize the ROC rather than the PRC. The White House announced that this snub of Lai was "to enable trade talks with the PRC." China's suspension of the sale of rare earth minerals needed for computer hardware, cars and weapons has created enormous difficulties for U.S. imperialism. Trump's snub can be seen as part of his clumsy efforts to "split" China from its Russian ally, and to pressure India to distance itself from BRICS. All these efforts are backfiring.

Washington Escalates War Preparations on Taiwan's Soil

Despite his continuing failure to force China into submission to imperialism, Trump has only been emboldened to escalate military war preparation in Taiwan, with the full assent of the DPP government, but without support of Taiwan's residents.

On May 12, CNN reported:

Taiwan's Residents Reject Being Washington's Proxy

> "Taiwan on Monday test-fired for the first time a new US-supplied rocket system that has been widely used by Ukraine against Russia and could be deployed to hit targets in China if there is a war with Taiwan...
>
> ...Taiwan has bought 29 of Lockheed Martin's precision weapon High Mobility Artillery Rocket Systems, or HIMARS, with the first batch of 11 received last year and the rest set to arrive by next year.
>
> With a range of about 300 kilometers (186 miles), they could hit coastal targets in China's southern province of Fujian, on the other side of the Taiwan Strait, in the event of conflict."[160]

The U.S. is doing more than just training. With the bulk of U.S. missile shipments going to its proxy war in Ukraine, it has fallen behind with such shipments to Taiwan. Therefore the U.S. has "persuaded" Taiwan to build its own long-range offensive missiles. As *Taiwan News* reported on June 7:

> "Taiwan has reportedly produced 100 Hsiung Sheng surface-to-surface missiles with a range of up to 1,200 kilometers.

---

[160] Reuters, "Taiwan test-fires new US-supplied HIMARS rocket system," *CNN*, May 12, 2025, https://edition.cnn.com/2025/05/12/world/taiwan-test-fires-himars-rocket-system-intl-hnk.

An unnamed senior military official told Liberty Times on Saturday that the Hsiung Sheng missile system has already completed its initial mass production phase.

The official was quoted as saying the production model of the Hsiung Sheng missile has a range of 1,200 km, and National Chung-Shan Institute of Science & Technology researchers are working to push this further. 'Naturally, the goal is the range of the latest US and Japanese missiles.'"[161]

The military website SOFREP reported in June that there are now more than 500 U.S. military personnel in Taiwan. Since the Pentagon lists only forty-one soldiers there, it can be assumed that most are expert contractors, who are there to ensure that all the missiles and other high-tech weapons will be fired if Trump, not Taiwan, gives the order.[162]

It should be noted that Taiwan's government is using bribery to convince the populace to go along with this arms buildup. The news outlet *Taiwan Plus* reported on August 2: "Taiwan's government is set to make cash payments of over US $300 per person by the end of

---

161 Keoni Everington, "Taiwan produces over 100 Hsiung Sheng missiles," *Taiwan News*, June 7, 2025, https://www.taiwannews.com.tw/news/6129229.

162 Guy D. McCardle, "500 US Military Trainers Now Reportedly Operating in Taiwan," *MSN*, May 27, 2025, https://www.msn.com/en-us/news/world/500-us-military-trainers-now-reportedly-operating-in-taiwan/ar-AA-1FAxpx.

Taiwan's Residents Reject Being Washington's Proxy

October, after President Lai Ching-te enacted an economic relief bill passed by the legislature in July."[163]

Of course, the 800,000 heavily exploited migrant workers in Taiwan from Indonesia, Vietnam and the Philippines[164] won't see a penny of that money.

* * *

> *Chris Fry is a long-time activist in the revolutionary socialist movement, first as a member of the Students for a Democratic Society (SDS) in Ann Arbor, Michigan, and then with the Workers World Party, which he joined in 1970. In 1972 he was elected a UAW union steward and bargaining committee member at the steel warehouse where he worked in Detroit. In 1973, he helped lead a successful six-week strike. He then worked for six years at the Chrysler Lynch Road Assembly plant where he was active in anti-racist and working class struggles both inside and outside the plant, such as the All Peoples Congress and the People's Takeover of Big Oil. Fry became a writer for* Workers World *and then for the* Fighting Words *newsletter of the Communist Workers League. He is retired and living in the Albany, New York area.*

---

163 Taiwan Plus, "Taiwan's Government Set To Make US$300 Cash Payments," *Taiwan Plus*, August 2, 2025, https://www.taiwanplus.com/news/taiwan-news/politics/250802005/taiwans-government-set-to-make-us300-cash-payments.

164 Michael Beltran, "In Taiwan, migrants flee oppressive workplaces for life on the periphery," *Al Jazeera*, July 8, 2025, https://www.aljazeera.com/economy/2025/7/8/in-taiwan-migrants-flee-oppressive-workplaces-for-life-on-the-periphery.

An Analysis of the Escalating U.S. Threats Toward China

by Mick Kelly

The United States is on a collision course with socialist China. People's China is promoting and pursuing peace while Washington, DC is encouraging separatism in the province of Taiwan. The U.S. has embarked on a unprecedented arms buildup that the Pentagon says is aimed at Bejing, and measures to decouple or delink the two economies, accompanied by President Trump's inflationary tariffs on China, are another aspect of the preparations for war.

No matter how strange it might seem, scholarly international relations journals—for example, *Foreign Affairs*—regularly carry articles about a coming U.S. war with the People's Republic of China (PRC), and debate issues like whether this war will be long or short in duration, or what sort of weapons systems will be deployed. The planners of wars take themselves seriously; advocates of peace and progress must do so as well.

The Decline of the U.S. Empire

In our rapidly changing world, People's China is ascending, and the United States is being left behind. In the post-World War II era, a period when the U.S. was able to dictate many of the rules for global trade and commerce, the U.S. had about 50% of the world's GDP. Today, it accounts for only one quarter of the world's GDP. The U.S.

Analysis of the Escalating U.S. Threats Toward China

share of world trade has also decreased, by about 40% since 1970.

A plurality of the world's steel was once produced in the U.S., and in 1955, it dominated about 40% of the world market. By 2019 the U.S. had become one of the largest steel importers, only producing about 5% of the world's steel. The same pattern can be shown in industry after industry, be it automobiles, electronic devices, or other manufacturing.

China's rapid development is a great contrast to the deteriorating economic position of the U.S. Using the measure of purchasing power parity, which allows a comparison of which commodities and services can be purchased with a given currency, the World Bank concluded that the Chinese economy was 23% larger than the U.S. economy in 2022.

Directly linked to the decay of U.S. monopoly capitalism is the abandonment by successive administrations of the economic architecture that was created by Wall Street in the aftermath of World War II. The World Trade Organization is paralyzed due to the refusal by both the Biden and Trump Administrations to allow judges to be appointed to the international institution's dispute resolution mechanism. U.S. policymakers invested immense amounts of time and treasure to create the Trans-Pacific Partnership, and then in 2016 withdrew from the free trade project shortly before Congressional consideration. The U.S. long-term commitment to the International Monetary Fund and World Bank is now shrouded by uncertainty, as foreign policy pundits lament the "post-American world."

The bellicose war threats from Washington are a sign of weakness, not strength. The U.S. departure from multilateral institutions and the construction of a tariff regime unseen since the 1930 Smoot–Hawley Tariff Act will bring about a fragmentation of the world economy, sharpen the rivalry between economic blocs, particularly between the

U.S. and Europe, and take the U.S. on a course towards war in the Pacific. In the long run, politics always follow economics; less economic power translates into less political power.

"Decoupling" from China

For the last decade, the Biden and Trump Administrations have imposed excessive tariffs on goods made in China. Promoting himself as the "tariff man," Trump has vacillated on his proposed tariff rates, but at times they have been high enough to amount to a trade embargo on China. While the trade and industrial policies of Trump and Biden differ, they have a important point in common—to "decouple" or "delink" the U.S. and Chinese economies.

Trump says that this will lead to a resurgence of U.S. manufacturing and generate well-paying manufacturing jobs. This will not happen. Tariffs are in essence a tax on consumers, and workers take the brunt of the blow. Much of the job losses in recent decades can be attributed to technology, and the utilization of advanced productive forces in the U.S. will lead to additional job losses in industries such as automobile production or steel. Putting impoverishment and a potential rise in unemployment aside, the Trump administration is determined to push ahead with decoupling, even at a high cost—for example, the tariffs on China have decreased the demand for U.S. agricultural products, thus causing a downturn in the production of farm equipment.

The process of economic decoupling is designed to hurt China, but the U.S. is likely to be hurt more. China exports more goods to more places that the U.S. does, so it has the advantage of diversification, and it has pulled ahead in many branches of industry, especially with respect to green technology. Delinking from China does not make sense as a program of economic development. At best, it is a way to manage U.S. decline.

Looking Back at U.S.-China Relations

From the victory of the Chinese revolution in 1949 until the early 1970s, U.S. foreign policy towards China was extremely hostile. Then came "ping pong diplomacy", and in 1972, both counties signed the Shanghai Communiqué agreeing that "all Chinese on either side of the Taiwan Strait maintain there is but one China and that Taiwan is a part of China." This One China principle was reaffirmed when Wahington recognized Beijing in 1979 and formal diplomatic relations were established.

In the following decades, the U.S. followed the strategy of "peaceful evolution", the theory that by using political, economic, and cultural ties, it would be possible to foster forces in China antithetical to socialism, capitalism would prevail, and a Western-style government would be established. The application of this strategy was played out in the late 1980s when the U.S. did everything it could to encourage turmoil in China and the other socialist countries. In China, however, socialism continued to not only survive, but to thrive, creating incredible social achievements such as the elimination of extreme poverty.

With Trump's election in 2016, the Cold War rhetoric, which had been part of the foreign policy background noise, came to the fore. This hostility towards China was open and raw, a toxic brew of national chauvinism combined with anti-Asian racism—for example, how of Covid was frequently called the "China virus" in the U.S. The Trump and Biden Administrations returned to trying to weaken China and prepare for war.

Mick Kelly

Preparations for War

In the Pentagon, real, concrete preparations for a war with China are underway. The Department of Defense budget for Fiscal Year 2026 is aimed at "[d]eterring China in the Indo-Pacific by prioritizing combat credible military forces and capabilities postured forward in the Western Pacific." This is just part of the military encirclement of China; given that even the coastal city of Shanghai is well over 6,000 miles west of Los Angeles, it is evident that the U.S. is going a long way to pick a fight.

The political establishment and the Pentagon have multifaceted plans. The U.S. is trying to put together alliances—formal and informal—against China. Of note is the Philippines, where the U.S.-backed Marcos regime has enlisted in the coming war on China. American and Filipino troops train together and carry out counter-insurgency operations against the national democratic movement, and plans are underway to construct a huge ammunition-making facility at Subic Bay.

The White House is looking to fund war-related manufacturing and expand naval capacity. Industrial policy will now have big money for submarines (a proposed $5 billion for the submarine industrial base), ship building, advanced aircraft, and munitions such as hypersonic missiles.

Finally, U.S. military bases, ships, and missile systems in the region are nothing less than the provocative encirclement of China. U.S. vessels violate Chinese territorial waters in the Taiwan Strait, and the Pentagon complains when military aircraft are confronted in the PRC Air Defense Identification Zone. All these things take place thousands of miles from the U.S. mainland. Fair-minded people might ask, who is it that really needs to be "deterred"?

Analysis of the Escalating U.S. Threats Toward China

Taiwan Province

Achieving reunification with Taiwan is the great unfinished business of the Chinese revolution. A part of China since ancient times, Taiwan was partially colonized by the Dutch in 1624. In 1662, the heroic Chinese General Zheng Chenggong led the fight to successfully drive out these invaders.

In 1949, the defeated American puppet Chiang Kai-shek decamped from the mainland and fled to Taiwan, where he still claimed be the ruler of all of China. His backers in Washington stood in the path of Taiwan's liberation and referred to Taiwan as their "unsinkable aircraft carrier."

Though the U.S. now acknowledges that Taiwan is part of China and that there is only one China, it also encourages separatism. The Pentagon's 2026 budget contains a proposal to send more weapons into Taiwan, and both Biden and Trump have contradicted the long-standing policy of "strategic ambiguity", suggesting that the U.S. might intervene to block reunification.

In his 2024 New Year's speech, President Xi Jinping stated, "We Chinese on both sides of the Taiwan Strait belong to one and the same family. No one can ever sever the bond of kinship between us, and no one can ever stop China's reunification, a trend of the times."

Reunification will happen. Those of us here in the U.S. who oppose imperialism and demand peace with justice must insist the Pentagon stays out of the way.

China: Peace and Progress

Socialist China is a beacon of progress. Its existence demonstrates that socialism brings peace and prosperity, while the United States controls a declining empire that is continuously at war. The difference between the two roads these respective counties offer could not be starker. When U.S. warmongers talk about "modernizing" nuclear weapons, in the next breath they mention China. Progressives and revolutionaries in the United States must do everything in our power to stop them, and join with people around the world who want to do the same.

* * *

Mick Kelly is the political secretary of the Freedom Road Socialist Organization and editor of FightBack! News. *He is a long-time labor and anti-war activist, and has written numerous articles on the international situation and the role of socialist China.*

6.

China's Impact on the World

Around the World, China is Turning on the Lights

by Gregory Dunkel
edited by Natalia Burdyńska

When the sun goes down, half of the people on the African continent—about 700 million people—have to live in the dark. They don't have reliable access to electricity, and thus have limited access to modern education, economic growth, or ways to improve their quality of life. Of the dozens of countries in the world where more than a third of the population still has no access to electricity, only a tiny few, such as Haiti and Papua New Guinea, are *not* in Africa.

This lack of access is largely the legacy of colonialism. The European great powers of the late nineteenth century, in their insatiable quest to enrich themselves by dominating the world, neglected to build infrastructure in their colonies that was not directly necessary for the cultivation of cash crops and the extraction of resources for profit.

While a few countries on the continent, like Egypt and Tunisia, now have 100% access, they are considering, along with the African countries with low access rates, installing low-priced Chinese solar panels to harness Africa's tremendous potential for using the sun to produce electricity. Importing China's renewable energy technology, which produces electricity from widely available and extremely inexpensive inputs—sunlight and wind—has become far more attractive to the post-colonial world than importing fossil fuel technology from the United States.

China: World Leader in Solar Power

During the 2000s, the nascent Chinese solar industry was a minor player, both on the world stage and domestically. Solar panels were too expensive for the Chinese market and were thus only viable as an export commodity. This led to disaster in 2012, when China lost access to the European market for solar power following the Great Recession and the subsequent eurozone debt crisis. SunTech and LDK Solar, two of China's largest solar energy firms at the time, went bankrupt. The government's efforts to develop solar technology were widely considered wasteful; according to Chinese economist Dr. Lan Xiaohuan, the solar industry was heavily criticized in the media as "a byword for the failure of state-led industrial policies and government subsidies" during the early 2010s.[165]

Nevertheless, according to Lan, subsidies and industrial policy were essential to the subsequent expansion of China's solar industry and the country's rise to become the undisputed world leader in solar power a decade later.[166] Subsidies, when employed properly, allow competing industry players the latitude to undercut each other, effectively lowering the price of their products. Since 2012, the price of solar energy has fallen like a stone, while the expansion of solar capacity in China has risen at an unprecedented rate. In May 2025, in a rush to take advantage of lucrative government subsidies, Chinese solar firms installed nearly a hundred gigawatts of new solar capacity domestically—more than any other country had installed in all of

---

165 Xiaohuan Lan, *How China Works: An Introduction to China's State-Led Economic Development*, English, trans. Gary Topp (Horizon Media Co., Ltd., 2024), 142.
166 Lan, *How China Works: An Introduction to China's State-Led Economic Development*, 149.

2024—and set the world record for the most solar installations in a single month.[167]

Today, China is on track to account for over half of all the world's renewable energy capacity by the end of the decade.[168] It also manufactures "over 80 per cent of capacity and production in all stages of the solar [photovoltaic] supply chain including polysilicon, wafers, cells, and modules," according to Chen Wei, executive deputy director of China's Photovoltaic Industry IP Operation Center.[169] In other words, China not only produces solar panels but also their components, for other countries to assemble.

Solar Power in Africa

Because their own domestic market has become saturated and the U.S. market is blocked by confiscatory tariffs, Chinese solar firms have launched a major campaign to sell their products to African countries who need and want to expand their electrical production.

A recent report from Ember, a global energy think tank, describes how solar panel imports from China into the African continent jumped 60% in the 12 months preceding June 2025, setting a record that could transform many of the countries involved. Both small and

---

167 Bloomberg News, "China Solar Additions Surge to Record in May Ahead of Deadline," *Bloomberg*, June 23, 2025, https://www.bloomberg.com/news/articles/2025-06-23/china-solar-additions-surge-to-record-in-may-ahead-of-deadline.

168 James Darley, "China is Set to Produce Half the World's Renewables by 2030," *Sustainability Magazine*, December 11, 2024, https://sustainabilitymag.com/articles/how-china-will-lead-the-green-energy-expansion.

169 Xiong Weisheng, "China shifts from solar manufacturing giant to solar IP innovator," *Xinhua Baoye Wang*, September 21, 2024, https://www.xhby.net/content/s66ee8993e4b0458dc38c9f9d.html.

poor countries, like Mali and Malawi, as well as large, middle-income countries like Algeria, Nigeria and South Africa are importing Chinese solar panels.

According to Ember, the impact of installing these panels will be significant:

> "If all solar panels imported into Sierra Leone in the last 12 months alone were installed, they would be able to generate electricity equivalent to 61% of reported electricity generation in 2023, the latest available data. For Chad, it would be 49%. In five other countries, imports in total could add electricity equivalent to more than 10% of reported 2023 generation—Liberia (25%), Somalia (15%), Eritrea (15%), Togo (11%), Benin (10%). Altogether, 16 countries would see an increase of at least 5%."[170]

Chad, the country the report identified as potentially seeing the most dramatic effects from solar power imports, is a landlocked country in the turbulent Sahel region, at the crossroads of North and Central Africa. It has a population of around 20 million people, which, according to the International Rescue Committee, includes 1.5 million refugees, most of whom have fled civil conflict in Chad's eastern neighbor, Sudan.

Currently, only 6.4% of Chad's population has access to electricity. The government of Chad is planning to raise its electrification rate to 30% by 2027 and to 53% by 2030 using inexpensive Chinese solar

---

170 Dave Jones, *The First Evidence of a Take-off in Solar in Africa* (Ember, 2025), https://ember-energy.org/latest-insights/the-first-evidence-of-a-take-off-in-solar-in-africa/.

panels. It plans to build a solar park in N'Djamena, its capital, with batteries to store power for nighttime access.[171] Once this is done, it intends to take what it has learned in N'Djamena to the rest of the country, where it will construct three hybrid power stations in other cities (installations that combine solar, wind, hydro and fossil fuel power with battery storage).[172]

Nnanda Kizito Sseruwagi, a senior research associate at the Sino-Uganda Institute in Kampala, summed up the impact of China's exports of renewable energy technology in the following way:

> "As the leading global player in green/clean energy, China has played a pivotal role in Africa's green energy transition through its investments in exploring solar, wind, hydropower, geothermal energy, and nuclear projects at their early stages on the continent. Through FOCAC (Forum on China-Africa Cooperation), China has addressed Africa's pressing need for sustainable, accessible and reliable energy while at the same time aligning with both the global climate goals as well as its own strategic shift towards green energy development. Across Sub-Saharan Africa, China has reshaped

---

171 Benedicte Ngono, "Tchad: le chinois TBEA choisi pour réaliser un projet électrique de 7 milliards de Fcfa à N'Djamena (Chad: Chinese TBEA chosen to carry out a 7 billion CFA franc electricity project in N'Djamena)," *EcoMatin*, December 12, 2024, ecomatin.net/tchad-le-chinois-tbea-choisi-pour-realiser-un-projet-electrique-de-7-milliards-de-fcfa-a-ndjamena.

172 Jean Omer Eyango, "Infrastructure: Chad seeks companies for the construction of three hybrid power plants, financed by the AfDB," *EcoMatin*, April 17, 2024, https://ecomatin.net/infrastructures-le-tchad-recherche-des-entreprises-pour-la-construction-de-trois-centrales-electriques-hybrides-financees-par-la-bad.

the energy infrastructure, installing over 23 gigawatts of electricity capacity in 27 countries."[173]

The Chinese Solar Industry Goes International

Africa is not the only beneficiary of Chinese renewable energy exports. Throughout the Global South—Africa, Latin America and the Caribbean, and much of Asia—developing countries are experiencing solar revolutions as China's remarkably cheap solar panels and photovoltaic components flood in.

Recently, Cuba has seen its entire electrical grid fail multiple times as the country has struggled to maintain its aging infrastructure under the brutal U.S. trade embargo that has isolated the island country for generations, depriving it of fuel and system components. But now, as *Reuters* reported in June 2025, China is financing dozens of new solar electricity projects across the island, nine of which were complete and already producing 400 megawatts of power, with nearly twice as much new capacity expected to be online by the end of the year. These installations provide a lifeline to Cuba's electrical system: by 2028, they are projected to cover nearly two thirds of the present national demand for electricity, which could finally make blackouts a thing of the past.[174]

As summers in Pakistan grow hotter and hotter, demand for electricity has increased, putting immense strain on its similarly outdated infrastructure. The International Monetary Fund recently forced the

---

173 Nnanda Kizito Sseruwagi, "China's Role in Africa's Renewable Energy Transition," Development Watch Centre, August 3, 2025, https://www.dwcug.org/chinas-role-in-africas-renewable-energy-transition/.

174 Dave Sherwood, "China Is Quietly Supplanting Russia as Cuba's Main Benefactor," *Reuters* (Jatibonico, Cuba), June 30, 2025, https://www.reuters.com/business/environment/china-is-quietly-supplanting-russia-cubas-main-benefactor-2025-06-30/.

country to end its energy subsidies that had made electricity affordable to the population, and as a result, the price of electricity has doubled since 2022.[175]

Overwhelmingly, the Pakistani people have responded to the crisis by buying Chinese solar panels. Solar panels now adorn the roofs of homes, small businesses, and even neighborhood mosques throughout the country. An expert from the University of Oxford's Environmental Change Institute called the rate at which solar power is being adopted in Pakistan to be unmatched by anywhere else in the world.[176] In June 2025, *Reuters* reported that Pakistan had increased its solar energy capacity by over three times the global average so far that year, and is now one of fewer than twenty countries in the world that source more than a quarter of their electricity from solar power.[177]

Experts from Ember, in its 2025 review of China's energy transition, called China's clean energy development model a "key engine of economic progress" that, in addition to driving other countries away from fossil fuels,[178] is developing new technology, creating jobs, and delivering economic growth.[179] In 2022, China's share of patent appli-

---

175 Betsy Joles, "Pakistan Is Tapping into Solar Power at an 'unprecedented' Rate. Here's Why," *National Public Radio* (Islamabad), August 21, 2025, https://www.npr.org/sections/goats-and-soda/2025/08/21/g-s1-82369/solar-power-panels-boom-pakistan.

176 Betsy Joles, "Pakistan Is Tapping into Solar Power at an 'unprecedented' Rate. Here's Why."

177 Gavin Maguire, "Pakistan's Solar Surge Lifts It into Rarefied 25% Club," *Reuters* (Littleton, Colorado), June 17, 2025, https://www.reuters.com/markets/commodities/pakistans-solar-surge-lifts-it-into-rarefied-25-club-2025-06-17/.

178 Max Bearak, "'China Is the Engine' Driving Nations Away From Fossil Fuels, Report Says," *The New York Times*, September 8, 2025, https://www.nytimes.com/2025/09/08/climate/china-clean-energy-fossil-fuel-research.html.

179 Muyi Yang et al., *China Energy Transition Review 2025* (Ember, 2025), 37–38, https://ember-energy.org/latest-insights/china-energy-transition-review-2025/.

cations related to clean energy technology was over three times greater than the rest of the world combined.[180] The total solar manufacturing capacity needed globally by 2030 to meet the International Energy Agency's road map to net-zero emissions by 2050 has *already* been reached by China alone, and by 2030, China's solar manufacturing capacity is projected to exceed the IEA's goal by 65%.[181]

There is no question that the People's Republic of China is indispensable to any solution to global climate change, as well as the world's best and quickest pathway out of the colonial underdevelopment that has kept so much of it in darkness for so many years.

* * *

After getting a degree in applied mathematics, Gregory Dunkel worked in data processing until retirement. He is a contributing editor for Workers World *and occasionally writes for* Haïti-Liberté. *He is one of the authors of the book* Haiti: A Slave Revolution.

---

180 Muyi Yang et al., *China Energy Transition Review 2025*, 46.
181 Muyi Yang et al., *China Energy Transition Review 2025*, 44–45.

Lips and Teeth: Korea, China, and Northeast Asia's Long Revolution

by Ju-Hyun Park

75 years ago, in 1950, the People's Republic of China made the fateful decision to deploy over a million soldiers of the Chinese People's Volunteer Army in defense of the Democratic People's Republic of Korea. This was not a straightforward decision at the time. There were those within the Communist Party of China (CPC) who questioned the wisdom[182] of committing the nascent republic to a foreign military operation against an enemy as powerful as the United States—particularly at a time when China remained politically divided and economically backward, having only established its state in 1949.

To explain the necessity of the War to Resist U.S. Aggression and Aid Korea, Mao drew on an old Chinese proverb: "If the lips are gone, the teeth will be cold." This statement reflected a straightforward geopolitical logic—one which the various rulers of China and Korea alike have discovered time and again. At times referred to as a "peninsular island",[183] Korea's position at the intersection of Russia, China, and Japan makes it a crucial pivot point in Northeast Asia.

---

182 "Speech to the Cadres of the Chinese People's Volunteers," Peng Dehuai, Peng Dehuai [unshi Wenxuan (Beijing, 1988), pp. 320-26. Uncertain partners pg.284-289, https://www.commonprogram.science/documents/Pend%20Dehuai%20speech.pdf.

183 Cumings, Bruce. "Korea's Place in the Sun: A Modern History." *The SHAFR Guide Online*, October 2, 2017, https://doi.org/10.1163/2468-1733_shafr_sim200070107.

This geographical reality has shaped the historical development of the Korean nation and the wider region, and remains a crucial dimension of Sino-Korean relations in the contemporary era.

While Mao's observation most immediately concerned the question of mutual security, the phrase "lips and teeth" has taken on a life of its own to describe the closeness of the PRC and the Democratic People's Republic of Korea (DPRK), which to this day is still the only country to enjoy a strategic alliance with China. By the time of the Korean War, the Korean and Chinese Revolutions were bonded by decades of joint struggle against imperialism. Driven from the peninsula by Japanese repression, a generation of Korean revolutionaries fought for China's liberation during WWII (1931-1945) to achieve the international conditions necessary for the liberation of Korea and the world proletariat.

After Korea's liberation from Japan and the founding of the DPRK in 1948, 100,000 Koreans took up arms in China to defeat the Kuomintang.[184] The DPRK and border Korean communities in Manchuria provided an essential rearguard to the People's Liberation Army. When Chinese volunteers crossed the Yalu River in 1950, they were not only defending Chinese security or answering an abstract internationalist duty, but repaying the sacrifices of countless Koreans who had given their lives for China's liberation.

Yet the phrase "lips and teeth" alone cannot describe either the contemporary or historical dynamism of the Sino-Korean relationship. Historically, Sino-Korean solidarity and friendship was forged in the crucible of Northeast Asia's long encounter with capitalist expansion, from mercantilism to imperialism. Since the Korean War, the durability and depth of these bonds have been tested by shifting international

---

184 Donggil Kim, "Prelude to War? The Repatriation of Koreans from the Chinese PLA, 1949-1950," Cold War History, Vol. 12, No. 2 (2010), 227-244.

conditions and the divergent paths each state has taken in response to them. Today, a rampaging Washington and an increasingly unstable liberal international order have once again produced the conditions for the DPRK and PRC to stand shoulder-to-shoulder—analyzing this development, not from the standpoint of slogans alone but as a new chapter in Northeast Asia's long revolution, can provide the best understanding of the significance of this alliance and the possibilities it may open in the future.

From Feudalism to Socialism: Northeast Asia's Long Revolution

Before Northeast Asia's integration into capitalism, relations between various Korean and Chinese dynasties over millenia were marked by periods of collaboration, tributary domination, and even rivalry as peer competitors. As part of the Sinosphere, Korean kingdoms owed much of their development to economic and cultural exchanges with China, but it would be a mistake to view Korea's historical role as only a recipient or a secondary actor. The exchange of ideas, technologies, and culture was not one-directional, and periods of dynastic decline and disorder in China usually coincided with the golden ages of Korean kingdoms. Just as much as the bounty of the continent benefitted Korea, its existence also depended on repelling a melange of invading forces from the continent, which at various times included Chinese dynasties. The peninsular island and the Middle Kingdom were thus bound together in a historical dialectic that can be observed across millennia.

The gradual integration of Northeast Asia into the capitalist world over centuries would alter the former Sino-Korean dynamic, as the changing class composition of the region's societies necessarily altered its politics. The earliest sign of this came in the Japanese invasions of Korea from 1592-1598, known as the Imjin Wars. For Japan, the invasions of Korea came at the end of more than a century of brutal warfare among competing daimyo, an era known as the Sengoku Period. The arrival of the Portuguese in the region would influence the trajectory of the Sengoku Period. From their colonial ports in Malacca (1511) and Macau (1557), the Portuguese established a mercantile monopoly over regional trade, and in the process introduced European firearms to Japan and stimulated its silver mining industry.[185] These factors would contribute to Japan's unification, after which daimyo Toyotomi Hideyoshi set his sights on the conquest of Ming China by way of Korea.

As in Western Europe, a mix of mercantile accumulation and feudal expansion drove territorial consolidation in Japan. Japanese pirates, or wokou, had plagued East Asia's coasts for centuries,[186] but the Japanese armada that set sail for Korea marked a qualitative shift in the archipelago's regional role. For the first time, China was forced to intervene in Korea for the purpose of mutual security, rather than for conquest or to influence peninsular rivalries among competing Korean kingdoms. Though Japan was ultimately repelled, the Imjin Wars devastated Joseon Korea; a million people perished and hundreds of thousands were abducted by the invaders to be enslaved in Japan, or even sold as chattel to Europeans.[187] The Ming Dynasty's eventual collapse in 1644 was also in part the result of these wars.

---

185 Flynn, Dennis O., et al. "Born With a 'Silver Spoon': The Origin of World Trade in 1571." *Journal of World History*, vol. 6, no. 2, University of Hawai'i Press, 1995.

186 Though classically attested to as Japanese pirates, contemporary scholars believe the wokou were motley crews of varying origins.

187 De Sousa, Lúcio. *The Portuguese Slave Trade in Early Modern Japan Merchants, Jesuits and Japanese, Chinese, and Korean Slaves*. 2018.

Ju-Hyun Park

The maturation of capitalism into imperialism, or the monopoly stage of capitalism, in the nineteenth century would usher in even greater horrors to the region. It was in this era that the capitalist powers finally amassed the strength to subjugate China in the Century of Humiliation, removing the Middle Kingdom as a bulwark against capital in the region. Japan and Korea, which both adopted policies of isolationism in the wake of the Imjin Wars, became much more exposed to the deprivations of an aggressively expanding capitalism. Japan responded with its own rigorous pursuit of capitalist development, launching itself into the ranks of the imperialist powers.

The waning Joseon Dynasty of Korea eventually attempted to do the same, but was too late, and became swallowed up by inter-imperialist rivalry which ended in colonization by Japan. Once again, Korea became a battleground from which great historical changes that would alter the region's future emerged. Japanese commercial imperialism in Korea inevitably challenged Qing tributary rights under the Sinocentric system. The resulting First Sino-Japanese War, chiefly fought in the peninsula, led to the surrender of Taiwan as a colony of Japan. With the Qing out of the equation, Japan then faced off against Tsarist Russia for control of Korea and Manchuria. Japanese victory in this war directly contributed to the revolution of 1905, striking a nail into the coffin of tsarism, which would be interred for good by the revolutions of 1917. As in the Imjin Wars, Japan saw in Korea a bridgehead to achieve the conquest of China, using the peninsula as a base for its invasion of Manchuria in 1931, which would set the stage for the Second Sino-Japanese War.

Imperialism not only introduced new foreign actors into Northeast Asia—capitalist integration also altered the character of China and Korea's existing tributary or feudal classes, and caused the development of a native bourgeoisie. The ruling classes of Qing China and Joseon

Lips and Teeth: Korea and China

Korea, characterized by a fusion of landlordism and control of the tributary bureaucracy, were first weakened by overt imperialist assault, and then enlisted into the exploitation of the toiling classes by capital. The masses of the peasantry, now at the mercy of the world capitalist market, were driven to proletarianization as they gained debt and lost land. As the feudal classes became integrated into imperialism, nascent bourgeois leadership emerged to fan the flames of national consciousness, but would prove futile or duplicitous over time. These historical transitions created the conditions for the communist movement to flourish in China and Korea.

Though emerging from distinct national realities, China and Korea's experiences of capitalist integration occurred as part of a singular historical movement of the extension of imperialism into Northeast Asia. The revolutions in these countries therefore developed coevally, conjoined by practical reality, geographic proximity, and historical affinity. Early Korean leaders of the armed independence struggle such as Hong Beom-Do and Yoon Hee-soon based themselves in Manchuria after facing defeat in the annexation of Korea. The 1911 Revolution in China and its leader Sun Yat-Sen held significant sway among Korea's early independence movement;[188] in turn, in 1919, China's May 4th Movement, a high point of the New Culture Movement that would produce the future leaders of the CPC, took inspiration from Korea's March 1st Movement of the same year. Bourgeois Korean nationalists affiliated with the government-in-exile based themselves out of Shanghai, allied with the Kuomintang; meanwhile, Korean and Chinese guerrillas, including Kim Il Sung, waged war against Japan from the jagged mountains of Manchuria. Koreans and Chinese did not make

---

188 Min, Tu-Ki. "Sun Yat-sen in Korea: Korean View of Sun Yat-sen's Idea and Activities in 1920s." 동아문화, vol. 30, December 1992, pp. 225–41.

their revolutions separately, but together—and it was among the communists that this partnership ran deepest.

Communists from both nations found common cause in a joint struggle against imperialism and domestic reaction, shedding blood alongside each other. Korean revolutionaries, impeded from advancing the struggle on the peninsula by vicious colonial repression, turned to the revolution in China as a battleground to turn the tide against Japan. China's revolution thus also became a Korean revolution. In Yan'an and beyond, figures such as Zheng Lucheng (Chong Ryulsong), Mu Chong, Ho Jong Suk, and Kim San dedicated themselves to China's liberation as the path to realize Korea's liberation. In Manchuria, Kim Il-Sung and countless other Koreans waged war alongside their Chinese comrades under the banner of the Northeast United Anti-Japanese Army. For a time, more than 90% of CPC cadres in Manchuria were Korean.[189] As previously mentioned, once Korea was liberated in 1945 and the dictatorship of the proletariat realized in the founding of the DPRK in 1948, mass Korean participation in the final days of the Chinese Civil War helped ensure the victory of the CPC and the founding of the People's Republic.

Sino-Korean solidarity in the Korean War was simply the latest chapter in a longer history of joint revolution. Once again, the struggle against imperialism in Korea had a lasting effect on the course of Northeast Asia's historical destiny; the war never formally concluded, and a state of territorial fragmentation persists in both China and Korea to this day. The DPRK and PRC's relationship since the signing of the 1953 Korean War Armistice therefore continues to be shaped by the conditions of Northeast Asia's long revolution.

---

189 Hongkoo Han, "Wounded Nationalism: The Minsaengdan Incident and Kim Il Sung in Eastern Manchuria" (Ph.D. diss., University of Washington,) 10.

Forks in the Road

The great sacrifices of the Chinese People's Volunteers have never been forgotten by the DPRK. Still, the Sino-Korean relationship has continuously evolved, and at times, the lips and teeth have been at odds. The Sino-Soviet Split,[190] and later, the Reform and Opening Up Era precipitated various diplomatic and political conflicts between the two states.

Undoubtedly, the relationship reached its nadir in the 1990s, when the fall of the Soviet Union left the DPRK without its largest trading partner, and more vulnerable than ever to U.S. sanctions. In 1994 and 1995, calamitous once-in-a-century floods devastated its agricultural base and led to a period of famine known as the Arduous March.[191] At the time, China's friendship with the DPRK was restrained, and socialist Korea was largely abandoned to face its crisis alone.

While the DPRK survived the Arduous March, relations with the PRC remained strained for some time, and are still not without their contradictions. Diplomatically, the PRC continued to support and enforce UN Security Council sanctions on the DPRK until 2019, when it proposed partial reductions of sanctions in a joint resolution with Russia.[192] The DPRK's nuclear weapons program has also,

---

190 The DPRK adopted a non-aligned position in the Sino-Soviet Split, and increasingly turned to the Non-Aligned Movement in the 1970s and 1980s.
191 Meredith Woo-Cumings. The Political Ecology of Famine: The North Korean Catastrophe and Its Lessons. 2002, www.adb.org/sites/default/files/publication/157182/adbi-rp31.pdf.
192 North Korea, China, Russia Converge Positions | Arms Control Association. www.armscontrol.org/act/2020-01/news/north-korea-china-russia-converge-positions.

at times, been another source of tensions.[193] Acknowledging these contradictions is crucial to understanding the historical ambit of the PRC-DPRK relationship; simultaneously, they should not be over-emphasized, or reduced to simple ideological explanations. These contradictions arose from material differences between the two states' respective positions in the contemporary world-system, as divergent conditions compelled the two states to pursue divergent interests in accordance with divergent strategies.

During Reform, China reintegrated into the capitalist world-system in order to massively develop its own productive forces—albeit without surrendering socialist command of politics. This changed the country's strategic calculus regarding many of its foreign relations, including with the DPRK. Whereas the DPRK underwent a generation of crushing ostracization and vilification by the U.S.-dominated international order, the PRC's economic rise became contingent upon its cooperation within that very order. Divergent strategies between the two states are therefore a reflection of divergent interests and conditions.

A Common Destiny?

Yet today, a new dispensation is forming. China's rise has encountered its opposite in heightened U.S. belligerence in East Asia and around the world. This growing aggression takes the form of expanded militarization and the formation of a new U.S.-led military bloc in the region, composed of constituent alliances such as AUKUS (Australia-UK-U.S.), JAKUS (Japan-Republic of Korea-U.S.), and the SQUAD (India, Japan,

---

193 Slavney, Natalia. "Quick Take: North Korea Jabs at China in Reaction to Trilateral Summit - 38 North: Informed Analysis of North Korea." *38 North*, May 28, 2024, www.38north.org/2024/05/quick-take-north-korea-jabs-at-china-in-reaction-to-trilateral-summit.

Philippines, Australia, U.S.). The 2026 National Defense Authorization Act, which is being debated in the U.S. Senate at the time of this author's writing, includes plans for the creation of "the Partnership"—a vaguely defined defense industrial free trade consortium including Japan, the Republic of Korea (ROK), Australia, the Philippines, India, and New Zealand.[194] The growth of new alliances is also accompanied by the acceleration of U.S.-led military exercises, particularly but not exclusively in Korea, where according to independent journalist Jang Chang-jun,[195] U.S. Forces Korea (USFK) has conducted 200 days of military drills in 2023 and 275 days of military drills in 2024—with a new record expected to be broken in 2025.

Plagued by military overreach and the tendency of the rate of profit to fall, Washington now seeks to internationalize military Keynesianism by pressuring its vassals to open the spigots of military spending, including Japan and the ROK. The DPRK's recent comprehensive strategic partnership with Russia must be viewed in this light. The fault lines of the old Cold War, which never truly ended in Northeast Asia, are now deepening as a consequence of this New Cold War.

Today, Washington sees little meaningful distinction between the DPRK and the PRC as antagonists. In a study published in May 2025,[196] the Atlantic Council branded the two states "a rising nuclear

---

194 "Text - S.2296 - 119th Congress (2025-2026): National Defense Authorization Act for Fiscal Year 2026." *Congress.gov*, Library of Congress, September 11, 2025, https://www.congress.gov/bill/119th-congress/senate-bill/2296/text.

195 "[신년특집]2024년 한미·한미일 군사 연습의 실체." 현장언론 민플러스, January 29, 2025, www.minplusnews.com/news/articleView.html?idxno=15777.

196 Aroh. "A Rising Nuclear Double-threat in East Asia: Insights From Our Guardian Tiger I and II Tabletop Exercises - Atlantic Council." Atlantic Council, May 12, 2025, www.atlanticcouncil.org/in-depth-research-reports/report/a-rising-nuclear-double-threat-in-east-asia-insights-from-our-guardian-tiger-i-and-ii-tabletop-exercises.

double-threat," arguing that the U.S. must prepare for "simultaneous" conflict with both—even if it would mean limited nuclear war. U.S. military leadership has already come to see the vast "Indo-Pacific" as a singular battlefront, one which pivots on the Korean Peninsula. Recent revelations from South Korean media found USFK using an inverted map[197] of the region placing Korea in the center, with lines of distance drawn to the major cities and capitals of Russia, China, Taiwan, the Philippines, and Vietnam. In a keynote address to the U.S. Army Land Forces Pacific Symposium in May 2025, General Xavier Brunson, commander of USFK, spelled out the value of Korea to imperialism in explicit terms:

> "What immediately stood out to me as I looked at the map was the position of the Korean Peninsula, and the fact that it's on the Asian continent, has a sizable U.S. force posture, is inside the first island chain and is the closest allied presence to Beijing....At night from a satellite image, the Republic of Korea looks like an island or like a fixed aircraft carrier floating in the water between Japan and mainland China."[198]

Beyond his brutishly utilitarian description of Korea as an "aircraft carrier," Brunson's comments also signalled a new vision for the US-ROK alliance. In a push to "modernize" the alliance, Washington

---

197 Hyo-Jin, Lee, and Bahk Eun-Ji. "Washington May Weigh Shake-ups of Top US Commanders in South Korea, Japan." *The Korea Times*, July 9, 2025, www.koreatimes.co.kr/southkorea/defense/20250710/washington-may-weigh-shake-ups-of-top-us-commanders-in-south-korea-japan.

198 "US Forces Korea Leader Says His Troops Deter China, Guard 'Freedom's Front Yard.'" *Stars and Stripes*, May 16, 2025, www.stripes.com/branches/army/2025-05-16/brunson-south-korea-china-lanpac-17807125.html.

now seeks to redefine USFK's mission from primarily containing the DPRK to containing China, breaking with the original terms of the US-ROK Mutual Defense Treaty and other core documents governing the U.S. occupation of Korea. This pivot would allow for USFK to be flexibly deployed beyond the Korean peninsula, and thereby make Korea into a battleground for U.S.-China war by default. Once again, imperialism seeks the subjugation of China by way of the Korean Peninsula—consequently, the DPRK and PRC's strategic interests now align more closely than at any time since the fall of the Soviet Union, and a revitalization of revolutionary solidarity and fraternity is underway.

At the recent 80th Anniversary of the Victory of the Chinese People's War of Resistance Against Japanese Aggression and the World Anti-Fascist War, Kim Jong Un was given pride of place in the celebrations, and exchanged important statements of friendship with Xi Jinping. In his statement to Kim, Xi called for greater "friendly cooperation", not just between the two countries but between the CPC and the Workers' Party of Korea, stressing the fields of security, economics, and governance to enhance "our socialist causes."[199] It has yet to be seen how the relationship will continue to evolve. While the imperialist intelligentsia is given to braying about the existence of a China-Russia-DPRK bloc, the real formation of such an alliance is still in development. As U.S. hostility in the region intensifies, China and the DPRK will face mounting existential pressures to find strategic unity. Contradictions and challenges will no doubt persist, but if the history of the Chinese and Korean Revolutions offers anything to the present, it is that the destinies of these two great historical processes

---

199 陈子琰. "China, DPRK Reaffirm Friendship." *China Daily*, September 5, 2025, www.chinadaily.com.cn/a/202509/05/WS68ba153ba3108622abc9eea9.html.

are shared, and can only be strengthened through collaboration. Just as lips and teeth must coordinate to speak, so too will the revolutionary forces of Northeast Asia seek unity to articulate a common future of peace and prosperity into the annals of history.

* * *

Ju-Hyun Park is a writer and organizer with Nodutdol for Korean Community Development, an anti-imperialist Korean diaspora organization based in the U.S. which coordinates the U.S. Out of Korea campaign. Ju-Hyun's writing on Korea and U.S. imperialism in the Pacific has appeared in Public Radio International, The New Inquiry, Funambulist, People's Dispatch, *and other publications. Ju-Hyun is the Web Editor at* BreakThrough News.

Is China's Foreign Policy 'Good Enough'?

by Danny Haiphong

The question in the title may seem hyperbolic, but it is one that comes up in one form or another across the U.S. political spectrum.

U.S. elites slam China's foreign policy as riddled with "debt traps" for poorer countries in the Global South. The Western corporate media asserts that China is pursuing its own kind of empire and has a target on its own province of Taiwan as well as on its neighbors in the South China Sea. For the U.S. ruling circle and its European vassals, China is an imperial competitor seeking to destroy the West's "rules-based" international order (actually a euphemism for U.S. imperialism).

There are also plenty on the political "left", even some communists, who view China in the exact same light. They consider China to be "state-capitalist" and therefore pursuing profits at the expense of humanity. And then there are those who, even if they rebuke this criticism and uphold China's socialist foundation, are profoundly disappointed in China's foreign policy. To these critics, China falls short of the global solidarity required in this historical moment and is not aggressive enough in the pursuit of justice.

The truth is, they're all wrong. First, the debt trap narrative has been debunked again and again. John Hopkins University political scientist Deborah Bratigaum tore apart this myth as nothing more than a fabrication that obfuscates a grimmer reality: the primary holders of the Global South's debt are private Western lenders, the IMF, and the World Bank.

Though there has been an uproar in Western media over a mythical Chinese seizure of Sri Lanka's Hambantota port, 81 percent of Sri Lanka's debt resides with U.S. and Western financial institutions as well as Japan and India. In November 2021, U.S. and Western media spread the fiction that China had seized Uganda's Entebbe International Airport after the country was said to have defaulted on its loan. The story, it turns out, was entirely fictional. The Uganda Civil Authority Aviation Spokesperson himself felt compelled to dispel the lie on Twitter: "I wish to make it categorically clear that the allegation that Entebbe Airport has been given away for cash is false…there isn't an ounce of truth in it."

Beneath these fictions is an important fact: China's cooperation with other countries is nothing at all like it's been characterized in Western media. When U.S. and Western elites demonize China as an agent of "debt-trap diplomacy", they not only project their own crimes onto China, but also smear a historic global project currently sending waves of fear down their spines.

This project is the Belt and Road Initiative (BRI), which China launched in 2013. Its primary aim is to develop connectivity amongst participating countries, thereby cementing economic trade routes and cultural exchanges between them. As of 2023, the BRI included over 150 countries, over 200 BRI cooperation agreements, and over thirty international organizations. As of 2025, overall trade volume between BRI countries and China reached over 22 billion RMB, a 6.4 percent increase year-on-year.

Infrastructure development is the key to the Belt and Road Initiative. BRI cooperation has led to land-locked Laos launching its own high-speed railway in 2021 with Chinese assistance. This train travels up to 220 km/h between Laos' southern and northern border, and from there to Kunming, one of China's economic hub cities. In 2023, Indonesia's Jakarta-Bandung high-speed rail, built as a joint venture with Chinese railway companies, began commercial operations. From Pakistan's first metro system to Greece's most critical port, the BRI has brought modern infrastructure to nations that have been historically robbed by the cruel exploitation of Western colonialism, imperialism, and financial coercion.

It's important to note that China's foreign policy via the BRI is not "aid" per se. China frames all of its cooperation with partner countries as "win-win." The Global South needs China's expertise and resources to develop infrastructure, and the construction of this infrastructure has also created hundreds of thousands of jobs in BRI countries, from the thousands of projects underway or completed. Along with the infrastructure, these jobs lead to a higher standard of living, which allows countries around the world to purchase and obtain higher-value added goods from China. Through positive relations, China also gets to expand the network of connectivity worldwide, even to Europe and "high-income" countries. Everyone wins.

However, when Americans and Westerners think of foreign policy, they think of military interventionism. After all, the U.S. and its European vassals have known nothing but war. Trillions have been spent on U.S. and NATO wars since 1945, and trillions more will be spent in the coming years for as long as U.S. imperialism stands. But what about China?

Despite loud condemnations from the U.S.-led West that China is "aggressive" and even "imperial", China's foreign policy follows strict adherence to what the Communist Party of China (CPC) refers to as non-interference. This means that China seeks neither expansion nor dominance, but rather follows the principles of the UN Charter in all

Is China's Foreign Policy 'Good Enough'?

respects. China opposes unilateral sanctions, military or other forms of intervention in the affairs of other countries, and hasn't fought a war since 1979. While China's military possesses hypersonic missile capabilities, the largest navy on the planet, drone technology, electronic warfare, and much more, it only spends around 1.7 percent of its GDP on defense, or about half of the 3.5 percent of total GDP spent by the U.S.

Unlike the U.S., however, China faces very real threats to its sovereignty. The U.S. military-industrial complex has supplied arms and munitions to China's province of Taiwan in the amount of tens of billions. In the last fifteen years, the U.S. has pivoted over half of its enormous military arsenal to the Asia Pacific region with the explicit intent to "contain" China. This includes moves such as sending anti-ship missiles to the Philippines, building an extensive network of around 400 bases from Japan to Singapore that completely surround China's only coast, and creating alliances like "AUKUS" (Australia, the U.S., and UK) to prepare the way for war.

Under these conditions, China has every right under the UN Charter to use military force to defend itself. But that isn't happening. Instead, China's response to U.S. aggression has been characterized by a staunch commitment to a different set of principles all together: peace, win-win cooperation, and multipolarity.

This approach has earned China the status of top trading partner to over 145 countries. Rather than dictate conditions to other countries, China promotes a model of cooperation that focuses on mutual benefit. For example, China has made trade with fifty-three countries on the African continent completely tariff-free, while the Trump administration imposes widespread tariffs as a means to punish countries over dubious claims of "unfair" and "imbalanced" trade with the U.S. During the economic shockwaves of the COVID-19 pandemic, China cancelled loans and outstanding interest owed by fifteen African countries.

China also acts as a proactive force for peace and multipolarity. China is the only nuclear-armed state to possess a no first use policy. Furthermore, China is second in direct funding and participation in international peacekeeping missions despite still being a developing country. Perhaps most significantly, China is one of the most important, if not the most important, economic and political anchor of an emerging alternative to U.S. hegemony. China's direct leadership in BRICS, the Shanghai Cooperation Organization, and in other multilateral initiatives as a whole is indispensable to the development of what international relations experts are calling a multipolarity, in which a world no longer dominated by U.S. financial, military, and cultural imperialism is becoming more and more possible.

This just scratches the surface of China's foreign policy and its significance. But is it good enough? After all, Gaza is being subjected to a brutal U.S.-Israeli genocide, which the world overwhelmingly opposes. Shouldn't something be done? If China is the biggest economy in the Global South and anchor of the multipolar world, doesn't it have a responsibility to come to Gaza's aid?

Such a question assumes China is sitting back and watching Gaza burn. Nothing could be further from the truth. China has used its influence at the United Nations to not only condemn Israel's brutality and call for an immediate ceasefire, but also to uphold the right of the Palestinian people to armed resistance. In 2024, China hosted a historic summit in Beijing that convened all major Palestinian political organizations with the aim of forging unity toward the establishment of a future Palestinian state. The summit led to the Beijing Declaration signed by all parties outlining the steps required to achieve this goal.

Additionally, China has virtually closed its market to Israeli blood diamonds in favor of its own cheaper lab-produced diamonds. Israel's diamond industry contributes up to $1 billion annually to the military committing genocide Gaza. China-Israel relations have indeed reached an all-time low. Head of state visits have screeched to a halt, and the RAND Corporation has complained that China's position on Gaza, Iran, and Yemen has angered both Israeli officials and Israeli society.

China is also a staunch supporter of Palestine's most important allies in the region. Not only does China purchase over 90 percent of Iran's oil exports, It has also bolstered its defenses through provision of air defense and satellite technology instrumental in its successful counter to U.S. and Israeli aggression during the "Twelve-Day War" of June 2025. China brokered the normalization of ties between Iran and Saudi Arabia in 2023, leading the latter to refuse to allow Israeli and U.S. fighter jets to refuel on its bases during their attacks on the former. China was deemed a non-participant in the Gaza genocide by Yemen's Ansar Allah from the beginning of its blockade of the Red Sea in 2023, and Chinese ships have never been disallowed from using the key trade route.

Still, some in the West demand that China do more to tip the balance, such as cut all trading ties with Israel. These voices claim such an action would have no impact on China and send a stark message to the world that genocide will not be tolerated. This hypothesis, however, is fatally flawed.

First of all, the horrors in Gaza are not of China's making. The U.S. accounts for 70 percent of Israel's arms imports, and wields a political and diplomatic shield over Israel that is arguably more powerful than that provided to any of its other so-called "allies" around the world. The blame for Gaza's plight rests at the feet of the U.S., the West, and of course, Israel. Moving attention away from this is as unhelpful as it is dangerous.

Makers of U.S. foreign policy have shown the world time and time again that they are willing to go to any length to protect what they see as their most important military asset in the region. Any unilateral action taken against Israel will be met with serious consequences. While the U.S. empire is in marked decline and unable to arrest the development of a rising China and Global South, it has proven more than capable of spreading chaos and instability. The U.S. and Israel would undoubtedly move to cut China off from the entire region if it were to carry out a boycott of Israel on its own, and the genocide would continue, but under even more hostile global conditions than currently exist. This isn't to say that a boycott isn't correct in principle, but to put the onus of responsibility for leading such a boycott on China, a developing country that is itself the target of U.S. sanctions, moves the goalposts away from the U.S. empire.

Foreign policy and international solidarity are determined by more than just the moral values nations and people hold in their heads and hearts. The complex relationship between the social system of a particular country and its material conditions—both domestically within it and internationally outside of it—ultimately determines the shape of its foreign policy at a particular moment in history. China, for example, possesses a shared history with Palestine as a target of imperial aggression, and has itself suffered the most brutal conditions of poverty, war and plunder from multiple foreign aggressors for more than a hundred years. China was thus one of the first countries in the world to recognize the nation of Palestine and its national liberation movement, the PLO, in 1965.

Yet China's foreign policy in the current period is tasked with ensuring the development of the Global South while standing true to its commitments to international law. China has thus hewed to its policy of non-interference to complement the win-win cooperation mech-

Is China's Foreign Policy 'Good Enough'?

anisms outlined in this chapter. From the Belt and Road Initiative to its key role in developing multilateral institutions such as BRICS, China is already playing an indispensable role in building a brighter future for the Global South. China doesn't wage wars of aggression, commit genocide for the sake of expansionism, or seek hegemony of any kind. By committing itself to the core principles of international law such as respect for self-determination, and by developing win-win relations in all spheres, China provides an example to the entire world of what a future of global peace could look like.

This won't satisfy everyone, especially those in the U.S. and the West feeling hopeless and powerless about the genocide in Gaza. Years of protest have not compelled the U.S. to pressure Israel to stop. Some in the West, under the weight of guilt or panic, might ask themselves, if China is a leader, why won't it DO MORE?

Simply put, it's the wrong question, and it's one that is not being asked publicly by the forces of resistance leading the way in Gaza and beyond. There isn't a single statement from the Palestinian resistance organizations or from the entire Axis of Resistance demanding that China do more. In fact, these forces are building closer ties to China with the aim of strengthening their stability and therefore their effectiveness in resisting imperialism and colonialism. China's relations with Iran have grown tremendously, helping the biggest supporter of Palestine to survive and to even make military and industrial advances despite U.S. and EU sanctions.

From Gaza to the Democratic Republic of the Congo, the crisis of U.S. imperialism is filling mass graves in an attempt to hold onto its hegemony. The suffering of the Palestinian people has sent shockwaves across the world and has led to a surge in support for the liberation of Palestine. It has also led some into the depths of despair as the alienation of capitalism in the terminal stage of imperialism heightens.

And in the West, despair creates the conditions for U.S. elites and their lackeys to sow Cold War-like divisions, even within the Palestine solidarity movement.

Asking whether China's foreign policy is "good enough" on Gaza falls into this trap when answered within a vacuum. It is clear that China is operating within the contradictions of a decaying U.S.-led unipolar order, and by doing so can offer many tangible benefits to humanity. The real question we in the West should be asking is, how can *we* collectively strengthen our movements to put real pressure on the root cause of the genocide in Gaza: the U.S. empire. Once we do, new and ample opportunities will emerge, to end not only the horrors in Gaza, but also the entire system of empire from which they sprang.

***

Danny Haiphong is an independent journalist and author. He is host of the geopolitics YouTube channel "Danny Haiphong" and co-editor of Friends of Socialist China.

China, Yemen, and the Red Sea Passage

by Ché Marino

(**Note on terminology:** *Though Western outlets often use the term "Houthis," the Yemeni revolutionary movement's official name is AnsarAllah, and its military arm is the Yemeni Armed Forces.*)

Yemen and the People's Republic of China have built a steady, positive partnership based on sovereignty, non-interference, development, and pragmatic diplomacy. While maintaining their blockade of Israel, AnsarAllah and the Yemeni Armed Forces allow Chinese vessels to move safely through the Red Sea to the Suez Canal.[200] Meanwhile, China defends Yemen's sovereignty diplomatically on the world stage and supports a Yemen-led political process and recovery.[201] Their relationship rests on mutual respect, shared interests, and decades of positive diplomatic and economic relations.

---

200 VOA News, "Houthis Won't Target Chinese, Russian Ships in Red Sea," *Voice of America*, January 19, 2024, https://www.voanews.com/a/houthis-won-t-target-chinese-russian-ships-in-red-sea/7446893.html.

201 Ministry of Foreign Affairs of the People's Republic of China, Permanent Mission to the UN, "Remarks on Yemen by Ambassador Geng Shuang at the UN Security Council Briefing," June 12, 2025, https://un.china-mission.gov.cn/eng/hyyfy/202506/t20250613_11647557.htm.

China, Yemen, and the Red Sea Passage

The Red Sea Passage

Yemen sits on one side of the Bab al-Mandeb strait of the Red Sea, which is the gateway to the Suez Canal, the maritime link between Asia, Africa, and Europe. Since 2016, the AnsarAllah-led Supreme Political Council (SPC) in Sana'a has exercised de facto governing authority over Yemen's western seaboard. In late 2023, AnsarAllah and the Yemeni Armed Forces announced a targeted naval blockade to show material solidarity with Palestinians, impose real costs on Israel, and push to end the genocide in Gaza.

The Yemeni leaders laid out clear principles: Israeli-linked ships, or ships sailing to Israeli ports, would be blocked. Ships with no link to Israel could pass. On January 19, 2024, senior AnsarAllah official Mohammed al-Bukhaiti said lanes around Yemen were safe for Chinese and Russian ships so long as vessels were not linked to Israel. Omani-mediated talks then brought senior AnsarAllah representatives together with Chinese and Russian officials to concretize those assurances. The following spring, a U.S. sanctions notice described the same point from the other side of the table, noting that safe-passage commitments were conveyed directly to Chinese and Russian officials.[202]

China has heavy commercial stakes along the Suez corridor.[203] In keeping with its strict non-interventionist foreign policy, Beijing

---

[202] Gary Howard, "Houthis Guaranteed Safe Passage to Russian and Chinese Ships, Says OFAC," *Seatrade Maritime News*, March 6, 2025, https://www.seatrade-maritime.com/security/houthis-guaranteed-safe-passage-to-russian-and-chinese-ships.

[203] Joe Cash, "Explainer: Houthi Attacks Expose China's Commercial Stakes in Red Sea," *Reuters*, January 15, 2024, https://www.reuters.com/world/middle-east/houthi-attacks-expose-chinas-commercial-stakes-red-sea-2024-01-15/.

maintains dual-track communications with both Sana'a and the Western-backed Presidential Leadership Council (PLC) headquartered in Aden, to support a Yemen-led peace process and plan for post-war reconstruction.

At the UN Security Council, Beijing has tied Red Sea tension to the genocide in Gaza, called to protect civilian ships, and stressed respect for Yemen's sovereignty and territorial integrity. Chinese officials have also criticized U.S. and UK airstrikes on Yemen as escalatory.

While many commercial shipping fleets detour around Africa, China-associated ships, including major automobile carriers, keep using Suez, saving time and cost in tight markets.[204] The U.S. has complained bitterly about this "unfair competition," and "restriction of trade," and in early 2025 initiated a series of savage bombing attacks against Yemen, which failed to end the blockade.[205]

Foundations of the China-Yemen Partnership

Yemen was the first country on the Arabian Peninsula to recognize the People's Republic of China on September 24, 1956.[206] In the 1950s, Beijing helped build the 266-kilometer Sana'a-Hodeidah highway, a backbone for trade and services. Over time, they added clear rules for investment; in 1998, China and Yemen signed a bilateral treaty that

---

204 Keith Bradsher, "China's Automakers Are Taking a Shortcut to European Markets," *New York Times*, August 11, 2025, https://www.nytimes.com/2025/08/11/business/china-electric-vehicles-red-sea.html.

205 Nicholas Kristof, "The $7 Billion We Wasted Bombing a Country We Couldn't Find on a Map," *New York Times*, May 17, 2025, https://www.nytimes.com/2025/05/17/opinion/yemen-war-trump.html.

206 Ministry of Foreign Affairs of the People's Republic of China, "China and Yemen," https://www.fmprc.gov.cn/eng/gjhdq_665435/2675_665437/2908_663816/.

lowered risks for investors and encouraged the influx of long-term capital.[207]

Economic ties deepened in the 2000s. Chinese firms began oil exploration and production. Huawei opened in Yemen in 1999. Joint ventures like the Chinese-Yemeni Star steel company expanded local industry. To tackle power shortages, the China National Corporation for Overseas Economic Cooperation agreed in 2012 to develop three natural gas-fired power plants. Yemen also selected a Chinese contractor for a major expansion of container terminals in Aden and Mokha, in line with national trade goals.[208]

Then, in March 2015, following the popular revolution that brought AnsarAllah to power, a coalition led by Saudi Arabia and backed by the United States and the United Kingdom intervened militarily in Yemen. The war and the blockade that followed caused a severe humanitarian crisis. Essential imports were strangled, and the country ran short of food, fuel, and clean water. Cholera spread. Reporting at the time showed that Washington elites hoped the Saudi war and blockade would force AnsarAllah to concede. Instead, they exacerbated the suffering by starving the Yemeni people and devastating their economy.[209]

---

207 EDIT (Electronic Database of Investment Treaties), "China – Yemen BIT (1998)," 1998, https://edit.wti.org/document/show/718c3112-dd74-4efb-91ae-053807d18e20.

208 Muhammad Zulfikar Rakhmat, "Why Is China Interested in a Volatile Yemen?," *The Diplomat*, June 4, 2014, https://thediplomat.com/2014/06/why-is-china-interested-in-a-volatile-yemen/.

209 Ryan Grim, "To Help End the Yemen War, All China Had to Do Was Be Reasonable," *The Intercept*, April 7, 2023, https://theintercept.com/2023/04/07/yemen-war-ceasefire-china-saudi-arabia-iran/.

China's support for Yemeni sovereignty remained steady. It supported a diplomatic solution, emphasized territorial integrity, and engaged in negotiations with both sides.[210] It also delivered targeted relief for food and health needs and widened development commitments. In April 2019, Yemen signed a Belt and Road memorandum of understanding in Beijing, which will pave the way for industrial investments with increased regional connectivity in the long term.

China's Support for Peace and a Yemen-Led Political Process

In March 2023, Beijing hosted a summit between Saudi and Iranian officials to restore diplomatic relations, making room for de-escalation in Yemen, where Iran has supported AnsarAllah against the Saudi assault. China followed with practical steps. The next month, its envoy met with PLC leaders to map political steps and post-war needs, then met China Harbor Engineering Company's Middle Eastern branch to connect those priorities to Belt and Road-linked projects.[211] In 2025, China announced tariff exemptions for Yemeni products and said it was ready to resume more than 100 Chinese projects in Yemen after the conflict.[212] In a meeting with the PLC's foreign minister, the Chi-

---

210 Nora Bendary, "Will China Move to Resolve the Yemen Crisis in 2023?," *Arab Wall*, February 1, 2023, https://arabwall.com/en/will-china-move-to-resolve-the-yemen-crisis-in-2023/.

211 Ladislav Charouz, "After Iran–Saudi Mediation, China Angles for Another Diplomatic Victory in Yemen," *The Diplomat*, April 22, 2023, https://thediplomat.com/2023/04/after-iran-saudi-mediation-china-angles-for-another-diplomatic-victory-in-yemen/.

212 Yemen Monitor, "China Exempts Yemeni Goods from Tariffs," *Yemen Monitor*, April 13, 2025, https://www.yemenmonitor.com/en/Details/ArtMID/908/ArticleID/137628.

nese ambassador offered humanitarian assistance and expressed China's interest in helping with reconstruction.[213]

China treats Yemen as an equal partner. It listens and invests where it counts: power, ports, and roads that move goods and create jobs. Tariff-free entry to China will help Yemeni farmers and fishers increase exports. Modernizing ports at Aden, Hodeidah, and Mokha, rebuilding the highways that feed them, and adding industrial parks near the docks will all help Yemen operate as a shipping and light-manufacturing hub again, and connect with regional trade routes on its own terms when conditions permit.

Given that China has all this to offer Yemen, while the West has nothing to offer but war, it is little wonder that Chinese vessels and Chinese diplomats are so much better received in the region.

* * *

Ché Marino is an organizer with the Bronx Antiwar Coalition (bronxantiwar.org), and a frequent contributor to the Workers World *newspaper.*

---

213 Ministry of Foreign Affairs and Expatriates (Republic of Yemen), "Yemen and China Discuss Strengthening Bilateral Relations," July 13, 2025, https://www.mofa-ye.org/Pages/33159/.

Should the Renminbi Replace the Dollar? The Surprising Answer

by Radhika Desai

Just like it changes everything else, China is destined to change the international monetary system. However, exactly how China can and should change it deserves careful, historically informed consideration. The matter is not a simple one of following the path of the U.S. dollar, nor should it be.

Much of the discussion of de-dollarization assumes that it is. However, a consideration of the twin processes that occasion this discussion—the decline of the United States, which has been caused by the very financial system that the dollar's role in the world has required since 1971, and the rise of China, which has been powered by practically the opposite sort of financial system—should give us pause.

Since the growth slowdown of the 1970s, the neoliberal reform of the U.S. financial system has resulted in low growth, low investment, skyrocketing economic inequality, stagnant wages, and a radical weakening of production and technological innovation. The only sector that has grown significantly is the so-called FIRE sector of Finance, Insurance and Real Estate. By contrast, China's economic advance was based solidly on advancing its manufacturing prowess in terms of productivity and technological progress. Indeed, the latter has reached the point where, even according to many Western observers, China is leading on the overwhelming majority of critical technologies while the government is prioritising the reduction of poverty and inequality.

Should the Renminbi Replace the Dollar?

U.S. decline and China's rise have led many to suggest that the renminbi is now poised to replace the dollar as the world's money. Not so fast! The change that China is destined to usher in will be far more radical than that. It will involve rejecting the false ideas about world money that have accompanied the dollar system and will shunt the locomotive of the world's monetary relations from the wrong track it has been on to the right one.

The idea that the currency of any one country, even the most economically powerful, should be the currency of the world is simply wrong. The roots of this idea lie in the aspiration of U.S. ruling elites to replace the weakening British world dominance with U.S. dominance, if not by acquiring an empire comparable with Britain's, then at least by making the dollar the world's money on the model of the pound sterling. Theories about U.S. hegemony are little more than this aspiration in disguise, and moreover, the dollar system never actually worked.[214] Not only did the dollar's postwar link to gold need to be broken in 1971, but thereafter, the system required precisely the burgeoning of the FIRE sector as its foundation, and has subjected the U.S. to economic decline and the world to a series of destructive financial crises.

With U.S. decline becoming more palpable every day, talk of de-dollarization has migrated from the fringes of scholarship, where it had been kept by the mighty exertions of primarily U.S.-based scholarship on the dollar system—the purpose of which was to eternalise, naturalise, and promote it under all circumstances—to the highest-level policymaking meetings of our time, particularly those in which China plays a leading part. However, the radical transportation of these discussions must also be accompanied by a radical transformation.

---

214 Radhika Desai. 2013. *Geopolitical Economy: After US Hegemony, Globalization and Empire.* London: Pluto.

Radhika Desai

Today's Discussion of the Dollar System

In the face of clear U.S. decline, U.S.-based dollar-boosting scholars have taken to arguing that the dollar will nevertheless continue to dominate world payments because there is no alternative currency that can displace it.

This argument assumes that the currency of the economically most powerful and dominant country must be the currency of the whole world, and so the dollar can only be replaced by a rival currency, just as it once replaced the pound sterling. They even go out of their way to praise the UK and the U.S. for successively stabilising the international system by providing the "public good" of world money.

In particular, they point out that the renminbi is in no position to be such a successor. Chinese authorities, the argument goes, are either unable or unwilling to internationalise the renminbi on the model of the dollar and therefore cannot pose a challenge to it.

It would be understandable if many Chinese and China-sympathetic scholars reacted to such assertions by claiming that they are wrong, and that the renminbi can be, should be, or even is being successfully internationalised, just like the dollar. However, understandable though this reaction may be, it would be a dangerous error. If such a reaction led to the design and implementation of policies that would set in train an internationalisation of the renminbi on the model of the dollar, it would prove a disaster for China's economy, put a brake on its impressive growth and technological development, and render it the same sort of neoliberally financialized and productively weakened economy as the United Kingdom has long had, and as the U.S. has today.

The Historical Background: Two Models of Finance

Finance and money predate capitalism. Karl Marx had expected that, as it emerged and matured, industrial capitalism would take the inherited forms of money and finance, with their orientation to short-term commerce, predatory and usurious lending and speculation, and transform them to serve its own productive expansion.[215] The result would be a financial sector providing long-term patient capital for industrial expansion.

Marx's expectation was fulfilled, though in a rather unexpected manner, as Rudolf Hilferding showed.[216] Along with the works of Rosa Luxemburg and Nikolai Bukharin, his *Finance Capital* had provided a major theorization of capitalism and its relation to imperialism in the early twentieth century which many considered a "fourth volume" of Marx's *Capital* and upon which Lenin relied considerably when writing his own later and more famous work, *Imperialism: The Highest Stage of Capitalism*.

The industrial revolution that made Britain the first industrial country dominating nineteenth century capitalism was possible despite the archaic, short-term pre-capitalist form of finance it had inherited, because the sums needed at the time for industrial investment were relatively small. While most financial institutions remained focused on short-term finance for commerce and speculation, the accumulated wealth of rich families sufficed for the amounts of industrial investment that powered Britain's industrial revolution, while Britain's banks concentrated on commercial rather than industrial credit.

---

215 Karl Marx. 1894/1981. *Capital* (Vol. III). London: Penguin, 735.
216 Rudolf Hilferding. 1910/1981. *Finance Capital: A Study of the Latest Phase of Capitalist Development*. Edited with an Introduction by Tom Bottomore, Tr. Morris Watnick and Sam Gordon, London: Routledge.

It was in the countries to industrialise next, chiefly Germany, the United States, and Japan, that, as Hilferding explained, Marx's prediction of capitalism taming inherited financial forms for its own purposes was fulfilled. These countries industrialised in opposition to Britain's dominance over the world market. Their industrialization was, moreover, not a replication of the one that Britain had accomplished, but an advance over it, a veritable "second industrial revolution" to Britain's first. It involved the production not of consumer goods but of investment goods, requiring immensely greater amounts of capital, much more sophisticated technology, the concentration of more and more workers in firms, and vastly more energy. This required protectionism against British market dominance, industrial policy, and other such methods of state intervention, including the construction of financial systems capable of providing long-term "patient" capital for investment in large quantities and for long periods. This industrialization leapfrogged over British industry, leaving it behind. In these countries, the transformation of inherited institutions of money and finance into institutions that would serve industrial development had become imperative because the vast amounts of capital required could not come from individual fortunes. Banks were essential, a point Hilferding signalled by labelling the type of capitalism in these countries "finance capital".

Hilferding explicitly contrasted finance capital with Britain's more archaic financial system. While there were pressures for Britain to move towards the finance capital model, the financially and commercially inclined capitalist classes of Britain, which had retained their dominance over industrial capital[217] and whose inclinations were rein-

---

217 Ingham, Geoffrey K. 1984. *Capitalism Divided?: The City and Industry in British Social Development*. Basingstoke: Macmillan.

forced by the empire and the sterling system which rested upon it, resisted them.

Today's U.S. dollar-denominated financial system, upon which the dollar's world role rests, is not the "finance capital" sort of financial system geared towards facilitating industrial expansion. Rather, it is of the British type, geared towards short-term speculation and predatory lending—essentially, towards skimming off incomes generated in production, whether as wages, profits, or government revenues. This is because although *the United States had started life as an industrial power with the financial system that closely resembled Hilferding's finance capital model, and though this orientation was reinforced by Depression-era regulation of the U.S. financial system, it began, after the dollar's link to gold was broken, to transform its financial system into one resembling the arcane British sort in pursuit of its goal to keep the dollar as the world's money.*

The Dollar-Denominated Financial System and the Dollar's World Role

The dominant narratives of the dollar system portray the dollar as following in the footsteps of the pound sterling. However, they forget a critical difference: sterling was not a national currency, but an imperial one. Empire was central to its functioning. Britain extracted vast sums as surpluses from its *non-settler* colonies such as British India, Africa and the Caribbean and exported these funds—its famous "capital exports"—to *Europe and the white settler-colonies in Canada, the United States and Oceania, enabling their industrialization*[218] just as, in

---

218 On this point, see Radhika Desai, 'John Maynard Pangloss: *Indian Currency and Finance* in Imperial Context' in Sheila Dow, Jesper Jespersen & Geoff Tily (eds), *The General Theory and Keynes for the 21st Century*, Cheltenham:

a previous era, these surpluses had enabled British industrialization.[219]

When the U.S. sought to replace the sterling with the dollar, without colonial surpluses to export, it had to resort to providing the world with liquidity by running deficits. This was always problematic. It created the the famous Triffin dilemma;[220] the greater the deficits—that is to say, the greater the liquidity provision—the greater the downward pressure on the dollar's value, making it less desirable for the rest of the world to hold. Inevitably, the Europeans refused to accept dollars for their exports to the U.S. and demanded gold instead. This drained the U.S. of gold and left it unable to back the dollar with gold as early as 1961. After spending a decade exhausting all avenues for artificially preserving the gold link, the U.S. finally had to break it in 1971.[221]

After 1971, the U.S. has been able to maintain the dollar's status as the world's money only by promoting a succession of what we may call financializations: a series of discrete expansions of financial activity to generate demand for dollars and counteract the downward pressure that U.S. trade deficits put on the dollar. Each of these financializations has involved distinct assets, regulatory frameworks, borrowers, lenders, and speculators. Each has been more volatile than the one

---

Edward Elgar Publishing Ltd, 2018; Patnaik, Utsa; and Patnaik, Prabhat. 2016. *A Theory of Imperialism*. New York: Columbia University Press; and Patnaik, Utsa; and Patnaik, Prabhat. 2021. *Capital and Imperialism: Theory, History, and the Present*. New York: Monthly Review Press.

219 Patnaik, Utsa. 2006. The Free Lunch: Transfers from the Tropical Colonies and Their Role in Capital Formation in Britain during the Industrial Revolution, in K. S. Jomo (ed.) Globalization under Hegemony. Oxford University Press, New Delhi.

220 Triffin, Robert. 1961. *Gold and the Dollar Crisis; the Future of Convertibility*. Rev. ed. A Yale paperbound Y-39. New Haven: Yale University Press.

221 See Desai, *Geopolitical Economy*, pp. 103-123.

before and more destructive when it crashed. The U.S. financial system had been of the "finance capital" variety and heavily regulated to prevent speculation and predatory lending and promote productive investment, but starting with the lifting of capital controls in the 1970s, waves of deregulation transformed this system into one that more closely resembled the British style: archaic, short-term, speculative and predatory finance.[222]

Each financialization ended in a distinct disaster: the early 1980s Third World Debt crisis, various currency and financial crises of the 1990s, the 1997-8 East Asian financial crisis, the 2000 dot-com crash, the 2008 crisis, and the 2023 banking crisis, which is merely the herald of a much greater crash to come.

This is the background against which we must try to understand why internationalising the renminbi on the model of the dollar would be ill-advised in the extreme, and how China can and should change international monetary and financial relations to serve its own and the rest of the world's development, instead.

The Chinese Financial System and Developing World Economic and Monetary Sovereignty

China's financial system has come a long and complex way in the last several decades. Well into the reform period, it was essentially a banking system without asset markets, and Western analysts considered it to be nearly insolvent. Today, however, China is home to three of the world's five biggest banks, which enjoy a remarkably low rate of non-performing loans, and Western investors are lining

---

222 For a brief summary, see Desai, *Geopolitical Economy*, 239-241.

up to invest in them.[223] As the pace of liberalising reforms of China's banking system increased, so did Western interest. However, Western and Western-oriented scholarship on China ignores the fact that these liberalising reforms took place to achieve the goal of a more dynamic socialist economy, not that of ever-greater neoliberal financialization.

Such scholarship, as Guy Williams points out, judges the Chinese financial system "according to the degree of implementation of free market policies"[224] complete with the full paraphernalia of elements associated with neoliberal financialization of the sort that has transformed the U.S. financial system for the worse since the 1970s. They include:

- central bank independence, which amounts to regulatory capture of the regulators by those to be regulated;
- private ownership, which constitutes a licence to produce money for private gain;
- stock markets, which are arenas of speculation rather than sources of capital;
- unrestricted foreign ownership, which detaches finance from the needs of the domestic economy;
- and greater "financial inclusion", which simply extends the financial system to anyone who can be usefully indebted.

These scholars do not criticise the extensive damage done by the U.S.-dominated financial system to its own productive economy, not to mention to that of the rest of the world, nor do they discuss the

---

223 Guy Williams, *The Evolution of China's Banking System, 1993-2017* (London: Routledge, 2020), pp. 1-2.
224 Williams, *The Evolution of China's Banking System*, 3.

critical importance of long-term "patient finance" in China's spectacular industrialization and development.²²⁵

For instance, Walter and Howie praise the liberalising reforms that culminated in China's entry into the World Trade Organisation and criticise limitations and reversals on the way to full financialization. The resulting financial system, they say, is still largely confined to banks, with underdeveloped asset markets. It underserves "China's heroic savers" with low interest rates. Since China's large state-owned banks typically focus on financing the state-owned and/or closely monitored corporations that remain at the commanding heights of China's economy, it leaves many smaller businesses without any reliable source of capital. Further, not only do they fault the party-state for protecting this system from competition or failure, particularly by keeping foreign banks confined to a marginal role, but they complain that "the Party treats its banks as basic utilities that provide unlimited capital to the cherished state-owned enterprises" and that "at the end of each of the last three decades, these banks have faced virtual, if not actual, bankruptcy, surviving only because they have had the full, unstinting, and costly support of the Party"²²⁶ which resolves matters by the "traditional problem-solving approach of simply shifting money from one pocket to another and letting time and fading memory do the rest." This, they think, cannot go on forever. They look forward to the moment when, "[t]ied up as it is in financial knots, the system's size, scale, and access to seemingly limitless capital can [no longer]

---

225 William Byrd, *China's Financial System,* London: Routledge 1983 is an early example while Marlene Amstad, Guofeng Sun and Wei Xiong, eds., *The Handbook of China's Financial System* (Princeton, NJ: Princeton University Press, 2020) is a more recent one.

226 Carl Walter and Fraser Howie, *Red Capitalism: The Fragile Financial Foundations of China's Extraordinary Rise* 2012), New York: Wiley, 2012, pp. 27.

solve the problems of the banks." This would, they argue, provide the opening for further market reforms that were abandoned after 2005.

Such writers ignore many rather obvious facts. Stock markets have rarely provided long-term patient capital. High interest rates strangle industry. Public services and investment should obviate ordinary people's need for savings. Finally, providing small businesses with capital will likely require the expansion of China's financial system on its present basis downwards into the economy, and not its neoliberal reform. Above all, they blithely ignore the regularity with which Western countries have bailed out their own banks—which is precisely "shifting money from one pocket to the next", but done so in the aftermath of the bursting of socially, economically and politically destructive asset bubbles, and not, as in China, after some proportion of patient productive investment has gone sour, as it must.

China's banking system has historically had a very different role in its economy. The banking system was long dominated by a single bank, the People's Bank of China. After the official adoption of a socialist market economy in the early 1990s, market reforms were gradually introduced to liberalise it.[227] However, contrary to Western views, this liberalization did not have neoliberal aims.

To be sure, reformers have learned and borrowed a great deal from Western banking techniques as they introduced competition, reduced the inevitable moral hazards in a system ultimately protected by the state, allowed carefully calibrated private ownership, including some foreign ownership, and imposed prudential limits on lending and risk-taking.[228] However, reformers have proceeded with caution,

---

227 For the early history, see Chunxia Jiang and Shijie Yao, *Chinese Banking Reform: From the Pre-WTO Period to the Financial Crisis and Beyond* (London: Palgrave Macmillan, The Nottingham China Policy Institute Series, 2017), pp. 15-20.
228 *Ibid*, p. 35-38.

bearing in mind the Chinese adage about "crossing the river by feeling the stones." Their borrowings have been governed by the party-state's aims, usually articulated as principles arising from an understanding of China's history and economic needs. Reform has sought to "transform the banking system to a market-oriented one that is viable in the long run thereby better serving the economic development of the country",[229] that is, serving the needs of the productive economy rather than those of a tiny financial elite.[230] Unlike the neoliberal financialized banking systems, China's banks have played a critical role in maintaining the remarkably high investment rate that has been so critical to China's economic success.[231]

Internationalization of the Renminbi

Like the Chinese financial system, the internationalization of the renminbi is also found wanting by Western observers who measure it against the benchmark of the unstable, predatory and volatile dollar system.[232] Since the party-state is unable or unwilling to internationalise the renminbi in the same way, the dollar's position, we are told, is secure. Benjamin Cohen, for instance, assuming that currency internationalization is desirable in itself, finds that Beijing's internationalising

---

229 *Ibid*, p. 55.

230 Williams, *The Evolution of China's Banking System*.

231 John Ross, 'Why China maintained its strong economic growth,' *Learningfrom-China.net*, 2020. https://www.learningfromchina.net/why-china-maintained-its-strong-economic-growth/.

232 Cohen, *Currency Power*; Eswar Prasad, *Gaining Currency: The Rise of the Renminbi* (Oxford: Oxford University Press, 2017); Kai Guo et al., 'RMB Internationalization' in *The Handbook of China's Financial System*, eds. Marlene Amstad, Guofeng Sun and Wei Xiong (Princeton, NJ: Princeton University Press, 2020) are typical works.

ambitions are checked by episodes like the outflow of nearly a trillion dollars in 2015 that forced devaluation[233] and by the fear that it will undermine the Party's political hold. Thus, Cohen concludes that the dollar remains "the *indispensable currency*—the one money the world cannot do without" thanks to the "depth of [U.S.] financial markets"[234] along with the U.S.'s "still broad network externalities in trade, a wide range of political ties, and vast military reach." While Cohen is careful not to doubt China's ability to internationalise the renminbi and even agrees that it has "achieved tangible results, particularly along the trade track", he concludes that progress is doubtful: "On its own the gravitational pull of China's economic size will not suffice. Other factors—above all, *a well-developed and open financial structure*—must also come into play" and China is unlikely to be willing to engage in the necessary financial liberalization because it would entail "a significant modification of Beijing's authoritarian economic model".[235] For Cohen, the restrictions placed on private enterprise in all sectors, including the financial, to bend their efforts towards China's economic development are authoritarian, and he demands that China replace it with precisely the archaic, short-term, speculative and predatory financial structure sported by the U.S. and the UK—which would no doubt bring an end to the spectacular growth China has experienced thanks to its contrasting financial system.

The dollar system is reaching the limits of its viability, particularly with the recent rise in inflation. Inflation itself is a result of the diminishing ability of the U.S. to compel the rest of the world to

---

233 Daniel McDowell, 'From tailwinds to headwinds: The Troubled Internationalization of the Renminbi,' in *Handbook on the International Political Economy of China*, ed. Ka Zeng (Cheltenham: Edward Elgar, 2019), pp. 194.

234 Cohen, *Currency Power*, p. 6)

235 *Ibid*, 236, emphasis added.

yield primary commodities and consumption goods at low prices, and compels interest rate increases that imperil the multiple asset bubbles needed to keep money flowing into the system.[236] It is no wonder that, since at least the 2008 financial crisis, critical voices pointing to the costs the U.S. itself has had to pay for its financialized dollar internationalization are becoming louder.[237]

The real alternative to the dollar system is not a renminbi system, which would be subject to the same problems, but the sort of system John Maynard Keynes had proposed—based on a multilaterally created currency to be used exclusively for settling international imbalances while national monies continue to operate as national money. This system was envisioned to reduce imbalances, produce growth and, above all, secure economic sovereignty for all countries.[238] Barring that, regional, bi- and multi-lateral agreements will be the realistic options, particularly considering that only a fraction of the astronomical financial flows necessary for the highly financialised dollar system will be necessary to serve the trade and investment needs of the world's productive economy.

Indeed, financial systems of the finance capital type have historically been reluctant to internationalise their currencies in the same

---

236 See Radhika Desai, "Vectors of Inflation' and 'Soft Landing?', Sidecar, 2022 and 2024.

237 Fred Bergsten, 'The Dollar and the Deficits: How Washington Can Prevent the Next Crisis,' *Foreign Affairs* 88, no. 6 (November/December 2009); Fred Bergsten, 'Why the World Needs Three Global Currencies,' *Financial Times*, February 15, 2011. https://www.ft.com/content/d4845702-3946-11e0-97ca-00144feabdc0.

238 Radhika Desai. 2009. "Keynes Redux: From World Money to International Money at Last?" Wayne Anthony and Julie Guard eds. Bailouts and Bankruptcies. Halifax: Fernwood Books.

manner[239] and for good reason. The internationalization of the renminbi is therefore proceeding according to the domestic and international needs of China's productive economy, as it should, and it is likely to proceed further along the same path, rather than the radically different and destructive path taken by the dollar.

* * *

Radhika Desai is a professor of political studies at the University of Manitoba, and is currently serving as visiting professor at the London School of Economics. She is the director of the Geopolitical Economic Research Group, and a founder of the International Manifesto Group. She is the author of numerous books, including Geopolitical Economy: After US Hegemony, Globalization and Empire (The Future of World Capitalism) *and* Capitalism, Coronavirus and War (Rethinking Globalizations).

---

239 See, for instance, Randall C. Henning, *Currencies and Politics in the United States, Germany and Japan* (Washington, DC: Institute for International Economics, 1994); Eric Helleiner and Anton Malkin, 'Sectoral Interests and Global Money: Renminbi Dollar and the Domestic Foundations of International Currency Policy,' *Open Economic Review* 23 (2012): 33-55. For a good overview, see Hyoung-Kyu Chey and Yu Wai Vic Li, 'Chinese Domestic Politics and the Internationalization of the Renminbi,' *Political Science Quarterly* 135/1 (2020): pp. 37-65.

7.

Looking Back & Looking Forward

The Rise of China and the Crisis of U.S. Imperialism

by Gerald Horne, Anthony Ballas,
Aspen Ballas, and PM Irvin

In September 2024, as a response to the profound summit between the People's Republic of China and over four dozen heads of state and government from Africa taking place in Beijing, Kamala Harris's plane touched down in East Africa. What is often overlooked about this curious confluence of events is the irony that on each and every leg of her journey, from Ghana to Zambia to Dar es Salaam, Tanzania, Harris's plane landed in an airport that was either designed or constructed by Chinese interests. Had Harris decided to extend her stay on the continent and visit Angola, Uganda, Namibia, Sudan, Ethiopia, Mozambique, or the Republic of Congo, she would have encountered much of the same. Or, if the former vice president had decided to travel by rail, she and her entourage from Washington would have encountered various transportation projects such as the trains from Mombasa to Nairobi, Kenya and from Ethiopia to Djibouti, among others—infrastructures which also bear China's fingerprints.

This curious fact is indicative not only of the importance of China to African development, but also of the role that China has played more broadly to fill the infrastructural vacuum left in the wake of Euro-American colonial and neo-colonial underdevelopment of the continent. With no scarcity of irony, this fact also reveals the reality that U.S. imperialism may be quickly losing altitude, forced to cede dominance due to China's meteoric rise as well as the contradictions that fomented the present crisis of U.S. imperialism. While it ought to be clear that the People's Republic of China is poised to replace the United States as the dominant economic force on planet Earth, evinced not least by strides in green energy technologies, quantum computing, artificial intelligence, space exploration, and alike, what is perhaps less clear are the historical forces which propelled China's rise in the first instance, and the latter's impact on the current crisis of U.S. imperialism.

During the early years of the Cold War, and as a sequel to the Red Summer and the Palmer raids following the Russian Revolution of 1917, the United States was again gripped by Red Scare hysteria. In tandem with the effects following the confrontation between Chinese and American forces on the Korean peninsula between 1950 and 1953, Washington pushed for a total ban on cultural exchanges and monetary transfers with China, while also barring U.S. citizens from traveling to the People's Republic. Although these particular restrictions were relatively short-lived, they were nonetheless of great consequence, especially for the hundreds of Chinese-Americans who were seized, arrested, deported, imprisoned, and who suffered loss of employment as the result of U.S.-style anti-communist and anti-Chinese fervor at midcentury. However, neither were the travel ban nor the subsequent persecutions historically unprecedented—far from it. By the 1950s, various anti-Chinese policies had already been passed and put into practice in preceding decades, including, *inter alia*, the Chinese Exclusion Act of 1882, which was in effect for over 60 years until 1943, as well as the Immigration Acts of 1917 and 1924, both of which were consequential for people of Chinese descent.

After the years of compounding anti-communism and enforced anti-labor legal machinations which lead to the repression and persecution of such luminaries as various as Paul Robeson, William L.

Patterson, Benjamin Davis Jr., W.E.B. Du Bois, and alleged fellow travelers alike, tensions with China were mounting.[240] By the early 1950s, however, Washington's barring of American citizens from traveling to China would have had little effect on W.E.B. Du Bois, for instance, against whom anti-Communist forces in Washington had already imposed a targeted travel ban, revoking his passport under the specious charges that he was working as the agent of a foreign government—namely, Moscow.[241] For Du Bois, already well acquainted with the events of October 1949, the Chinese Revolution caused such a rupture in the imperialist world order that "the moon fell out of the heaven of Big Business," dealing a mighty blow against global white supremacy.[242] Prior to 1949, China was a semi-colonial nation that consisted of a fifth of the world's population, and it was long subjected to white European colonial domination.[243] Viewing China as "the end

---

240 See Horne, Gerald, *Black Liberation / Red Scare: Ben Davis and the Communist Party*, (University of Delaware Press, 1994); Burden-Stelly, Charisse, *Black Scare / Red Scare: Theorising Capitalist Racism in the United States*, (University of Chicago Press, 2023).

241 See Horne, Gerald, *Black & Red: W.E.B. Du Bois and the Afro-American Response to the Cold War 1944-1963*, (SUNY Press, 1986).

242 Du Bois, W. E. B. (William Edward Burghardt), 1868-1963. "A History of the Last Forty Years," March 31, 1958. W. E. B. Du Bois Papers (MS 312). Special Collections and University Archives, University of Massachusetts Amherst Libraries, 10.

243 On Du Bois' analysis of China, particularly its history as a semi-colony of Western imperialism, see Li, Dai, "Du Bois's Intellectual and Political Significance for China," in *The Oxford Handbook of W. E. B. Du Bois*, Oxford Handbooks, Morris, Aldon D., and others (eds), (2025; online edn, Oxford Academic, May 19, 2022); Gao Yunxiang, *Arise, Africa! Roar, China! Black and Chinese Citizens of the World in the Twentieth Century*. University of North Carolina Press, (Chapel Hill, 2021); and Yunxiang Gao, "W. E. B. and Shirley Graham Du Bois in Maoist China." *Du Bois Review: Social Science Research on Race* 10, no. 1: 59–85.

and aim of all imperial planning, from America to Japan," Du Bois lauded the Chinese Revolution all the more.[244]

The feeling was mutual: as a response to Washington's revocation of Du Bois's passport, China protested, evinced by an outpouring of "letters of support," with Shanghai's *China News* "join[ing] media worldwide in publishing supportive articles," while the *People's Daily* "proclaimed that people around the globe, including citizens of the Soviet Union and China, protested 'this baseless behavior of the U.S. government.'"[245] After Washington's travel ban was lifted and Du Bois's passport restored, the eminent nonagenarian sociologist, along with Shirley Graham Du Bois, traveled to China in 1959 to meet with Mao Zedong and other Chinese officials. In the same year, Du Bois would celebrate the Chinese Revolution once again in "I Sing to China," a poem which emphatically urged China to partner with Africans in the struggle against global imperialism and white supremacy.[246] 1959 also saw the fruits of Du Bois's internationalism as translations of his books *John Brown* and *The Souls of Black Folk* were published in Beijing, marking a significant achievement in African American and Chinese relations, given their shared histories as the victims of atrocity

---

244 Du Bois, W. E. B. (William Edward Burghardt), 1868-1963. *Russia and America: An Interpretation*, 1950. W. E. B. Du Bois Papers (MS 312), Special Collections and University Archives, University of Massachusetts Amherst Libraries, 133.

245 Gao Yunxiang, *Arise, Africa! Roar, China!*, 35.

246 Du Bois, "I Sing to China: Dedicated to Kuo Mo-Jo, May 1, 1959," in Creative Writings by W. E. B. Du Bois: A Pageant, Poems, Short Stories, and Playlets. Ed. Herbert Aptheker. White Plains, NY: Kraus-Thomson, 1985. 47-51; see also Chiu, Jeannie, "Imaginary Neighbors: African American and Asian American Writers' Visions of China During the Cold War" (2008). *Global Asia Journal*. 2, 2008.

and humiliation executed at the hands of colonial and fascist forces in the United States and Europe.[247]

The "century of humiliation" endured by China which came to a screeching halt in October 1949 was fueled in no small measure by what we might refer to as the *centuries of humiliation* endured by peoples of African descent at the hands and at the behest of the unlamented African slave trade perpetrated by what amounts today to the North Atlantic powers. Although it is no mystery that the wealth that fueled the rise of Great Britan and the United States, as well as France and Spain, was driven in no small measure by the African slave trade, the confluence of globalized, extraterritorial anti-Blackness[248] and anti-Chinese hysteria is not often mentioned in this context. For instance, the series of anti-Chinese pogroms in the late 19th century, from Denver, Los Angeles, San Francisco, Tacoma, Rock Springs, and Seattle to the curiously named Chinese Massacre Cove in Oregon, which saw the murder of thirty-four Chinese workers in 1887, overlapped in time with the period in which Black people were en route to being denaturalized, numerous anti-Black pogroms were taking place in Dixie, and white supremacist terrorism, headed by the Ku Klux Klan, was on the rise. Also witnessed in this period was the end of the Kingdom of Hawai'i, held at ransom by the Bayonet Constitution of 1887, and the coup to oust Queen Liliuokalani that followed in

---

247 See Li, Hongshan, "Building a Black Bridge: China's Interaction with African-American Activists during the Cold War," *Journal of Cold War Studies*, Volume 20, Number 3, Summer 2018, 123; as well as Yunxiang Gao, "W. E. B. and Shirley Graham Du Bois in Maoist China," *Du Bois Review: Social Science Research on Race* 10, no. 1: 59–85.

248 Horne, Gerald, *The Capital of Slavery: Washington D.C., 1800-1865*, (International Publishers, 2025), 55.

1893.[249] Collectively, these events resulted in voter repression laws that enabled only those with European ancestry to vote, ensnaring descendants of African and Chinese people in the machinations of repressive liberalism that greatly affected the lives of Chinese workers and African workers alike. Through these maneuvers and others, the sons and daughters of missionaries established what amounted to an apartheid regime in the Pacific, harmful to those of African and Chinese ancestry.

It is no coincidence, thus, that the events of October 1949 witnessed a turning point in world history for peoples of African descent, and the wave of anti-colonial and national liberation movements which flowed from the end of World War II. Neither is it coincidental that the events of 1949 provided inspiration and assistance to the embattled workers' movements in the United States, as well as the Civil Rights movement, culminating in the erosion of some of the more egregious aspects of Jim Crow, which reflects a certain confluence as well between the events of October 1949 and the retreat from the agonizing horrors of U.S. Apartheid.

What this conjuncture reveals is the way U.S. imperialism responded to the perceived tripartite threat of the "Red Menace," the "Black Bolshevik," and the "Yellow peril" domestically and abroad. Not only is the history of this grotesque triptych vital for understanding the period of the Cold War at midcentury, but indeed, the contradictions of U.S. imperialism generated throughout this period have proven to be consequential in our present era of Cold War 2.0[250] as U.S. imperialism once again renews and recalibrates its political and

---

249 See Horne, Gerald. *The White Pacific: U.S. Imperialism and Black Slavery in the South China Seas after the Civil War*, (University of Hawa'ii Press, 2007).

250 "Why Does Xi Keep Purging Loyalists? Look to Stalin and Mao for the Answer," *The New York Times*, August 20, 2025.

economic standoff with the People's Republic of China. In order to understand the current iteration of this renewed Cold War (perhaps more aptly dubbed a "Hot Peace") and the current crisis of Western imperialism, as well as the impact of China's meteoric economic and technological ascension post-October 1949 on the latter, it is vital to understand the role that China played for African Americans during the consequential post-World War II era.

Although Washington has faced great difficulty convincing not only African Americans, but any progressive forces in the United States and in the international community writ large, that the U.S. is, as it claims, a "paragon of human rights,"[251] few seek to understand how the United States encouraged economic and technological growth in China, arguably participating directly in the ascension of the global juggernaut we see today. Leonard Woodcock, former president of the United Auto Workers and U.S. ambassador to China urged Washington to temper relations with the People's Republic of China in the late 1970s. Woodcock's efforts included calls to cease supplying Taipei and Beijing with arms as part of the process to normalize relations[252] while also opening up and maintaining trade between the U.S. and China.[253] What often goes unremarked is Woodcock's strat-

---

251 "US guilty of myriad human rights abuses," *China Daily*, May 30, 2024. https://epaper.chinadaily.com.cn/a/202405/30/WS6657b6fea310df4030f51e75.html.

252 "A Labor Voice Urges China Trade," *Washington Post*, March 7, 2000. https://www.washingtonpost.com/archive/politics/2000/03/08/a-labor-voice-urges-china-trade/9464a4b2-8fd4-4d67-aa31-0dd59b3c0f6e/.

253 Walte, Juan J.,"Leonard Woodcock, former American ambassador to China, told a...," *United Press International* (archives), May 28, 1981. See also "Memorandum From the President's Assistant For National Security Affairs (Brzezinski) to President Carter," Carter Library, National Security Affairs, Staff Material, Far East, Oksenberg Subject File, Box 56, Policy Process: 1–4/78. Secret. Sent for action. The date is handwritten. At the top of the first page, Carter expressed his approval for the proposed studies (on Korea, China nor-

egy to engage in the transfer of technology with Beijing in lieu of direct arms sales; unbeknownst to the U.S. at the time, and what has often gone unacknowledged in the decades hence, is the way that the United States assisted and encouraged the rise of China through direct foreign investment and technology transfer, which China utilized in their broader efforts to fill the infrastructural vacuum left in the wake of Euro-American colonial and neo-colonial underdevelopment in the Global South.

While U.S. imperialism desperately seeks to turn back the hands of time, longing for a prelapsarian return to before Deng Xiaoping's sojourn to the United States in 1978, or before Richard Nixon's conference with Mao Zedong in 1972, or perhaps further still, to a time prior to the fateful events of October 1949 that saw the triumph of the Chinese Revolution, there will be great difficulty redeeming U.S. imperialism and the North Atlantic bloc more generally, which got fat and happy on the plundering of Africa without leaving behind much infrastructure. And this is precisely where China's influence and role in the region has been paramount. The various Belt and Road projects on the continent have provided a counterweight against French imperialism, which has historically been the major bloodsucker on the continent, and against British imperialism, which explains the pro-Soviet stance of Africa during the Cold War, which is now manifesting in the PRC's recent reluctance to sanction Russia and the expulsion of French mining from the Sahel, among other intersecting phenomena.

The fervor directed at Cuba, for instance, by Senator Ted Cruz of Texas, and by Senator Marco Rubio, another son of a Cuban expat, is part of this same anti-communist and anti-China constellation. In

---

malization, and arms sales to Taiwan) by writing, "First 3 studies ok—needed. J." In the margin next to the paragraphs summarizing each of these topics, Carter wrote, "OK.," April 18, 1978.

early 2025, Rubio viciously promised the expulsion of 6,000 Chinese students from U.S. universities,[254] only for President Donald Trump to pull a dramatic about-face just months later, instead promising to allow 600,000 Chinese students into the U.S. out of fear of U.S. universities facing economic difficulties otherwise. Trump's characteristically vulgar admission that the "schools would go to hell"[255] is a stunning, and telling, riposte to not only his own administration's previous policies regarding Chinese student visas, but the long-standing, bipartisan hostilities against the PRC out of Washington. This fact is indicative of the China-centric swerve that is currently taking place, unprecedented even in the annals of Western hegemony, with similar signals, too numerous to mention, abounding at every level of U.S. politics.

One need only take a perfunctory glance at the emergent powerhouse hailing from the Global South as economic trading partners composing the BRICS nations ascend at breakneck speed and at global scale, challenging the hegemony of the U.S. dollar, while portending a process of de-dollarization which may well be imminent. Although this ascendant economic coalition should not come as a surprise to astute analysts and historians of U.S. imperialism, there remains nonetheless archaic bipartisan efforts to foment anti-China hysteria. Indeed, few issues unite the two major bourgeois parties in the United States than kneejerk hostility to Beijing. This position is reflected in the fact that the notorious Central Intelligence Agency has an entire Center

---

254 "Marco Rubio: US to 'aggressively' revoke visas of Chinese students," *Politico*, May 28, 2025. https://www.politico.com/news/2025/05/28/rubio-revoke-chinese-students-visas-00373835.

255 "Trump saying 600,000 Chinese students could come to the US draws MAGA backlash," *AP*, August 26, 2025. https://apnews.com/article/chinese-student-visas-trump-maga-dce4e064ea61a4df090865668ca48cde.

devoted solely to undermining Beijing, which is quite unusual, by the bipartisan resolution "denouncing the horrors of socialism" in the U.S. House of Representatives in 2023,[256] as well as by Nancy Pelosi's bizarre pageantry in 2022 when she flew across the Pacific to Taipei.[257] These strange paroxysms of a flagging U.S. imperial order ought also give us pause, and ask us to consider how these and other ideological shows of force directed at the PRC appear actually as dramatic signs of decline and imperial weakness in retrospect. Only weeks after Pelosi's peculiar U.S. foreign policy sideshow, former Secretary of State Antony Blinken was forced to retreat with his tail between his legs and publicly profess the United States's commitment to its long-standing One China policy.[258] This particular retreat exposes a fissure in Washington's ideological edifice, revealing how vapid and ineffectual its various anti-China strategies truly are.

Such fissures appear to quickly be turning into gaping wounds, indicative of U.S. imperial overreach, which, as of 2025, is exemplified not least by the Trump regime's attempts at exacting punitive tariffs against China and its trading partners around the globe. However, bulwarked by the rise of the BRICS nations, and complemented by the Shanghai Cooperative Organization, China appears likely to parry Trump's attempts at a trade war. As one U.S. analyst put it, China maintains "escalatory dominance" over the United

---

256 "H.Con.Red.9: Denouncing the horrors of socialism," *GovTrackUS*, February 2, 2023.
https://www.govtrack.us/congress/votes/118-2023/h106.

257 "Pelosi's flight to Teipei took a circuitous route. Here's why," *The New York Times*, August 3, 2022. https://www.nytimes.com/2022/08/03/world/asia/pelosis-widely-watched-flight-to-taipei-took-a-circuitous-route-heres-why.html.

258 Blinken, Anthony, "The Administration's Approach to the People's Republic of China," May 26, 2022. https://2021-2025.state.gov/the-administrations-approach-to-the-peoples-republic-of-china/.

States, rendering Washington's leverage against the PRC nonexistent. The recent dumping of U.S. treasury bonds held by China have only made Washington's efforts all the more futile; as one *China Daily* commentator put it, China's bulwarking of the U.S. economy by purchasing treasury bills suggests that the U.S. "is increasingly dependent on surplus foreign savings to fill the void"[259] in its own coffers, which has increased dramatically during the second iteration of the Trump administration, making the dumping of these bills all the more consequential for U.S. imperialism. In a similar vein, we might also look to China's ban on cryptocurrency, and the shuttering of coal-powered digital currency "mining" operations as blows against new forms of fictitious capital currently vying for financial and commercial purchase in the West, whilst public and private institutions[260] in the United States have come to rely on digital currencies as ill-fated and perhaps even fantastical attempts to decelerate the decline of their economic dominance.

We can also interpret Trump's stated desire in early 2025 to eventually rid the U.S. of income tax altogether and implement his tariff regime on the rest of the world as signs that the curtain may be closing on U.S. imperialism: not only has Trump's tariff regime faced an uphill battle domestically in the federal courts, but has faced stiff competition

---

259 *China Daily*, March 23, 2006; Horne, Gerald, *Blows Against The Empire*. (International Publishers, 2008), 14.

260 See, for instance, Ganea, Teddy, "UChicago Lost Money on Crypto, Then Froze Research When Federal Funding Was Cut," *The Stanford Review*, March 19, 2025, https://stanfordreview.org/uchicago-lost-money-on-crypto-then-froze-research-when-federal-funding-was-cut/; and Golumbia, David, *The Politics of Bitcoin: Software as Right-Wing Extremism*, (U of Minnesota Press, 2016); and John, Alun, et al. "China's Top Regulators Ban Crypto Trading and Mining, Sending Bitcoin Tumbling," September 24, 2021, reuters.com/world/china/china-central-bank-vows-crackdown-cryptocurrency-trading-2021-09-24/.

at a global scale, and even caused economic whiplash for the United States, resulting in a flailing U.S. empire seeking to expand its borders in a Monroe Doctrine-style effort by once again seeking to annex Canada and vying for control of Greenland via surreptitious means. Likewise, we might look to renewed aggression with China's trading partner, Venezuela, as part of the broader effort to deport Venezuelan migrants from the United States while also sending Naval ships to the coasts of Latin America, and placing a $50 million bounty on the head of President Nicolas Maduro.[261] Given this kind of gunboat diplomacy[262]—and especially in the context of Trump's recent proposal to rename the Pentagon the "Ministry of War"[263]—it is evident that, like an animal lashing out after being backed into a corner, the Trump regime is signalling that the U.S. imperialist project may be in a steep and ignominious decline that shows no signs of abating.

Like one scene in a film cross-dissolving into another, we are currently witnessing the transition into a new global correlation of forces, with Beijing and the 100 million-strong membership of the CPC in

---

261 The Trump regime's refusal to negotiate with Brazil, another trading partner of the PRC, despite numerous entreaties on the part of President Lula da Silva, ought to remind us why the right wing coalition of international forces has erected ramparts against Latin American socialism. Trump has also called for the release of Jair Bolsonaro, currently on house arrest awaiting trial for his role in plotting the attempted overthrow of Lula da Silva in 2022 as a sequel to the attempted coup of January 6, 2021.

262 Philips, Tom, "Trump's Venezuela gunboat diplomacy: sabre-rattling or prelude to invasion?" *Guardian,* August 29, 2025, https://www.theguardian.com/world/2025/aug/29/venezuela-gunboat-diplomacy-trump-maduro/.

263 Trump expressed a desire to rename the US Department of Defense to the "Ministry of War," Известия, August 26, 2025; and "Trump pushes to rename Department of Defense to the 'Department of War,'" Международная жизнь, August 26, 2025, https://en.interaffairs.ru/article/trump-pushes-to-rename-department-of-defense-the-department-of-war/.

the director's chair.[264] The rise of China may well bring the curtain down on a half-century if not more of Western hegemony, forcing the West to take a back seat and become an economic minority.[265] The prospect of this emergent reality is causing equal parts delirium and panic within the Trump regime in Washington,, indicated not least by its flailing and vacillating foreign policy initiatives. This panic, sown by China's meteoric rise, will soon be reaped by Western European nations and the North Atlantic bloc as well; China's refusal to capitulate to the aging Western hegemon's attempts to pressure the PRC and provoke a rebuke of Moscow allowed for even greater expansion of the China-Russia relationship following the Shanghai Cooperative Summit in 2022.[266] If the warming relations between India and China are any indication, then a similar process may already be underway there in late 2025; as the result of the Trump administration enforcing its capricious tariff regime on India, Prime Minister Modi met with Chinese Foreign Minister Wang Yi in New Delhi and with President Xi Jinping in Beijing in 2025, exposing a weakening U.S. imperialism if not a full-blown imperial crisis altogether.

Just as the Alaska summit between President Putin and Trump in August 2025 may well signal a Moscow-centric drift away from the North Atlantic bloc, so too the attendance of President Xi in Red Square in commemoration of the 80-year anniversary of victory over fascism suggests the possibility of a similar realignment of global

---

264 "The CPC grows stronger as membership exceeds 100 million," *Beijing Review*, July 7, 2025.

265 *Asia Times*, January 28, 2006; Horne, Gerald, *Blows Against The Empire*, (International Publishers, 2008), 7.

266 "SCO summit did not show what you think it showed," *Asia Times*, September 21, 2022. http://asiatimes.com/2022/09/sco-summit-did-not-show-what-you-think-it-showed/.

forces. If this so-called "Asian Pivot" is any indication, then, along with the role that China has played in the Caribbean and in Africa, as we go forward in this century we should continue to salute Beijing and in particular its assistance to socialist Cuba, as this aid, among other factors, is indicative of a brighter future for the bulk of humanity.

* * *

Gerald Horne is the John J. and Rebecca Moors Professor of History and African American Studies at the University of Houston.

Anthony Ballas is a PhD student in the Program for Literature at Duke University.

Aspen Ballas is a PhD student and teaching fellow in English at the University of North Carolina Chapel Hill.

PM Irvin is a PhD Candidate in the Department of Philosophy at Stanford University.

Shoulder to Shoulder: British People's Solidarity with the Chinese People's War of Resistance Against Japanese Aggression

by Keith Bennett

During his state visit to the United Kingdom in 2015, the 70th anniversary year of victory in the global anti-fascist war, President Xi Jinping recalled in a speech at Buckingham Palace how our two countries had once stood together as allies and fought shoulder to shoulder.

Saying that the Chinese people would never forget this help during their hard time, he mentioned one individual in particular.

George Hogg died of tetanus aged just 30 on 22 July 1945 after devoting the last nearly eight years of his tragically short life to the Chinese people and their struggle for liberation, initially as a journalist and finally as headmaster of the Shandan Bailie School, caring for children orphaned by Japan's brutal war of aggression. He is perhaps best remembered for leading his pupils on a month-long 1,100 kilometre (700 miles) journey, most of it on foot and over snow-covered mountain paths, to the relative safety of Gansu.

Long acclaimed as a national hero in China, Hogg remained almost entirely unknown in his native country for decades. This began to be partially rectified with the 2008 publication of James MacManus's biography, *Ocean Devil*. The same year saw the release of the perhaps overly fictionalised feature film, *The Children of Huang Shi*, also called *Children of the Silk Road* or *Escape from Huang Shi*, starring Jonathan Rhys Meyers as Hogg and Chow Yun-fat as the legendary Chinese communist Chen Hansheng.

George Hogg came to China as a young idealist. Although from a privileged background, he had a strong family background in pacifism, specifically in the Fellowship of Reconciliation, and rooted in non-conformist Christianity. However, he not only served China. His world outlook was transformed by China, as is well expressed in the title of his book, *I See a New China*.

In his 1954 book, *The People have Strength*, his mentor, the New Zealand internationalist Rewi Alley wrote:

> "The sixty-odd peasant and refugee kids who carried him out to his grave in what has now become a playing field in a school training new technicians for a new China, will not forget the day. For them it meant the passing of a comrade who was very close to them. It is not given to everyone to live with heroic disciplined revolutionary armies. George had had inspiration from his tour, as correspondent, with the Eighth Route Army and then he came at my bidding, to work with Gung Ho [the Chinese Industrial Cooperatives], where there was little glory, many problems and a simple grave at the end of the trail.

As he fought with tetanus in his last days of the summer of 1945, he asked to have the 'Communist Manifesto' read to him. I read it and he said, 'That makes sense.'"

Whilst there were also other British friends who made their contribution to China's struggle against Japanese militarism in China itself, such as Michael Lindsay, later 2nd Baron Lindsay of Birker, whose expertise in radio engineering was much appreciated and personally commended by Mao Zedong, and the Friends Ambulance Unit, organised by the Quakers and composed of conscientious objectors, roughly 200 of whom, with the British contingent being the largest group, served in China, including by providing medical supplies to the Shandan Bailie School, this was obviously an option that was open to relatively few. But the solidarity of people in Britain with China's war of national salvation, as a vital, and the first, front of the world peoples' struggle against fascism was by no means confined to those who made that journey.

By far the most important and effective organisation in this regard was the China Campaign Committee (CCC), which was founded in late August or early September 1937, scarcely two months after the July 7 Lugou 'Marco Polo' Bridge Incident that heralded Japan's full-scale invasion and the start of China's nationwide resistance.

Seven days later, on July 14, the *Daily Worker*, the newspaper of the Communist Party of Great Britain (CPGB), described this as a "plain case of aggression" in its editorial, adding: "The Chinese people must be backed up."

In an August 20 resolution passed by its Executive Committee, the CPGB stated:

> "The cause of peace throughout the world depends to a considerable extent upon the success of the heroic Chinese people... Unless peace forces can be rallied the Japanese attack on Central China will be followed by a German fascist outbreak in Central Europe... The defence of China is the defence of peace."

Although it operated on an unprecedented scale and with unprecedented breadth of support, the China Campaign Committee did not emerge from a void or a vacuum.

Jenny Clegg, writing for the Society for Anglo-Chinese Understanding (SACU), noted that the "roots of this activism are to be found in Chartist opposition to the first Opium War" and refers to the 'Hands off China' Campaign (1925-27) and the 'Friends of the Chinese People' (1927-37), founded by the British Section of the League Against Imperialism.

Her father, Arthur Clegg, who served as the CCC's National Organiser practically from the campaign's inception, traces the roots of such solidarity back even further in his memoir, *Aid China – 1937-1949*, published in 1989:

> "Movements like the China Campaign Committee have long been part of the democratic tradition in Great Britain. They date back to the English Revolution [of the 1640s] when the Levellers took a stand for Irish independence and the end of English interference in Ireland."

Arthur Clegg details the extraordinary range of forces mobilised by the CCC. They included church and missionary societies, businesses, leading intellectual and cultural figures, members of the House of Lords, the Chinese community, people with a specialised interest in China and Chinese culture, and many others.

On one occasion he even personally received a financial donation from a Colonel Younghusband. Only years later did he realise that it was the same Younghusband who had led the 1905 British invasion aimed at separating Xizang (Tibet) from the rest of China. He writes: "The only explanation I can find was that he was trying to make amends for his past efforts to weaken China."

Support was forthcoming from many members of the Labour and Liberal parties and even from the occasional Conservative MP. However, Clegg is at pains to point out:

> "Our greatest and most consistent supporter was the Communist Party, both directly and indirectly, for in those days it had influence far beyond its small but increasing membership. It was the first party to take a position defending China, the first to issue a pamphlet for China, the first to organise a Hyde Park meeting, where on August 23 [1937], J.R. Campbell demanded a Japanese withdrawal. Its branches and members loyally supported our meetings, distributed our handbills, posted our posters and saw in this a reinforcement for, rather than any rivalry with, the similar work they were doing for Spain. We all knew the issue of Spain and the issue of China were one and the same, the issue of preventing a world war."

A clear example of how such direct and indirect support worked in practice is provided by the South Wales miners. Through much of its history, the miners and the mining communities may be considered to have constituted a key vanguard of the British working class. The 1926 general strike lasted for just nine days, but the miners fought on for a further six months, despite facing hunger, destitution and repression, just as they did throughout their great strike of March 1984–March 1985.

In 1937, the communist-led South Wales Miners Federation adopted a resolution which read in part:

> "This Council of the South Wales Miners' Federation, representing 120,000 members, expresses its deep-felt horror at the savage and inhuman massacre of defenceless men women and children in China by the invading forces of Japan. We urge the Trades Union Congress Council to make every effort through the International Federation of Trade Unions and other working class organisations, particularly in European countries, Australia, United States and Canada, to adopt a policy of refusing to handle any goods and materials for export to or imported from Japan and to create a worldwide movement to boycott all Japanese goods, until the Japanese have left Chinese territory."

The next year, while making a donation for the provision of medical supplies to China, it passed the following resolution:

> "This Executive Council of the South Wales Miners' Federation expresses the strongest indignation and protest against the ruthless war of aggression which Japanese imperialism is waging on China, accompanied

as it has been by the systematic barbarous and pitiless massacre of the Chinese civil population.

It hopes that the victories of the Chinese armies over the Japanese armies will continue and that they will have the effect of wearing down and ultimately smashing the power of the Japanese military clique, thus opening the way of peace, freedom and democracy in Japan as well as liberating China from the danger of foreign domination.

This Executive Council therefore calls upon the members of the South Wales Miners' Federation to do whatever they can to assist the Chinese people in their struggle, particularly in regard to boycotting Japanese goods and creating a public opinion to force the British government to adopt a more positive policy in aid of China and against the present imperialist rulers of Japan."

Today, as the new cold war waged against China and other countries edges the nuclear clock closer to midnight, and as the genocidal war waged against the Palestinian people in Gaza ever more brutally recalls the horrors perpetrated by the Japanese militarists and German Nazis in the 1930s and 1940s, we need to remember and promote this history of anti-imperialist solidarity, peace and people-to-people friendship.

Writing in memory of Dr. Norman Bethune, who went from the battlefields of Spain to the battlefields of China, Mao Zedong explained:

"What kind of spirit is this that makes a foreigner selflessly adopt the cause of the Chinese people's liberation as his own? It is the spirit of internationalism, the spirit of communism."

Today, as we commemorate and celebrate the 80th anniversary of the victory of the people of China and the world against fascist aggression, and when the choice facing humanity is ever more starkly whether to go forward to a community of shared future or backwards to barbarism and even possible extinction, these words are surely more cogent than ever.

* * *

Keith Bennett is a co-founder of Friends of Socialist China. He studied Chinese history and politics at SOAS University of London, and upon graduating, worked full time for the Society for Anglo-Chinese Understanding. He has been visiting China and the Democratic People's Republic of Korea regularly since the early 1980s. He writes and lectures on China extensively and is co-editor with Carlos Martinez of People's China at 75: The Flag Stays Red. *He is also deputy chairman of the 48 Group Club, whose 1953 "Icebreaker Mission" was the first Western trade delegation to the People's Republic.*

200+ Years of U.S. Military Deployments in and around China

by Michael Kramer

U.S. ground, air and naval forces from a Jim Crow-era segregated military occupied and patrolled Chinese cities, coastal waters and rivers from the 1820s until 1949. This brutal and racist occupation was always resisted by the Chinese people.

This historic chronology was originally prepared for a workshop given in 2020 by the Veterans For Peace–China Working Group. Since 2020, aggressive and provocative naval deployments and maneuvers off the coast of the People's Republic of China (PRC) by the U.S. Navy 7th Fleet and its NATO allies have continued.

U.S. Army Special Forces from the 1st Special Forces Group maintain a presence on the large island of Taiwan and on the smaller Kinmen Islands, which are located just six miles off the coast of mainland China. All of these islands are an integral part of the PRC. In testimony to the U.S. Congress on May 15, 2025, retired U.S. Navy Rear Admiral Mark Montgomery disclosed that around 500 U.S. military personnel are stationed on Taiwan.

U.S. Air Force reconnaissance flights off the coast of the PRC have been reported by *Newsweek*.[267] These spy planes are RC-135V/W

---

267 Ryan Chan, "Map Shows US Military Plane off Chinese Coast," *Newsweek*, August 20, 2025, https://www.newsweek.com/map-shows-us-military-plane-off-chinese-coast-2116115.

Rivet Joint aircraft and are flown by the 55th Wing, 38th Reconnaissance Squadron out of Kadema Air Base on the Japanese-occupied island of Okinawa.

Chronology

May 16, 1820: The USS *Congress*, a three-masted, wooden-hulled heavy frigate with 38 guns and a crew of 340, docks unannounced and uninvited in Guangzhou on the Pearl River.

1835: The U.S. Navy East India Squadron is established.

1854: The East India Squadron forms the Yangtze River Patrol Force to protect U.S. citizens, U.S. property and Christian missionaries. It operates between Shanghai and Chongqing, a distance of over a thousand miles, until 1949.

April 4, 1854: Marines and sailors from the USS *Perry* land in Shanghai to protect U.S. and European commercial interests in a joint operation with Great Britain. They do not withdraw until June 1854.

May 19, 1855: Marines and sailors from the USS *Powhatan* land in Shanghai to protect U.S. citizens.

August 4-5, 1855: The USS *Powhatan* along with British allies seize 17 Chinese ships and destroy another in the Battle of Ty-ho Bay off the coast of Hong Kong. The U.S. demonizes the Chinese as pirates. Hundreds of Chinese are killed and over a thousand are taken prisoner.

October 22, 1856: Marines and sailors from the USS *Portsmouth* land in Guangzhou to protect U.S. interests. This force is continuously reinforced over the next few weeks.

November 16-24, 1856: The USS *Portsmouth*, USS *San Jacinto* and USS *Levant* bombard and occupy Chinese forts on the Pearl River in an alliance with British drug dealers during the Second Opium War.

June 24-26, 1859: The Second Battle of Taku Forts takes place during the Second Opium War. U.S., British and French forces are defeated as they fail to seize forts from Chinese defenders on the Haihe River in Tianjin.

July 31, 1859: Marines and sailors from the USS *Mississippi* deploy to Shanghai with British help to protect U.S. interests.

June 20, 1866: Marines and sailors from the USS *Washusett* land at Yingkou on a punitive expedition after the U.S. consul is allegedly assaulted. The force is reinforced five days later. Tens of Chinese are tried and punished by the U.S. Navy before the USS *Washusett* withdraws.

June 18, 1867: Marines and sailors from the USS *Wyoming* and USS *Hartford* land on Taiwan to conduct a punitive expedition. Within six hours the expedition is forced to retreat after meeting fierce resistance and its leader, Lt. Commander Alexander Slidell MacKenzie, is killed.

1868: The East India Squadron is disbanded and the Asiatic Squadron is formed. In 1902, it is upgraded to the Asiatic Fleet.

December 4, 1894: Marines from the USS *Baltimore* deploy to Tianjin. They remain there until May 1895.

November 4, 1898: Marines from the USS *Baltimore*, USS *Boston* and USS *Raleigh* establish bases in Beijing and Tianjin to protect U.S. diplomatic missions. The Marines withdraw in March 1899.

May 24, 1900: The first U.S. ground forces land at Taku on the Haihe River in northeastern China and join with eight other countries to put down the anti-foreign occupation uprising known as the Boxer

Rebellion. The so-called China Relief Expedition grows to over 19,000 soldiers before it occupies the Imperial City in Beijing on August 15, 1900. Most military units are withdrawn from Beijing on September 28, 1900. The U.S. Army 9th Infantry Regiment remains to guard the U.S. legation.

September 12, 1905: Marines from the Philippines arrive in Beijing to replace the U.S. Army 9th Infantry Regiment.

December 20, 1905: Marines and sailors from the USS *Baltimore* land in Shanghai to "help preserve order" in response to anti-foreign demonstrations. They are joined by British, German and Japanese troops.

November 4, 1911: Marines from the USS *Albany* and USS *Rainbow* land in Shanghai to protect U.S. interests. They withdraw on November 14, 1911.

January 18, 1912: Less than three weeks after the Republic of China is established, the U.S. Army 15th Infantry Regiment deploys to Tianjin. It does not leave China until March 2, 1938.

July 7-August 17, 1913: Marines from the USS *Baltimore* and USS *Rainbow* land five times in Shanghai to protect U.S. interests.

April 28, 1922: Marines from the USS *Baltimore* deploy to Beijing to strengthen forces guarding the U.S. legation.

May 5, 1922: Marines from the USS *Huron* deploy to Shanghai to protect U.S. interests.

October 6, 1924: Marines from the USS *Asheville* form the First Expeditionary Force and land in Shanghai. They then proceed to Tianjin and do not withdraw until February 8, 1925.

January 22, 1925: Marines form the Second Expeditionary Force and deploy to Shanghai from the Philippines. Numerous other Marine deployments take place throughout the rest of the year.

February 24, 1927: The 4th Marine Regiment commanded by Brigadier General Smedley Butler arrives from San Diego aboard the USS *Chaumont*. The ship docks at the Standard Oil Company terminal in Shanghai. U.S. military forces in China now total 6,000 troops and 44 naval vessels in Chinese waters. Butler later writes, "In China in 1927 I helped see to it that Standard Oil went on its way unmolested."

March 4, 1927: Marines from the USS *Pittsburgh* seize a ship being held by Chinese authorities and return it to the Standard Oil Company.

March 25, 1927: Marines from the USS *Pittsburgh* begin patrolling the main waterfront boulevard in downtown Shanghai. Marines from the USS *Sacramento* begin guarding the property of the Universal Leaf and Tobacco Company.

April 25, 1927: Marine aviation units VF-3M and VO-5M arrive from San Diego and Guam. Chinese pasture land 35 miles from Tianjin is seized and occupied by the Marines to facilitate the building of an airfield for the aviation units.

May 2, 1927: The 6th Marine Regiment arrives in Shanghai on board the USS *Henderson*. It withdraws in March 1929.

February 4, 1932: The U.S. Army 31st Regiment arrives in Shanghai to reinforce the 4th Marine Regiment. It withdraws to the Philippines on July 5, 1932.

November 27-28, 1941: The 4th Marine Regiment withdraws to the Philippines.

September 30, 1945: Operation Beleaguer begins with the 1st Marine Division arriving in China and deploying to Shanghai and Beijing. It is followed by an additional 50,000 Marines from the III Amphibious Corps, warships from the 7th Fleet, the 14th Air Force and two Navy Construction Battalions. The stated mission is to facilitate the surrender and repatriation of 600,000 Japanese soldiers after the end of World War II.

October 6, 1945: The 14th Air Force begins airlifting 50,000 Kuomintang troops around China for three weeks as they fight a losing battle against the People's Liberation Army (PLA).

July 13, 1946: PLA forces capture seven Marines guarding a bridge in Hebei Province.

July 29, 1946: PLA forces ambush a Marine patrol outside the village of An Ping on the Beijing-Tianjin highway in a battle that lasts four hours. Four Marines are killed.

April 4, 1947: The last major clash occurs between the PLA and the Marines, who suffer five killed and sixteen wounded.

May 26, 1949: Operation Beleaguer ends with the USS *Manchester* departing Qingdao. The U.S. occupation of China has finally ended.

1958-1974: The CIA Tibetan Program trains thousands of Tibetan Chinese at Camp Hale in Colorado to wage war against the People's Republic of China. The program includes airdrops and support for a low-intensity guerrilla war that is defeated by the PLA.

July 2020: Carrier strike groups from the 7th Fleet organized around the USS *Nimitz* and USS *Ronald Reagan* conduct aggressive maneuvers off the coast of China in the South China Sea.

Sources

Captain Harry Allanson Ellsworth, USMC, *One Hundred Eighty Landings Of United States Marines 1800-1934* (History and Museums Division Headquarters, U.S. Marine Corps, 1974).

U.S. Department of the Navy, *Yangtze River Patrol and Other US Navy Asiatic Fleet Activities in China 1920-1942* (Annual Reports of the Navy Department, 1920-1942).

"The China Marines: Dedicated to Documenting the United States Marine Corps China Experience 1818-1949," 2014, http://chinamarine.org/.

＊ ＊ ＊

Michael Kramer is a member of Veterans For Peace/Chapter 021 (Northern New Jersey) and is the co-coordinator of the national Veterans For Peace-China Working Group. He has travelled in China and has long been inspired by the Chinese Revolution and the heroism of the People's Liberation Army.

Defend the Socialist Countries, and Stand with the Peoples of the World Against Imperialism

by Carlos Martinez

I've been involved in the Marxist movement in the West in some way or another since I was a teenager, but thankfully have never got particularly close to Western Marxism.

The political tradition I grew up in emphasised the importance of supporting the socialist states, and always prioritised the struggle against imperialism, colonialism and racism. To support China, to support the DPRK, to support Cuba, to support the national liberation struggles of the Irish, Palestinian, Zimbabwean, Vietnamese and other peoples were very much part of that tradition.

So despite being a Marxist in the West, I haven't had all that much exposure to the Western Marxist academics described by Domenico Losurdo, and haven't had to go through that extremely difficult "unlearning" process that many others have. I've read a lot of Lenin; I've read very little Adorno, Zizek and Perry Anderson.

Nevertheless, Losurdo's book *Western Marxism: How it was Born, How it Died, How it can be Reborn* was really clarifying for me, and helped me understand the ideological roots of some of the objectively reactionary positions that you come up against all the time. Because although Western Marxism exists mainly in an academic ivory tower, it seeps into the wider movement for revolutionary change, which it seems to find quite fertile soil.

Marxism Moves East and South

Marxism is, obviously, Western by birth. The first line of *The Communist Manifesto* is after all: "A spectre is haunting Europe—the spectre of communism." The nascent communist movement was geographically limited to Europe and North America, and focused almost exclusively on the industrial working class.

But from the beginning, it's been on a journey to the East and South, including in Marx's own lifetime.

First, the phenomenon of imperialism, which was studied systematically by Lenin but which Marx and Engels started to take note of in the 1860s and 1870s, expanded capital's geographical sphere of operation. Capitalism was becoming a global system, and with that came the creation of a proletariat—a class of propertyless workers—from Mexico City to St. Petersburg to Shanghai.

Second, Marx and Engels, as their own thinking developed, came to understand the inextricable link between the struggle of the working class in the capitalist countries and that of the oppressed nations against their colonial oppressors.

For Marx and Engels, this intellectual journey started with the Irish question. Of course Ireland is not in the South or the East! But it was England's first colony, and had suffered for hundreds of years under a system of brutal colonial oppression.

Marx had originally considered that socialist revolution in Britain would bring national liberation to Ireland. In 1869, however, 21 years after the publication of *The Communist Manifesto*, he wrote that "deeper study has now convinced me of the opposite. The English working class will never accomplish anything before it has got rid of Ireland."

He went on: "A nation that oppresses another forges its own chains" and called on his followers to "put the conflict between England and Ireland in the foreground, and everywhere to side openly with Ireland." He pointed out that "the national emancipation of Ireland is no question of abstract justice or humanitarian sentiment, but the first condition of the English working class's own social emancipation."

So over 150 years ago, the founders of scientific socialism were already pointing to the indispensability of the struggle against colonial and national oppression.

Importantly, that understanding also extended to the struggle against national oppression within the capitalist heartlands. Hence that memorable sentence in Volume 1 of *Capital*: "Labour in the white skin can never free itself as long as labour in the black skin is branded."

The development of imperialism gained pace towards the end of the 19th century.

Lenin noted that concentration of capital had reached a point where monopolies were increasingly driven abroad in pursuit of profit. As a result, more and more of the world was brought into the capitalist system, but not on equal terms. Rather, this was "a world system of colonial oppression and of the financial strangulation of the overwhelming majority of the people of the world by a handful of 'advanced' countries."

Lenin further noted: "Imperialism is leading to annexation, to increased national oppression, and, consequently, also to increasing resistance."

The strategic implication of this is that the working class in the advanced capitalist countries must unite with the broad masses of the oppressed around the world against their common enemy: the imperialist ruling classes. Hence at the second congress of the Communist International in 1920, the slogan "Workers of the world unite" was updated to "Workers and oppressed peoples of all countries, unite".

To return to Marx's point that this is "no question of abstract justice or humanitarian sentiment": while imperialism is strong, the ruling class is powerful and the possibilities for socialist advance are extremely limited. National independence and sovereignty for the oppressed nations means the ruling class becomes weaker, and the relative position of the working class becomes stronger.

That's why Lenin said in 1921 that "the outcome of the struggle will be determined by the fact that Russia, India, China, etc account for the overwhelming majority of the population of the globe… It is this majority that has been drawn into the struggle for emancipation with extraordinary rapidity, so … there cannot be the slightest doubt what the final outcome of the world struggle will be. In this sense, the complete victory of socialism is fully and absolutely assured."

So we can say that by a hundred years ago, Marxism had developed a clear global applicability. It had transformed from being a liberatory framework for the industrial proletariat in Western Europe and North America to being a liberatory framework for the working and oppressed peoples around the world. And with Marxism's global applicability came its global application: the success of socialist and national liberation revolutions in Russia, Korea, China, Vietnam, Cuba, Nicaragua, Zimbabwe, Mozambique, Guinea-Bissau, Angola and elsewhere. All these practical experiences have contributed to the broadening and deepening of Marxism.

Carlos Martinez

Western Marxism Resists

The Western Marxism described by Losurdo essentially rejects this whole process of globalisation of class struggle.

Firstly, it near-comprehensively rejects the experiences of actually existing socialism. The Western Marxist trend has consistently distanced itself from the process of building socialism in reality: in the Soviet Union, in China, in Korea and elsewhere.

Wherever these academics and groups do support a socialist process, that support is highly conditional. For example, there was reasonably broad support for the first "pink tide" in Latin America at the beginning of this century, in large part because it was a form of socialism being built within the limits of bourgeois democracy.

However, once the U.S. stepped up its destabilisation and propaganda campaign, and once countries like Venezuela and Nicaragua were forced to use the repressive machinery of the state in defence of their revolutionary processes, Western Marxism became disillusioned and withdrew support.

Some Western Marxist thinkers were for a time inspired by the Cultural Revolution in China, with its extreme emphasis on class struggle. But when the Communist Party de-emphasised domestic class struggle and found a place for capital within its development process, Western Marxism wrote China off as having restored capitalism. In fact, with Western Marxists we always find what Losurdo called "the dogmatic rejection of actually existing socialism"; if a socialist project doesn't look like what they imagine socialist projects should look like, it's rejected.

This is combined with, and closely related to, a downplaying of the role of anti-colonial and anti-imperialist struggles; a rejection of the notion that the primary contradiction in today's world is that between imperialism and the oppressed nations; a rejection of the ideas of national liberation Marxism, in a historical context where the vast majority of socialist experiments thus far have had a major national liberation component. In Cuba, China, Korea, Venezuela, Laos, Vietnam, Mozambique, Nicaragua, the struggle for socialism has been very closely connected to the struggle against imperialism and the struggle for sovereignty.

Why is Western Marxism Like This?

Western Marxism has many different trends and contradictions, but its essence is these two rejections: of actually existing socialism and of national liberation. Both are a function of Eurocentrism and dogmatism.

But it's also important to bear in mind that there is a clear material basis for a Western left that minimises the national question. In their introduction to Losurdo's book, Gabriel Rockhill and Jennifer Ponce De Leon mention how the academic mainstream encourages a dogmatic, Eurocentric and essentially inert Marxism, creating a situation whereby success in academia more or less relies on taking positions that don't fundamentally threaten the interests of imperialism.

This is a microcosm of a trend Lenin recognised over a century ago, whereby the "high monopoly profits for a handful of very rich countries" opens up "the economic possibility of corrupting the upper strata of the proletariat", creating a privileged layer of the working class that benefits from imperialism and therefore has a material interest in its success. Therefore, I argue that the distortions of Western Marxism really represent the extension of this trend of opportunism and social chauvinism into the realms of academia.

Carlos Martinez

Where Do We Go From Here?

Now, it's important to recognise that the Western Marxist trend has produced some extremely valuable insights, and in many cases has expanded Marxism into a range of academic fields, from gender studies to cultural studies and a good deal more. Being based in the advanced capitalist countries, it generally addresses itself to the problems faced by people in those countries, and on that basis has played a valuable role in moving human understanding forward. But there are some things we must absolutely insist upon if our movement is going to make any real progress.

First is the primacy of anti-imperialist struggle, of solidarity with peoples fighting *our* ruling classes, and of playing our part in a global united front against imperialism. Since today is the 50th anniversary of Cabo Verde's independence, it seems apt to cite Amilcar Cabral: "If imperialism exists and is trying simultaneously to dominate the working class in all the advanced countries and smother the national liberation movements in all the underdeveloped countries, then there is only one enemy against whom we are fighting."

Second is the leadership of socialist countries. It should be obvious that it's the socialist world that is the vanguard of the project of developing Marxism; that it's the states, movements and parties engaged in the process of building socialism that are doing the most to build humanity's collective understanding of how to carry out the task that history has placed before for us: completing the transition to world socialism.

As Mao Zedong famously put it in his essay 'On Practice', "if you want knowledge, you must take part in the practice of changing reality. If you want to know the taste of a pear, you must change the pear by eating it yourself."

Additionally, it is absolutely crucial to understand, support and learn from China—the largest and most advanced socialist country, that is at the core of an emerging multipolarity. Indeed, as China develops, we should increasingly be showcasing China as an example of what can be achieved under socialism.

China simply cannot be understood through a lens of Western Marxism—a lens of purism and dogmatism. In the course of over a century of fierce and constant struggle, the Chinese leadership have developed a socialist path that is suited to the traditions of the Chinese people and adapts to the ever-changing material reality they face.

Outside an academic ivory tower, the questions of whether people have food on the table, whether they have access to healthcare, whether they have a roof over their heads, and whether their children get a good education are more important issues than whether China has billionaires, or whether there are branches of Starbucks and KFC in Shanghai. Deng Xiaoping's insistence that "development is the only hard truth" and that "poverty is not socialism" may have been dismissed as revisionist or capitulationist by well-fed intellectuals, but they reflected the actual needs of the Chinese people.

Domenico Losurdo of course understood all this.

On the question of inequality in China, Losurdo pointed out that China's rise constitutes a most extraordinary contribution to the fight against global-scale inequality—the inequality between developed and developing countries. He also pointed to the existence of an "absolute inequality that exists between life and death" which Chinese socialism has addressed with extraordinary success, "eliminating once and for all the absolute qualitative inequality inherent in starvation and the risk of starvation."

That's what a Marxist, dialectical analysis of inequality in China looks like.

Carlos Martinez

On the question of China's role in the world, China's support for sovereignty and development in Africa, Latin America, the Middle East, the Caribbean and the Pacific is more important than whether people think China should do more aid and less trade, or China should pursue a more militant foreign policy. Suffice to say that the slogan 'Neither Washington Nor Beijing' is not often heard in Palestine, in Iran, in Venezuela, in Cuba, in Eritrea, in Zimbabwe.

And again, Losurdo understood this very well, describing China as "the country that more than any other is challenging the international division of labour imposed by colonialism and imperialism, and furthering the end of the Columbian epoch—a fact of enormous, progressive historical significance." Any Marxist that refuses to understand this enormous, progressive historical significance is, frankly, not actually a Marxist.

So we have a plan of action: reject dogmatism and purism, reject Eurocentrism and chauvinism, and get back to playing our part in a global united front composed of the socialist countries, the oppressed nations, and the working classes and progressive forces in the imperialist countries. That's what will get us on the path to a socialist future.

* * *

Carlos Martinez is an author, researcher and political activist from London, Britain. He is author of The East is Still Red: Chinese Socialism in the 21st Century *(Praxis Press, 2023) and* The End of the Beginning: Lessons of the Soviet Collapse *(LeftWord, 2019), and co-editor with Keith Bennett of* People's China at 75 – The Flag Stays Red *(Praxis Press, 2024). Carlos is a co-editor of the Friends of Socialist China platform and a coordinating committee member of the International Manifesto Group.*

He writes regularly for the Morning Star, Beijing Review *and* Global Times, *and has published several articles in the academic journals* International Critical Thought *and* World Review of Political Economy.

Resources for Additional Information

Friends of Socialist China, socialistchina.org/
The East is Still Red: Chinese Socialism in the 21st Century, by Carlos Martinez
People's China at 75 – The Flag Stays Red, by Keith Bennett
Darker Than Blue *on WPFW 89.3 FM*, with Jaqueline Luqman
Capitalism on a Ventilator – The Impact of COVID-19 in China and the U.S., and *Sanctions – A Wrecking Ball in a Global Economy*, by Sara Flounders
China's Revolution and the Quest for a Socialist Future, and *From Yao to Mao: 5000 Years of Chinese History*, by Kenneth Hammond
FightBack! News, Mick Kelly, Editor
The Progressive International, Pawel Wargan, coordinator, *https://progressive.international/*
Workers World, workers.org, Monica Morehead, Sara Flounders and Betsey Piette, Editors
Popular Resistance, popularresistance.org/, Margaret Flowers, Director
Why the World Needs China, by Kyle Ferrana
United National Antiwar Coalition, *Blog: https://unac.notowar.net/,* Judith Bello, Editor
U.S. Peace Council, *uspeacecouncil.org,* Roger Harris, Board Member
Befriending China: People-to-People Peacemaking, and *A Realistic Path to Peace,* by Dee Knight
Geopolitics Newsletter, us9.campaign-archive.com/ Arnold August, Editor
CodePink's China Is Not Our Enemy Campaign, *www.codepink.org/china,* Megan Russell, Campaign Coordinator

Resources for Additional Information

Black Agenda Report, *www.blackagendareport.com/,* Margaret Kimberley, Executive Editor
The China Report, *www.youtube.com/playlist?list=PLwZtBKjG-SMzWROz7Dbxc-vZDgVfEhENmN* K.J. Noh, Co-Anchor
Fighting Words: Journal of the Communist Workers League, fighting-words.net/
Nodutdol for Korean Community Development, *nodutdol.org/*
The Danny Haiphong Show, *www.patreon.com/c/dannyhaiphong/posts*
Geopolitical Economy Research Group, *geopoliticaleconomy.org/people/radhika-desai/,* Radhika Desai, Director
The Dawning of the Apocalypse: The Roots of Slavery, White Supremacy, Settler Colonialism, and Capitalism in the Long Sixteenth Century, by Gerald Horne

Captions and credits for front cover pictures (from bottom to top)

Map: Projects of China's Belt and Road Initiative in Asia, Africa, and Europe as of 2018, Credit: Lena Appenzeller, Sabine Hecher, Janine Sack, in Brake, Michael, ed., (2020) *Infrastrukturatlas: Daten und Fakten über öffentliche Räume und Netze*, (1st ed.), Lahr: Druckhaus Kaufmann, p. 43, ISBN 978-3-86928-220-6.

Carrying water from a cave, Credit: China News Service, 2022

The Three Gorges Dam, Credit: Author, *Le Grand Portage,* https://commons.wikimedia.org/wiki/File:ThreeGorgesDam-China2009.jpg,

BRICS logo, Credit: Adobe Stock

Chinese Rail Bullet Train Beijing Station, Credit: WorldHistoryPics.com, Gary Lee Todd, Ph.D., Creative Commons: Zero https://www.flickr.com/photos/101561334@N08/9870869793/

Wind Turbines, Dongbai Mountain, Jinhua, Zhejiang, China, Credit: Shutter Stock https://www.shutterstock.com/image-photo/wind-turbines-on-summit-dongbai-mountain-2676863999, Lanhang Ye, Confirmation Number: CS-0D615-D641

DeepSeek Logo, Credit: https://lobehub.com/icons/deepseek, @lobehub/icons

Captions and credits for front cover pictures (from bottom to top)

Chinese solar farm, Credit: shutterstock_1731943456, EIN: 80-0812659, *https://www.shutterstock.com/image-photo/aerial-view-solar-power-panels-clean-1731943456*

Students attend class at a rural primary school in sheqi county: USN: GM1E5B31C5T01 https://www.reutersconnect.com/ detail?id=tag%3Areuters.com%2C2009%3Anewsml_GM1E-5B31C5T01%3A679724706) Media date: 2 Nov 2009 Headline: 2009-11-03T000000Z_679724706_GM1E5B31C5T01_RTR-MADP_3_CHINA-EDUCATION.JPG
Source: REUTERS

www.ingramcontent.com/pod-product-compliance
Lightning Source LLC
Chambersburg PA
CBHW071855290426
44110CB00013B/1154